DANGEROUS WOMEN

Gender and Korean Nationalism

≡

DANGEROUS WOMEN
Gender and Korean Nationalism

Edited by
**Elaine H. Kim
and Chungmoo Choi**

Routledge: New York and London

Published in 1998 by
Routledge
29 West 35th Street
New York, NY 10001

Published in Great Britain by
Routledge
11 New Fetter Lane
London EC4P 4EE

Library of Congress Cataloging-in-Publication Data

Dangerous women : gender and Korean nationalism / edited by Elaine H.
   Kim and Chungmoo Choi.
         p. cm.
   Includes bibliographical references and index.
      ISBN 0-415-91505-8 (hb : alk. paper). — ISBN 0-415-91506-6 (pb :
alk. paper)
         1. Women—Korea—History. 2. Sex roles—Korea—History. 3.
Women—
Korea (South)—Social conditions. 4. Korea—Civilization.
5. Korean American women—Social conditions. I. Kim, Elaine H.
II. Choi, Chungmoo.
HQ1765.5.D36   1997   96-49259
                                                                      CIP

Table of Contents

Acknowledgments

Interest in Korean and Korean diasporic gender politics has been surging in recent years. Indeed, this book emerges from the participation of Korean and Korean American women in three conferences, all held in 1994: the "Articulations of Korean Women" conference, sponsored by the Asian American Studies program and the Center for Korean Studies at the University of California at Berkeley; the "Women in South Korea" conference at the University of British Columbia in Vancouver; and the "Gender, Culture, and Politics in the Korean and Korean American Communities" conference in New York, organized for the International Society for Korean Studies in America.

We wish to acknowledge some of the many individuals who have helped bring *Dangerous Women* into being. In particular, Professor Hyun Sook Kim of Wheaton College not only organized the ISKSA conference in New York, which provided an initial venue for some of the work in this volume; she also helped conceptualize the book, suggesting contributors and commenting on early drafts of their work. Likewise, we thank Professor Hong Yung Lee, Director of Berkeley's Center for Korean Studies, and Professor Ling-Chi Wang, head of Asian American Studies at Berkeley for generously supporting the "Articulations" conference. Finally, we are grateful to Professor Yun Sik Chang of the University of British Columbia for organizing the Vancouver conference. For their expert critiques of the manuscript, we wish to thank Norma Field, Eithne Luibheid, Lisa Rofel, and Lisa Yoneyama. We are also grateful for the encouragement of Marlie Wasserman, and for the guidance and support of Alan Wieder and David Auburn, all formerly of Routledge. For all sorts of technical and logistical help, we are indebted to Eric Fong of Berkeley's Asian American Studies office.

ELAINE H. KIM & CHUNGMOO CHOI

Introduction

Korea's relationship with various colonial powers provides a backdrop to all the essays in this book. Recent writings on gender and colonial discourse tell us a great deal about the workings of gendered colonialism and its legacies. But although these studies are useful, they have focused almost exclusively on European colonialism. Hardly any work has been produced on multiple colonialisms in East Asia. This elision skews our understanding of gender in the colonial and post-colonial context, centering and even privileging European colonialism as a universalized subject of intellectual inquiry. The erasure of Japanese colonialism in Asia racializes the production of knowledge and colonizes the critical terrain.

The essays in *Dangerous Women* enrich and diversify the critique of colonial discourse by filling a critical lacuna with discussions and analyses of the postcolonial challenges Korean and diasporic Korean women face. Moreover, these essays clearly demonstrate that discussions of these challenges should not be ghettoized as being merely country-specific or as exclusive subjects of area studies. Instead, the issues grappled with in this book are inextricably connected to problems of the capitalistic world system and the military hegemony that underpins it.

The two main forces that have shaped nationalism and the directions of women's movements in Korea are the experience of Japanese colonial rule and the national partition engineered by the U.S. and the U.S.S.R., the two Cold War superpowers of the post-liberation period.

During the Japanese occupation (1910–1945), Korean feminism was entwined with the cause of national liberation. Indeed, the goal of the first organized women's movement under Japanese protectorship (1905–1910) was to raise funds to pay the debt to Japan that Koreans considered the direct rationale for the protectorship. Although the patriotic women's convention consisted mostly of gentry women, a large number of courtesans participated in the movement, which explains the importance of restaurants as message-relaying posts for the (underground) independence movement. During the massive March First, 1919 demonstrations, female teachers and student protesters led other women into the streets.

As in China at the turn of the century, enlightened male intellectuals in Korea during the Japanese colonial period preached about the importance of women's liberation and education to strengthening the nation. However, the nationalist position of the male elite did not separate women from nation and emphasized enlightenment for women only as mothers. Inevitably, the national liberation movement was hostile to the New Women's movement of the early 1920s, which stressed women's explorations of their own sexuality and emancipation from the patriarchal household, notions which certain educated Korean women learned from European liberalism via Japan. The short-lived New Women's movement was supplanted in subsequent decades by the largely Christian church–based nationalist women's movement and by socialist women's organized activities. The Japanese colonial government was intolerant of socialism, and many liberal women's organizations were co-opted by the colonial government. Even so, the socialist women's movement, especially the women's labor movement, reached its peak in the late 1920s into the 1930s and continued even during the Korean War. By the early 1950s, however, socialism had been brutally suppressed by the U.S.-backed South Korean government, and the Left had been all but obliterated in South Korea. The national partition and the terrors of the ideological war surrounding it created a long hiatus in the development of Korean feminism that lasted until the 1980s.

One of the fundamental sociopolitical problems in postcolonial Korea after the "liberation" has been the tenacity of colonialism, which has left an indelible imprint on many aspects of people's lives. Twentieth-century Korea is a palimpsest of multiple layers of Japanese colonialism and neo-imperial domination, especially by U.S. hegemony, which superimposed its systems on the political and social infrastructures of Japanese colonial rule. The informed reader will be reminded that behind every nationalist legitimization of military dictator Park Chung-Hee lies its counterpart, the drive to emulate the militaristic industrial capitalism of both Meiji and Showa Japan. Park had been, after all, an officer in the Imperial Japanese Army in Manchuria, the unit that participated in suppressing the Korean independence fighters. We are reminded of Frantz Fanon's warnings about the dangers of post-liberation nation-building by national elites trained by former colonizers to serve the interests of colonial rule.[1]

Because of the direct installation of the U.S. military apparatus at the end of World War II, South Korea, like many other former colonies, never had an opportunity to decolonize in the true sense of the word. Indeed, as Seungsook Moon points out in her essay in this volume, U.S.-sponsored military dictatorships combined with traditional Korean neo-Confucian patriarchy to construct modern South Korea as an androcentric nation. South Korea's androcentric nationalism helps explain the effacing of the "Comfort Women" (military sex slaves drafted by Imperial Japan during the Pacific War) issue that Hyunah Yang discusses in her essay. This silence occurs not only because of the "shame" associated with the raped woman in patriarchal discourse, but also because of the South Korean military government's efforts to "normalize" relations with Japan from the early 1960s onwards. Indeed,

Japanese colonialism was erased from public discourse as the reins of rule over Korea were passed to the U.S. from Japan because the U.S. needed, in order to maintain the East Asian border of its empire, a financially strong ally in the region, which would counter-balance an arrangement between the U.S. and the U.S.S.R. that guaranteed Soviet control over the northern corner of the world.[2]

The U.S. neo-colonial domination over South Korea reproduced already familiar gendered and sexualized relationships between the two countries. In her essay on nationalism and the construction of gender in Korea, Chungmoo Choi reveals that while a wide spectrum of South Korean cultural products claim Korean hyper-masculinity and vigilance about female chastity, Korean women's bodies are being offered up to the metropolitan male gaze while the bodies of white women are being privileged. Moreover, Katherine Moon argues that to address the entwined and conflicting projects of feminism and nationalism is to contend with the massive sex industry around U.S. military camptowns scattered all over South Korea, where a large number of Korean women serve U.S. military personnel under the jurisdiction of the two states. Whether forcibly drafted under colonial rule or driven by financial need in the neo-colonial, dependent economy, and despite shifting discursive constructions of the nation, these women are variously constructed as outcasts or as a trope of the suffering nation, as revealed in Hyun Sook Kim's essay on Korean prostitutes servicing the U.S. military.

Anti-colonial nationalism idealizes the self-sacrificing woman who is devoted to the national liberation struggle: mothers as asexual vessels of fertility dedicated to revolutionary husbands and sons. Hyun Ok Park's essay on North Korean revolutionary literature on women's struggles in Manchuria for Korean liberation highlights this theme. In her critique of the representation of female subjectivities in Hyŏn Ki-yŏng's novel *Paramt'anŭn sŏm* (*Island in Wind*), You-me Park points out how progressive contemporary South Korean writers and critics comply with such male-centered imaginings. Their patriarchal ideology confers neither anti-colonial revolutionary agency nor autonomous subjectivity to women. Instead, the boundaries are drawn and the terms set by a male elite, so that women, though always indispensable participants in political struggle, are relegated to the status of voiceless auxiliaries. Both

4

Hyun Ok Park's and You-me Park's essays point to the fact that the radicalization of women as revolutionary subjects does not emerge from desexualized motherhood but from the experience of migration from home and community as colonized women.

Hyun Yi Kang's reading of the work of various Korean American women artists interrogates, complicates, and extends the meanings of nation and "home" for Korean women, especially Korean diasporic women. Yong Soon Min's first visual essay, "Kindred Distance," features photographs of the display of North Korean apparel at the South Korean post near the DMZ. Min deploys text to create a triangulated relationship between North Korea, South Korea, and diasporic Koreans in the U.S. Mixing phoneticized broken Korean and English to spell "why?" and "where is our home?" Min confounds and contradicts commonly accepted notions of "home." As a "1.5 generation" Korean American, Min suggests that the answers are partly rooted in who is asking why. In her "personal genealogy" of Korean North American women's cinema, Helen Lee discusses how *kyop'o* (overseas Korean) women's art, including her own art, has been informed by race and gender identifications. She conjectures about the extent to which this work constitutes a hybrid, multivalent, "new visual culture." Elaine H. Kim's essay provides a specifically Korean American examination of South Korean cultural constructions of gender and sexuality. Kim's essay delineates the relationships between money and masculinity in the 1980s, an era of new economic power and stability in South Korea, when sexuality remains a troubled site of contestation and symbolic economics.

Anti-colonial nationalism reclaims masculinity, usually at the expense of women and their interest in sexuality. The unifying impulse of the masculine nationalist discourse homogenizes the nation and normalizes women and women's chastity so that they properly belong to the patriarchal order. Thus "Comfort Women" are constructed as national virgins. As Hyunah Yang explains when she analyzes the strategies of remembering Korean "Comfort Women," the discourse of the violation of national virgins mobilizes the Korean sense of shame, which in turn serves to unify the nation. In other words, the exchange value of shame for national unity is the basic capital that circulates in the symbolic economics of nationalism. Katharine Moon extends this notion of sexual economics as she examines the official but local discourse that defines camptown prostitutes as dollar-earning patriots. By exploring the regulation of Asian female bodies through disease control and the objectification of Korean women as prostitutes in U.S. military camps, Moon suggests how the internalization of white privilege and its discontent and the medicalization of Korean prostitutes' bodies are embedded in a deep-rooted discourse of race and sexualized racial relationships.

While contestations between Japan and Korea about masculinity are not explored in the essays presented here, there are indications that the subjugation of women to the anti-colonial masculine national imaginary is inextricably linked to the masculine imperial discourse, especially the discourse of the U.S. Chungmoo Choi suggests that the double discourse of South Korean nationalism persists despite and because of multiple distortions under colonialism and internalized racial hierarchy in South Korea.

Yong Soon Min's "Kindred Distance" invokes the metropolitan construction of the Othered Self as internalized by South Koreans. These images demonstrate the South Korean construction of North Korean alterity as the estranged Self who is Othered and who lags behind in the capitalist time line. The items displayed in the showcase invoke both nostalgia for things left behind or destroyed in the South's rush toward modernity and a smug sense of technological superiority that renders the North Korean objects worthy of touristic curiosity. The exoticization of things North Korean is not exactly an instance of "imperial nostalgia," that strange longing for the "primitive" or the "backward" things imperialism has permanently destroyed. Instead, it suggests the former colony's feelings of pride at still belonging to the imperial power. The Othered Self is sexualized by a display that contains mostly women's apparel, all the way down to brassiere and panties, marked with North Korean renderings of the items' names on the name plates, as if the items were museum pieces. This deepens our suspicion of how closely South Korea emulates the gendered imperial relationship it imagines with its Northern sister.

Min's second visual essay, "Mother Load," features the *bojagi*, or wrapping cloth, a traditional handicraft and utilitarian custom associated with women. The first two parts of this sequential sculpture refer

6

to the past and present of colonized, divided, and militarized Korea. The current diasporic and Korean American experience is suggested by the third part, in which a scarf, torn in half, contains neatly folded items of underwear and everyday clothing, each of which has also been severed in half. The final *bojagi* cloth is a collage of color snapshots from Min's personal collection of photographs, including images of Korean businesses destroyed during the Los Angeles "riots" and a photo of a Los Angeles Korean American demonstration demanding disclosure of the U.S. government's role in the Kwangju massacre. The final *bojagi*, a weighty bundle tied up and ready to go, suggests both action and a future.

Feminism and nationalism are the antinomic offspring of modernity. Feminism as a project of modernity stands at odds with nationalism, which imagines a fraternal community. On the one hand, nationalism, while emphasizing liberal democratic notions of individual differences, has in fact reconstituted the class hierarchy of the *ancien regime.* On the other hand, it is these very liberal democratic notions that have been used to segregate gender and race in the interests of a unifying ideology of the nation-state.

Feminism in the colonies, having inherited this double legacy of discriminatory gender and race politics, has either been subsumed under or subordinated to the greater cause of national liberation, which usually imagines the liberation of men. Women who brave these conflicting forces are at once endangered by and dangerous to the integrity of the masculinist discourse of nationalism. From this dangerous position, the essays in this collection critically interrogate and intervene in the workings of nationalism in the arenas of gender and sexuality in post-colonial Korea and in diasporic Korean communities, whether in northern China or North America.

NOTES

1. Frantz Fanon, "The Pitfalls of National Consciousness," *The Wretched of the Earth,* New York: Grove Weidenfeld, 1968.

2. Immanuel Wallerstein, "The Agonies of Liberalism," *New Left Review,* 204 (March–April, 1994).

2

CHUNGMOO CHOI

Nationalism and Construction of Gender in Korea

Driving on the Pacific Highway one glorious afternoon, I spotted, in the rear view mirror, a military vehicle being driven by a young soldier in a khaki uniform.[1] Momentarily, I caught myself in the act of preening, but at the same time straightening my back and holding my chin up. At first I was at a loss to explain my actions, which were but the long-forgotten habits of another time. I felt overwhelmed and confused. The pounding of my heart was clearly audible. Then inexplicable anger welled up inside me. I suddenly realized that my reaction to this encounter with the specular image of an American soldier was the reified *habitus* of a woman who had endured foreign domination in "postcolonial" Korea. I chastised myself, as many Koreans would do under such circumstances, in order to overcome that persistent specter. I muttered to myself, "Wait! You no longer need to act like this. You are not a young girl. You are a professor. Besides, this is America." It was as if my age and social standing—living in a metropolis as a professional—would protect me from the painful memories of ambivalent female subjectivity. These are memories that have been so deeply inscribed in me that they threaten to expose my vulnerability at the slightest provocation. That the soldier behind me may not have even recognized that I was a Korean, among all the Asians in California, did not occur to me until later. He would not have known what a Korean meant to American military servicemen stationed in postwar Korea or what it meant to be a Korean woman in that occupied space.

Fetishism of Power

What compelled me to react with the intractably subtle yet very contradictory behavior of preening, which may be deemed a seductive gesture, and straightening, which is a gesture of defiance, may be indices of the complexity of my female subjectivities when forced to face this representation of hegemonic U.S. militarism that exerted colonial authority over the occupied Koreans. At the same time, the fact that I chose to live in America, seeking what were considered to be better opportunities, whether driven by political or economic motivations under the socio-historical conditions of South Korea in the 1970s, further complicated my feelings and drove me to a debilitating impasse on that highway. As a woman who spent her childhood in the immediate post–Korean War period, I felt that the power relationship between colonizer and the colonized had been deeply inscribed in my psyche. The relationship had long been translated into not only gendered and sexualized terms but also into material terms. The power of the U.S. and its material representations were irresistibly seductive and at the same time repulsive to many South Koreans, who harbored a hidden sense of shame for their self-contradictions, which were repressed by the totalizing discourse of anti-colonial nationalism. Many post–Korean War male writers such as Ch'oe In-ho or An Chŏng-hyo[2] painfully recall the seductive taste of powdered milk and chocolate that children in the post–Korean War received either

10

from the U.S. government or from passing U.S. soldiers. Rob Wilson captures the complexity of Koreans' memories of American occupation:

> When the Korean War was finally over, three little Korean orphans from Pusan huddled to share a Roy Rogers comic—"Parents! Look! Free Christmas gifts!" In their little boots from Texas and thick sweaters from the Lower East Side, the boys smiled at this new ideogram of a triumphant, happy cowboy. Orphaned Korean children received money, chocolates and toys contributed by thousand of Americans. "I hated those chocolates," said a drunken novelist.[3]

This ambivalence may be attributed to a postcolonial denial of the status of the materially deprived recipient. In addition, chocolate is embedded in the history of colonial conquest: cocoa was Mayan ambrosia that the conquistadors took to Europe, where it was transformed into one of the most popular commodity items, the chocolate candy bar. The chocolate candy bar that the American soldier handed out to the Koreans was of course not ambrosia but a sensuous signifier of colonialism. Can we imagine a Korean's refusal to take that signifier as an act to avoid the historical contagion, and the danger of swallowing and embodying the history of conquest that would have a contagious effect on layers of colonialism on Korean bodies?

The sensuousness of the sweet, smooth chocolate on the palate and the warmth of sweaters upon the skin were at once irresistible and burdensome to the dispossessed and dominated people in the war zone. I too share such memories of longing and refusal. I remember a bright red-and-green checkered winter coat that my mother brought home one day. It was unusually beautiful, with a tapered waist and a warm hood, unmistakably a "relief supply *(kuhomulja)*" item from America. The beautiful flea market coat posed a dilemma for me: my own sense of dignity and my sympathy towards my mother, who had swallowed her pride as a descendant of eminent scholars in a fallen country and, for the first time in her life, rummaged through the flea market—*Yangki* (Yankee) Market it was called—to protect her daughter from the harsh Korean winter. I resolved the dilemma by wearing the coat until I could no longer be seen from my house. Then I carried it inside out the rest of the thirty-minute walk to school on crisp winter mornings.

Resistance to the warmth of the wool weighed heavily on a ten-year-old girl in destitute post-war Korea. That was the burden of history.

Historical awareness here, vague as it may be, stems from a power differential that was reified into thingness, and in the form of a charitable gift. Charitable gifts require the recipient's self-degradation and surrender of dignity to the power that not only produces the fine commodity but affords a luxury surplus to be dispensed, thereby garnering symbolic capital from the recipients. According to Pierre Bourdieu, symbolic capital is disguised profit drawn from the ideological labor of honor rather than from direct economic exchange. It often takes the seemingly disinterested form of a gift or a feast, such as a potlatch with no expectation of direct reciprocity. The investment or display of material power anticipates obligatory reciprocation from the recipients, which often allows the gift-giver's political and economic domination.[4] Therefore, in the gift economy one is suspended between the sense of dignity and desire, between indebtedness and self-pity, agonizing in ambivalence.

As I discussed elsewhere,[5] in the occupied space the gift economy works its way into the sexual economy, which firmly establishes the relationship between the colonizer and the colonized as a gendered and sexualized relationship, not only in the metaphorical sense but also at the level of corporeality, which institutes military sexual services.

The capitalistic modernization project that the South Korean military regimes carried out attempted to emulate the metropolitan materiality. At the same time, these modernization projects demanded the sacrifice of South Korean workers in the name of the nation. Such capitalistic nationalism was legitimatized by the anti-colonial discourse, which paradoxically claimed spiritual superiority and masculine integrity, while imposing chastity upon its women.

What disturbed me on the Pacific Highway that day was not that I still felt anxiety towards US military servicemen but the way in which the Korean ideology of chastity still dictated my behavior from deep down in my own consciousness. My own ambivalent behavior of preening and straightening my back may be seen as a defensive reaction—a refusal to humble myself before an American soldier. All the same, making myself look feminine for the visual consumption of a "foreign" soldier was a humbling act. In the eyes of Korean men, who have obsessively disciplined and regulated women's bodies as metaphors for their uncontaminated, uninterrupted homonational (or homosocial) identity and imposed on women the ideology of chastity and self-censorship, my preening would have been a sign of their own cultural and national defilement.

This very ideology of chastity has silenced hundreds of thousands of former and present "comfort women" who fear that they might be stigmatized as the emblem of promiscuity: *hwanhyang nyŏ*. The term, *hwanhyang nyŏ*, which in its written form is composed of Chinese characters—the language of Confucian male rulers—simply means "homecoming women." The etymology of the term precisely illuminates the position of Korean women victimized by their own history of foreign dominations and homonational misogyny. The "homecoming women" were initially sent to Qing China in the mid-seventeenth century as tribute items for Qing's suzarainty over Korea. Some of the mostly lower-class women were returned home after their usefulness was exhausted and their youth had withered. The returned women were stigmatized as defiled women and labeled promiscuous. The "promiscuous" "homecoming woman" signified a nomenclature that constructs Korean men as the victims of the emasculation of the Korean nation. In a similar context, upper-class women often carried a small dagger as a part of their attire as a reminder for them to take their own lives, if and when their bodies were violated by men other than their husbands, especially by invading foreign soldiers.

The ideology of chastity, while exempting men of their self-appointed responsibility to defend the nation, safeguards masculine authority at the expense of women's lives. The "comfort women" drafted by the Japanese military for sexual services who returned from the war fronts have lived for half a century carefully guarding their past. Their existence had been completely erased even in the most fervent anti-colonial nationalist narrative in Korea, until 1991 when three women took the issue into their own hands and sued the Japanese government.[7] Ironically, in South Korea the "comfort women" issue has been cast as an emblem of a nationalistic discourse in the trope of a violated and colonized victim.

These are not the only women who have lived under the self-censorship imposed by the ideology of chastity. All Korean women, as the discourse of homogeneous single-nation (*tanil minjok*) mandates, are expected to be chaste and vigilant against foreign males and, by extension, masculine foreign power. My preening act was not a simple infringement or defiance of such an imposition. It had an added meaning. It was a bid for recognition, recognition of the feminine subjectivity that had been denied by and subordinated to the constructed idea of national subjectivity. In Korea's long history of colonial and neo-colonial domination, this national subjectivity has been exclusively a male subjectivity.

bell hooks perceptively argues that women of the colonized nation are doubly colonized by the colonizers and by men of the same race. Drawing from the experiences of Black nationalism, she asserts that colonized males adopt the stance of the colonizer as a way of recuperating their masculinity. In that process of mimicry, colonized Korean men not only deny feminine subjectivity but oppress Korean women, to shed their emasculated and infantilized image and prove their masculinity to a degree of exaggeration that may include violence against women. Thus colonized men and the colonizers unite against the colonized women. In other words, in the sacred mission of anti-colonial nationalism, the object of which is often to restore national masculinity, women of the colonized nation are doubly oppressed.[8]

Sexualized Nation and Gendered Nationalism

A woman's subject position in the social and historical reality of colonial or neo-colonial space has often been constructed as a sexualized one. The West has constructed the Orient and the non-West as a feminine or primitive Other to define the West as a center of masculine civilization. A wealth of feminist literature has demonstrated that this differential relationship between the metropolitan Self and the colonized Other has often been articulated in terms of gender. These gendered relations in turn are represented in sexual metaphors.[9] In other words, two axial equations have been constructed onto which the West and the non-West are respectively inscribed: the civilized (enlightened) vs. primitive and masculine vs. feminine. The axial binary, of course, intersects with an indigenous patriarchy that has been at work for centuries.

This metaphoric relationship was often embodied in postcolonial South Korea. In the 1950s, on the streets of a residential area of Seoul, Koreans used to hear American soldiers calling indiscriminately for "*saekssi* (young woman)" from the passing military trucks to all passers-by. The call was a public declaration of the soldiers' intention to violate Korean women. If this was not an indiscreet threat of metaphorical rape of the nation, it was clearly a display of masculine domination over the women and men of Korea, constructing all Korean people as the sexualized feminine Other.

A striking number of South Korean works of fiction, films, protest theater performances, and even military textbooks thematize this gendered and sexualized international relationship. The image of postcolonial South Korea envisaged in these works is often a raped woman or prostitute who struggles to survive under colonial rule. This presupposes the helpless impotence of Korean males. In his short story "Nalgae" ("The Wings") published in 1936, Yi Sang depicts the colonized Korean male precisely in these terms, sketching the lopsided relationship between a working wife and her dependent and infantilized husband, both of whom live in a warren of prostitutes. The husband is confined to the inner section of their quarters, while the wife conducts her business in the outer section, reversing the conventional inner/outer division of labor between the husband and wife. Even while the wife earns an income entertaining her clients in the external part of the couple's crowded living quarters, the husband shows no sign of jealousy. Instead, he innocently lies in the inner part of their quarters. When he is let out, he is shown to be absolutely incompetent to deal with daily life. This inverted image invokes what Partha Chatterjee describes as the Indian national imaginary under British colonial rule. Indian nationalist discourse of the nineteenth century saw the necessity of fortifying the inner spirituality, which was the women's domain, against the colonizer who demonstrated material superiority, the realm of which should have belonged to the Indian male.

Yi Sang's story problematizes the absence of spirituality or materiality in the abject colonial situation of Korea. The husband in "The Wings" is a well-read intellectual, conversant in Russian and French literature as well as in Malthusian economic theories. However, in the colonial situation, the intellectual husband finds no room for himself in the society and realizes that he has been relegated to the status of a drone relying on the "queen bee" of a woman who, in turn, is already leading the life of a widow in the absence of a "masculine" male. In the course of the narrative, the emasculated and infantilized husband, who looked up to his wife as an angelic figure at the beginning, begins to compete with the wife who found an opportunity to make a living outside the confines of household. Finally, he suspects her of nursing a murderous intention: to poison her innocent husband with sleeping pills. This is the watershed moment when the lethargic husband imagines the possibility of growing wings to liberate himself. In other words, the economic power of women has to be vilified and denied in order to imagine a postcolonial world for men. In order for the masculine imaginary of the postcolonial world to work, the reverse hierarchy of the conjugal relationship must be rejected as futile, and the wife who occupies the male domain must be made a prostitute. In this construct, the wife not only violates the rules of chastity but is expected to betray conjugal trust. In a reading of "The Wings" as a national allegory, the figure of the prostitute wife disrupts national integrity and collaborates with the colonizer.

The official nationalism of the South Korean military government, however, denies such a feminine construction of a colonized nation. When Nam Chŏng-hyŏn's short story, "Punji" ("The Land of Excrement," hereafter "The Land") appeared in 1965, the South Korean government accused the novel and the author of violating the National Security Law on the grounds that the story misrepresented the U.S. military as a brutal force and distorted the facts about the wretched state of the victims. The novella, it was argued, inspired anti-American sentiment and instigated class consciousness.[10] "The Land" is written in the form of a confession by Hong Mansu, the narrator, to his deceased mother. Mansu reveals that his mother, wife of an underground guerrilla for Korean independence, was raped by an American soldier during the festivities welcoming the U.S. military that occupied Korea after liberation from Japan. This trauma of rape drives Mansu's mother insane and eventually to death. Mansu's insane mother forces him to witness the site of her humiliation, her genitalia. The horror of this experience deeply inscribed the mother in the son's memory as a metaphor of the occupied nation. The orphaned Mansu becomes a black marketeer of the goods smuggled from the U.S. military base and his sister a prostitute for the U.S. servicemen. One day Mansu rapes the wife of a U.S. military personnel, Sgt. Speed, who has been keeping Mansu's sister as his mistress. For the rape of Sgt. Speed's wife, Mansu soon meets a massive artillery assault from the U.S. military.

While "The Land" indicts the U.S. as a conqueror that rapes Korean mothers, the sacred emblem of the Korean nation, and turns its women into prostitutes, this anti-imperial novella reveals a surprising antinomy that may undermine the totality of the discourse of masculine nationalism. In the story, Mansu frequently hears Sgt. Speed's open complaints about the unsatisfactory body of his sister and her lack of sexual appeal. While Mansu sees his sister's body "as pretty as a blossoming flower bud" that satisfies men's viewing pleasure, he develops a sexual longing for white female bodies. Mansu claims that his sexual intercourse with Sgt. Speed's wife was not rape but worship of a "goddess-like superior white woman's body" that had indeed blessed him with heavenly sexual plenitude. From the perspective of Korean male sexuality and sexual desire, the colonized Korean male in this anti-imperial narrative is not fully resistant to the colonizer. Instead, the Korean male is complicit with the colonizer in disdaining Korean women. He submits himself to the colonizers in his sexual fantasies about the women of the colonizing race. The novel exposes the Korean male's split subjectivity which vigilantly controls the chastity of national woman on the one hand and desires and worships the oppressor's woman on the other. However, the anti-colonial nationalist narrative does not consider this multiplicity of the male subjectivity a threat to national integrity but rather a sign of heroism, as the novella "The Land" is firmly ensconced in the canon of South Korean national literature.

The South Korean government's denial of neo-colonial reality and its negation of the existence of the class gap—issues that were contended during the trial of "The Land"—paradoxically admitted the existence of both. The denial itself confirms the South Korean government's complicity with and internalization of U.S. hegemony. This is evidenced in the South Korean Army textbook, *Hanminjoggŭi yongtŭrim* (*The Dragon Rise of the Korean Nation*). In the textbook with a title graphically depicting militant masculinity, South Korean military authorities argue that the Korean military's bloodshed in the Vietnam War was an invaluable experience for the "maturity (*sŏngsuk*)" of the military state of Korea.[11] In other words, partaking in the oppression of another feminized former colony was opportunity for self-assertion that led South Korea through a rite of passage to recuperate its virility and join the ranks of the imperialistic order. Yet by joining this order, the South Korean government uncritically internalizes and reproduces the very hegemonic practices of the United States. In its celebration of masculinity, the South Korean government elides the fact that when the nation itself is emasculated or feminized, the symbolic rape of the mother nation and the real rape of its daughters by the fraternal blood-ally suggests an incestuous violation,[12] a fraternal violation that takes the insidious form of capitalistic penetration. The South Korean state fails to rescue itself from the universalizing forces of imperialism and remains subordinated.[13]

One such example can be found in the ideology of the 1988 Seoul Olympics. The opening ceremony of the Seoul Olympics was an auto-biographical narration of an archaic nation coming of age and modernizing, overcoming its colonial past. For instance, the Seoul Olympic Committee had septuagenarian marathoner Son Ki-jŏng carry the Olympic torch into the stadium. Son Ki-jŏng had won a gold medal at the Berlin Olympics in 1936, not as a citizen of Korea but as a colonized Japanese citizen. At the time, Korean language newspapers had whitened the Japanese flag on Son's uniform in the photo of his medal ceremony, and the newspaper companies were forced to shut down by the Japanese colonial government. Half a century after the humiliating experience in Berlin, the citizens of this partitioned country proudly reminded the world that they had gained not only sovereignty but also the power to host the Olympics.

Portraying the nation as having overcome its colonial past, the 1988 Olympics inevitably showcased a prelapsarian past. It was embellished with Korea's nuanced cultural nationalistic logos that are deeply embedded in archaism. The chief choreographer of the 1988 Olympic ceremony Yi O-ryŏng—a writer, publisher, and literary critic—imagined the opening ceremony as a utopian narrative that seeks harmony and humanistic progress, true to the Enlightenment spirit of nineteenth-century Olympism. Yi drew three cosmic principles—heaven, earth, and humans—from the yin-yang principles of the cosmos, which were also emblematized in the design of the Korean flag. This archaism is metaphorically transformed into universal humanism as it is interpreted in the language of several strands of European philosophies of transcendental existentialism and myth criticism. For instance, Yi explained his vision of the Olympic ceremony as follows:

> If we make the Olympic field a space like the archetype of God's city, it will become a place of common feeling for connecting our space with the world's. Moreover, modern people, who have lost the sense of vertical space, live only in secular horizontal space. By reviving the sublime, transcendental, and cosmological dimensions, we can make a sacred space as if the world were being created anew. People all over the world will harmonize with each other in the fresh morning of God's city.[14]

What kind of new history did he envision? The Olympic opening ceremony was deeply influenced by South Korea's official nationalist narrative, which valorizes shamanism as the essence of indigenous Korean culture. This idea is steeped in an Eliadean transcendental theology that anticipates the possibility of the regeneration of time. All of the opening scenes were dramatized around the Olympic flame holder as the symbolic world tree, or *axis mundi,* through which humans and deities were believed to communicate, and the first three scenes were choreographed and titled in ways that evoked Korea's archaic religious ritual: the Passage at Dawn, the Dragon Drum Procession, the Prayer of Blessings, and so on. In other words, this part of the opening ceremony was a narrativization of mythical Korea cast in the performative act of a shamanic ritual. This was followed by the creation of dramatized chaos in the scene entitled "Festival of Masks." The ritual solemnity of the previous scenes was broken as masks from many corners of the world danced in seemingly undisciplined chaotic dance movement.

In the theater of the Seoul Olympic ceremony, ritual chaos was enacted to introduce a new chapter of history or the birth of a new militant state. This new chapter was announced by a boy dressed in an athletic outfit turning a wheel from one corner and slowly covering the vast arena of the stadium. All the music had stopped, and the grounds were empty. The silence and disciplinarity were in dramatic contrast to the chaotic primitivity of the previous scene. The effect was a magnified sense of tranquillity and emptiness: a breathless Zen-like serenity. The turning of a wheel was impregnated with Buddhist symbolism: the turning of Samsara/karma, which anticipates reincarnation and birth of a new life or an Eliadean ritual/mythical regeneration of time.[15] Remarkably, this imaging of a new nation reinforced the patriarchal gender ideology of male domination. The idea of male dominance was further fortified with militarism. The new karma, a new history initiated by a male child, fully blossomed as hundreds of boys demonstrated Taekwondo, breaking bricks in disciplined unison. The Taekwondo demonstration confirmed the power of youthful, exclusively male, warriors, which was complicit with the official nationalist historiography of the military government.

During its thirty-year rule, South Korean official historiography has constructed masculine national identity by highlighting patriotic military activities through knowledge production apparatuses like the Korea Research Institute of Spiritual Culture (*Chŏngsin Munhwa Yŏnguwŏn*).[16] Such nationalist construction and inculcation of a militaristic masculinist identity for the nation not only occludes women but legitimizes further subordination of women for the benefit of the country's capitalistic development.[17] The Olympic opening ceremony reiterated this official militaristic narrative of the newly industrialized nation for global viewers.

Acknowledging this accomplishment, the Roh Tae Woo government bent its legislative rules and created the Culture Ministry in 1990, appointing as its first minister none other than the master architect of the Olympic ceremony, Yi Ŏ-ryŏng. The South Korean Culture Ministry was fashioned after its French counterpart. Unfortunately, the gesture was an unwitting tribute to a nineteenth-century French policy that imposed a unitary notion of "culture" over regional and popular culture and insisted on the universal use of the French language, while repressing regional languages.[18] This hallmark policy of high culture and the standardization of language was further imposed throughout the French colonies. Other imperial powers followed suit. According to the South Korean Culture Ministry, France boasts the greatest number of overseas cultural information centers: 168 French Cultural Services sites as compared to 126 U.S. Information Services centers, 120 Goethe Institute of Germany sites, 81 British Councils, and 28 Japanese Information offices throughout the world. Drawing on the masculine energy of the Seoul Olympic narrative, the South Korean Ministry of Culture internalized and replicated the metropolitan production of self-knowledge and its inscription onto the Other.

The internalization and mimicry of metropolitan imaging of the Other has been eloquently portrayed in the film *Sŏp'yŏnje*. This film has been received with an unprecedented hoopla of nationalistic self-congratulation for depicting the "essence of Korean beauty," its land and music. *Sŏp'yŏnje* is set in Korea's postcolonial period, when American mass culture had pushed its way deeply into the meager markets of the remote countryside and further marginalized the singers of *p'ansori*, a Korean popular art genre of the nineteenth century. Capturing the moment of Korea's intense industrialization, *Sŏp'yŏnje* presents a wide slice of everyday life from Korea's recent past, offering a visual tour of a time when things Korean were being replaced by commodities of Western origin and everyday life was marked by a confusing array of hybridity. These items of daily life are the sites of social memory. For the film's spectators, these nostalgic devices work, not because the past is seen as utopian but because it offers Korean spectators the place of safety, *Heimat*.

Social memory confers the aura of emotional spontaneity and moral certainty that the past is believed to have ensured. John Frow argues that what nostalgia seeks is the absence that generates the mechanism of desire. It is the desire for desire that lies in the ontological homelessness in an industrial world where the past appears to offer a sense of home and security.[19] This *Heimatlos*ness is represented by the homeless family of traveling singers lost in a capitalistic society. In fact, the film spectacularizes the Korean rural life surrounding the marketplace that was excluded from intense capitalistic development. For the film's urban viewers who are immersed in the ambiance of late capitalism, the uncritically received inequalities between the city and the country, between center and periphery, and the sense of now and the most recent past itself are a spectacle of alterity. This is the logic of tourism. The lack that stems from unequal development is precisely what makes an area/time attractive as a tourist site. The cinematic commodification of the Othered space resembles what Renato Rosaldo terms "imperialist nostalgia," the peculiar metropolitan sense of loss of the native culture that has been reduced to serve the metropolis.[20] This nostalgia is visually celebrated by the cinematography of the director, Im Kwŏn-t'aek. The homeless family, peregrinating and singing in beautifully tamed wild nature, offers a riveting visual feast. The film's aesthetic frame exoticizes Korea by rediscovering it as "the sacred, uncontaminated, that is, undeveloped and perhaps virgin land," hiding the intensely developed industrial country that lies outside the camera frame.

Sŏp'yŏnje projects the South Korean postcolonial split subjectivity that surveys and identifies the self but at the same time constructs and represents the self by mimicking and internalizing the surveying subject. In other words, the film takes the position of both a colonial male gaze and an Othered feminine subject responding to this colonial male gaze. Under this self-primitivizing, internalized colonial male gaze, a young woman is blinded and raped by her adopted father in the name of artistic perfection. The prediction of Yubong, the leading male character, that p'ansori, this dying art of another time, would be dominated, has been fulfilled outside the film frame.

Sŏp'yŏnje has been skillfully reproduced as an intangible cultural asset by the South Korean government and is disseminated as a mass cultural form of film. The possibility of intertextuality here between the male character's aspiration for his adopted daughter's artistic development and South Korea's drive for economic development is striking. The capitalistic development that deprived a nation of its voice and devastated its land in the name of nationalism is mirrored in the father's deprivation of his daughter's sight and in his violation of her body for the perfection of national art. In other words, the capitalistic development destroys a national body in the name of nationalism, while the spiritual essence of a nation is believed to be maintained only through the destroyed body. This creates a double-edged, paradoxical allegory of a postcolonial nation: anti-colonial nationalism can be achieved only through the self-construction of the feminine Other. The two discourses cancel each other out.

South Korean oppositional intellectuals, who diagnose the Korean national body as fragmented and penetrated by the world capitalistic system, offer an alternative image of a postcolonial nation. Their idea of the new nation celebrates the virility of the working class, represented by men who would rescue and protect both victimized and collaborating women. The protest play *Sorigut Agu* (roughly translated as "ritual cry of Agu"), which was performed mostly underground throughout the 1970s and 1980s, articulates a critique of transnational capitalism and its impact on South Korean life. South Korean protest theater of the 1970s and 1980s adopted the form of the carnivalesque mask-dance-drama of the precolonial period. In the street theater version, the Buddhist monk is replaced by a Japanese businessman who seeks the services of Korean women, and the two shamanesses are replaced by a college woman and a factory girl. Both women are drawn to the Japanese capital that the businessman may offer them. This blind worship of the material, represented in an implicitly sexualized relationship between Japan and South Korea, critically questions South Koreans' all-pervasive material fetishism spurred by recent capitalistic development. The seduction of the wealthy neighbor may be an obvious protest against sex tourism. But more critically, the play interrogates the complicity of South Koreans with hegemonic multinational capitalism. The servant in the mask-dance-drama is replaced by a male factory worker, Agu, who is of rural origin. Agu defeats the Japanese businessman and reclaims the two Korean women, thus prophesying the victory of the Korean workers, through their counter-hegemonic struggle, over the penetrating international capitalistic forces.

Here the oppositional cultural activists suspect the women of prostitution and collaboration. The late national poet, Sin Tong-yŏp, suspects women, especially prostitutes, to be mediators of postwar U.S. expansionism and sites of capitalistic penetration. In his poetry, prostitutes represent commodified bodies, and the purchase of these women's bodies metaphorizes the neo-colonial accumulation of capital and expansionism that replaces the archaic form of colonial invasion, especially that of Japan. In Sin's poem *"p'unggyŏng"* ("The Landscape," 1960), the commodified women, the bodies of the nations that are available at the mere price of gratuities, mark the vast borderline of the U.S. empire—from Korea and Japan to the Arab countries. Sin Tong-yŏp paints the landscape as follows:

> The soldier, who flew over Korea yesterday,
> may be walking on the dikes of rice paddy
> outside of Tokyo, today.
>
> The soldier, who put on the shirt that Suni washed,
> left Ŭijŏngbu yesterday.
> He must be giving tips today
> to a girl at a tavern by the Dead Sea.

In the mind's-eye of Sin Tong-yŏp, women, especially educated women, appear as high-class prostitutes. These are women who were educated in the postcolonial American school system that the U.S. military government superimposed over the Japanese colonial education system. Even the physical appearance of these women resembles that of Western women. In his epic poem, *Kŭmkang* (*The Kŭm River*, 1967), college women with long white *daikon* legs[21] carry *Life* magazine under their arms and hang around the U.S. military base, suggesting an image of high-class prostitutes. According to Partha Chatterjee, this hostility towards the Westernized women (and disdain of low-class women) was precisely what gave rise to the neo-patriarchy in the nationalist discourse of nineteenth-century colonized India. Neo-patriarchy idealized the patriarchal middle-class family as the site of cultural and biological production: it would provide a spiritually fortified stronghold of anti-colonial struggle against the materially superior British colonizer and produce the offspring of the future.[22]

As George Mosse, and to a certain degree Benedict Anderson, argue, nationalism is a masculine discourse *par excellence*.[23] Due to the sexualized construct of the colonial relationship, the discourse of anti-colonial nationalism demands moral purity, which is again sexually metaphorized. At the same time, since the focus of the decolonization effort is to recuperate an infantilized and emasculated nation, any power that may threaten male authority is suspected of undermining the national struggle. When that threat comes from women, these women are relegated to the status of "whores."

The South Korean male nationalists on the opposite side of the government thus turn misogynic eyes to educated women, not only because these women challenge traditional patriarchal authority but also because their familiarity with (materially superior, masculine) American culture may lead them to collaborate with the dominating foreign forces. Albert Memmi observed the relationship between the colonizer and colonized —the colonizer loses humanity by dehumanizing the colonized. Memmi's borrowing of this Hegelian image of the master-slave relationship for the relationship of colonizer and colonized also applies to the hierarchical relationship between men and women of the oppressed nation.

The postcolonial Korean discourse of nationalism, compounded by the Confucian patriarchal ideology of chastity[24] demands self-censorship from women not only because of the danger of real rape but because of the suspicion of conspiracy against the already disempowered Korean men. The women who come in close contact with the U.S. in the form of "American soldiers" are deemed dangerous to national integrity. These women are then relegated to the status of "prostitute." They are not only considered defiled but also traitors to the patriarchally constructed nation and outcasts at the boundary of that nation. What is it like to live as a woman in this postcolonial space permeated with masculine nationalism?

Decolonization and Multiple Subject Positions

I attended a girls' high school located next to the U.S. ambassador's residence. This residence occupies a large space next to the deserted building of the old Russian consulate, in which one of Korea's last rulers, Regent Taewŏngun, was taken hostage in 1896.[25] The area lies in the vicinity of the former headquarters of the Japanese colonial administration. Through this landscape of imperial contestation, high school girls clad in uniforms passed. The uniforms incarcerated female bodies aged between twelve and eighteen in navy blue tunics over *monpe* pants[26] donned with wide belts and shoulder pads that the Japanese colonial masters forced Korean girls to wear.[27] The uniform desexualized the teenage girls, who were emerging into womanhood, denied their femininity, and obliterated their individuality. Simply put, these uniformed girls were objectified. Here we need to remind ourselves that *chŏngsindae* girls were wearing the uniform of a similar design. *Chŏngsindae* or literally "the body-offering corps," were the Korean girls mobilized during the Pacific War under Imperial Japan's Manpower Mobilization Act. Promulgated in 1939, the Manpower Mobilization Act sent tens of thousands of Korean girls to Japan and other parts of Asia as a "voluntary" labor force working in various sectors of war industry. Soon the mobilization of girls extended to sexual slavery for the Japanese imperial soldiers at the war fronts. These were the so-called "military comfort women." The militaristic uniform that these girls wore, and that we, the female students in postcolonial South Korea inherited, was a signifier of mobilizable womanpower. The signifier of the colonial labor force, by extension, signified sex slavery. In this uniform we were herded by the roll call of our physical education teachers—those who were in charge of disciplining the girls' bodies—to line the streets of Seoul as the U.S. President Lyndon B. Johnson and his entourage, the U.S. Defense Secretary Dulles, and other dignitaries, passed. As if as part of our curriculum (as it was my mother's high school curriculum to carry human refuse to grow vegetables for the metropolis), we stood all day on the streets of Seoul, poised to wave the Stars and Stripes. As the procession of U.S. dignitaries divided the sea of red, white, and blue, we pledged our subordination and loyalty and demonstrated our gratitude to the U.S. for partitioning and making our land a Cold War fortress. Our uniformed bodies, as desexualized objects, were signifiers of a sexualized territory offered to the gaze of the dominating power. In this uniform we were also mobilized to "comfort" (notice the rhetoric!) the Blue Dragons or Fierce Tigers, the Vietnam-bound South Korean soldiers. Once again the uniformed, desexualized girls or unpolluted sacred (or sacrificial) prostitutes, the high school girls, were offered as a feast for the gaze of the soldiers. These mercenary soldiers were shipped to Vietnam for a monthly payment of a mere forty U.S. dollars and to confirm their sanguine allegiance (*hyŏlbang*) to the American soldiers.[28] Like the military prostitutes praised as nameless patriots for bringing foreign capital to the country, we uniformed high school girls were deployed to stimulate the soldiers earning the U.S. dollars and to fortify militant masculinity, while our sisters from the lower class were fulfilling their patriotic mission to develop the country by selling their labor and bodies[30] to bring in foreign capital. Yet this official offering of desexualized virgins for the visual consumption of foreign dignitaries and the encouragement of Vietnam-bound soldiers radically betrays the masculinists' own construction of the Korean female as a woman who should be available only for the Korean male and then only within the bounds of matrimony.

On the streets, the symbolic altar where the nation's daughters were offered, I used to encounter the "blue-eyed" American soldiers, the symbol of fetishized masculinity. These encounters were imbued with self-contradiction and ambiguity.. Wearing the brand of colonial objectification, I was fearful of being gazed at as a desired object, "*saekssi*," and gestured to display my dignity, de-signifying myself as an available object. At the same time, being desexualized in a uniform, I also felt a strong desire to be recognized as feminine: preening and defiantly straightening. I sensed, however, that regardless of my motivation, the act of preening itself could be suspected as a gesture of seduction, which evoked in me a sense of guilt and shame. This impasse was excruciating. While the nationalistic ideology of chastity demands that young women repress their sexuality, these same women were deployed by the state as *ersatz* prostitutes packaged in a desexualizing/objectifying uniform that was a sign of the colonial oppression of women. In this polyvalent field of significance, my urge to claim my feminine identity could never have been fulfilled in the sweeping postcolonial discourse of South Korean nationalism.

The theoretical homology of the colonizer as masculine and the colonized as feminine tends to obscure not only the multiplicity of subject positions of the colonized people, but also constructs women as purely sexualized objects, which is not to say that women are not objectified in the discourse of colonialism and nationalism. However, the critique of colonial objectification of colonized women itself complies with the discourse of alterity by eliding colonized women's multiple subjectivities.

Here one is reminded of Teresa de Lauretis's appropriation of "postcolonial" as a trope for feminism. She encompasses the postcolonial multiplicity of positions and histories that should include the difference between colonizer and the colonized. By the "postcolonial," de Lauretis means that "The female subject is one constituted across a multiplicity of discourses, positions and meanings which are often in conflict with one another and inherently historically contradictory."[31] However, De Lauretis's deployment of "postcoloniality" does not consider the positions of women who are differentially situated in global political and economic relations and overlooks the multiple subjectivities of women in the Third World who are caught in multivalent colonial relationships.

Such an oversight generates the often uncompromising tension between feminism and the discourse of nationalism developed in the "postcolonial" situation. The unifying impulse of nationalism demands moral purity, which is often articulated in gendered rhetoric. Nationalism represses ambivalence about and contradictions in women's subjectivity and therefore leaves no room to negotiate. Women of a postcolonial nation are denied an opportunity to decolonize their split (or multiple or hybrid) subjectivity, which is shaped under the colonial oppression. On that Pacific Highway, I was bedeviled by this specter of postcolonial schizophrenia and the nationalistic repression of feminine subjectivity. Postcolonial feminine subjectivity may be reified in a wide range of cultural fields: rejection and longing, denial and conformity, resistance and complicity. In this equivocality, inarticulate resentment breeds.

The dominant discourse of nationalism in postcolonial Korea strategically chooses to suppress women's equivocality to privilege the masculine subject of the nation. Gendered nationalism thus antagonizes women's self-contradiction and suspects women's desire for the recognition of multiple female subjectivities as a kind of whoring, while valorizing multiple male subjectivities as nationalistic and therefore heroic. The fraternal discourse that fails to address women's double subjugation is a fragmented discourse. A fragmented discourse of decolonization is a failed project in that it is destined to reproduce a totalizing colonial discourse, thereby hampering emancipation from oppression of any kind. A decolonization discourse must be a subversive project aimed at dethroning the universalizing hegemonic discourse.

NOTES

1. I thank Elaine Kim, Norma Field, Lisa Rofel, Lisa Yoneyama, Lauren Bryant, Chi Hyun Park, the participants of the "Colonialism and Modernity in East Asia" seminar at the University of California Humanities Research Institute, and the participants in the Gender and Society workshop at the University of Chicago, among others, for reading this essay and making helpful comments.

2. Ch'oe In-ho, *Tasi mannal ttaekkaji* [*Till We Meet Again*] in *Ch'oe In-ho* (Seoul: Samsung Ch'ulp'ansa, 1981). Ahn Junghyo [An Chŏng-hyo], *White Badge* (New York: Soho, 1989).

3. Rob Wilson, *Waking in Seoul* (Seoul: Minumsa, 1988), 113.

4. Bourdieu arrives at the notion of symbolic capital by way of the theory of gift economy developed by Marcel Mauss. See Pierre Bourdieu, *Outline of a Theory of Practice* (Cambridge: Cambridge University Press, 1977) and Marcel Mauss, *The Gift: Forms and Functions of Exchange in Archaic Societies* (New York: Norton, 1967).

5. See my "Transnational Capitalism, National Imaginary, and the Protest Theater in South Korea, "*boundary 2*, 22:1 (Spring 1995), 240–44.

6. This is an extension of Sedgwick's neologism, "homosocial." See Eve Kosofsky Sedgwick, *Between Men: English Literature and Male Homosocial Desire* (New York: Columbia University Press, 1985).

7. Much more detailed information will be presented in the special issue, "Comfort Women" *positions* 5:1 (Spring 1997).

8. bell hooks, "The Imperialism of Patriarchy," in *Ain't I a Woman* (Boston: South End Press, 1981).

9. Malek Alloula's *The Colonial Harem* offers a visual representation of sexualized colony. For a critique of cinematic construction of gendered relations Ella Shohat's analysis is very helpful. See Ella Shohat, "Gender and the Culture of Empire: Toward a Feminist Ethnography of the Cinema," *Quarterly Review of Film and Video*, Vol. 13 (Spring 1991), pp. 45–84.

10. Won Soon Park, *Kukka poanbŏp yŏngu* [*A Study of the National Security Law*] vol. 2 (Seoul: Yŏksa pip'yŏngsa, 1992).

11. The Republic of Korean Army, *Hanminjoggŭi yongtŭrim* [*The Dragon Rise of the Korean Nation*] (Seoul: Korean Army Headquarters, 1982).

12. I thank Bruce Cumings for this insight.

13. Seungsook Moon's chapter in this volume analyzes the national ethics textbooks that have been used as one of the most essential forms of ideological state apparatus and concludes that South Korean official construction of Korean identity is a masculinist discourse that valorizes and worships the warrior.

14. See Kim Mun-hwan, "Kae-p'yehoesiggŭi mihakchŏk sŏnggyŏk" ["The Aesthetic

Character of the Opening and Closing Ceremonies"] in *Sone son chapko, pyogŭl nŏmŏsŏ* [*Hand in Hand, Beyond all Barriers*] (Seoul: Hanguk pangsong saŏptan, 1988), 266.

15. See for instance Mercia Eliade, *Cosmos and Chaos: The Myth of the Eternal Return* (Princeton: Princeton University Press, 1957).

16. For more detail, see Seungsook Moon's essay in this volume.

17. Seungsook Moon, "Gendered State Nationalism," in *Economic Development and Gender Politics in South Korea (1963–1992)*, Unpublished Ph. D. dissertation, Brandeis University, 1994.

18. Brian Rigby, "From High Culture to Ordinary Culture," in *Popular Culture in Modern France* (New York: Routledge, 1991).

19. John Frow, "Tourism and the Semiotics of Nostalgia," *October* 57 (Summer, 1991), 136.

20. Renato Rosaldo, "Imperialist Nostalgia," in *Culture and Truth* (Boston: Beacon Press, 1989).

21. The adjective here is *hŏyŏn* rather than *hayan*. While the "a" sound of *hayan* projects lightness and cleanness, the "ŏ" sound of *hŏyŏn* evokes the feeling of opaqueness and uncleanness. The image of women with long straight (like *daikon*) legs of opaque and unclean complexion not only invokes Western women's long legs but also induces suspicion toward their opaqueness.

22. Partha Chatterjee, "The Nationalist Resolution of the Women's Question," in Kum-Kum Sangari and Sudesh Vaid eds., *Recasting Women: Essays in Indian Colonial History* (New Brunswick: Rutgers University Press, 1990).

23. George L. Mosse, *Nationalism and Sexuality: Middle-Class Morality and Sexual Norms in Modern Europe* (Madison: University of Wisconsin Press, 1985).

24. For a discussion on the brutality of Confucian ideology of chastity imposed on Korean women in general and the "comfort women" in particular, see my "Korean Women in the Culture of Inequality," Donald Clark ed., *Korea Briefing, 1992* (Boulder: Westview Press, 1992).

25. Agwanp'ach'ŏn. 1896.

26. *Monpe* are Japanese peasant women's pantaloons that tie around the ankles. Another variation of *monpe* was straight-legged slacks called *zubon* or *ssubon*, a Japanese loan word which was borrowed from the French word *jupon*. Here we see layers of colonial legacy imposed on Korean girls' bodies. The high school uniform was mandated in South Korea until 1980, thirty-five years after independence.

27. Most Japanese high school girls' uniforms of the prewar period were *serahuku* (sailor's clothes), that had wide (more feminine?) lapels decorated with white outlines and a short tie in the front, not the heavy tunic with a stiff collar matched with tied legs, which resembled the (Prussian derivated?) Japanese military's battle field uniform with puttees, which was imposed on Korean girls. Japanese high school girls' uniforms may be

discussed in the context of imposing on girls Japan's masculine national identity based on its naval force as evidenced in the prewar Japanese flag. In an American context, Peter Hulme points out that Europeans gave the newly discovered and conquered continent male derivative female names starting, with "America" from the name of its European male discoverer Amerigo, and thereafter, Georgia, Carolina, Virginia, etc. See Peter Hulme, "Polytropic Man: Tropes of Sexuality and Mobility in Early Colonial Discourse," in Francis Barker et al. eds., *Europe and Its Other*, volume 2, (Colchester: University of Essex, 1985). Norma Field's grandmother offers a personal narrative about the origin of the Japanese girls' *serahuku*: her father, who was an affluent drapery businessman, had it made for her fashioning after the British sailor's uniform that he had seen at the British Embassy in Tokyo. The *serahuku* attracted the eyes of her school principal, who adopted it as the school's uniform. Soon other schools followed the suit (personal communication with Norma Field). But why girls were homogenized in the uniform still remains to be answered. Morio Watanabe argues that the sailor uniform for girls began in the postwar Japan, which may indicate Japan's compensation fantasy in the war they could have won against the West. See Morio Watanabe, "The Images of War in Contemporary Japanese Popular Culture," presented at the conference on "The Politics of Remembering the Asia/Pacific War," East-West Center, Honolulu, September 7–9, 1995.

28. For a related discussion in more detail, see Katharine Moon's essay in this volume.

29. Diana Lee and Grace Yoon Kyung Lee, *Camp Arirang* (New York: Third World Newsreel, 1995).

30. Sex tourism was apparently part of the South Korean government's policy in the 1970s as a way of attracting foreign tourists to Korea. See Pyon Young-joo's documentary film, *Asiaesŏ yŏsŏngŭro sandanŭn kŏt* [*Living in Asia as a Woman*], (Seoul: P'unŭn Yŏngsang, 1993).

31. Teresa de Lauretis, *Technologies of Gender: Essays on Theory, Film, and Fiction* (Bloomington: Indiana University Press, 1987), ix–x.

3

SEUNGSOOK MOON

Begetting the Nation:
The Androcentric Discourse of National
History and Tradition in South Korea

Rapid economic growth in East Asia
in general and South Korea in particular has generated a body of literature attempting to formulate a "successful" model of economic development. Searching for factors contributing to this economic growth, scholars of economic development tend to emphasize such cultural factors as
Confucianism and nationalism.[1] By nationalism, I refer to a set of ideas
and practices designed to build an independent nation that is supposed
to be a unified community, distinguished from others by its essential
culture, tradition, and history. This definition suggests that there is more
than one type of nationalism, depending upon who produces the ideas
about a nation and how to build it. In this article I am concerned with
official nationalism (or state nationalism)[2] and its implications for

gender hierarchy in contemporary Korea. Specifically, I will focus on the discursive form of nationalism produced by the state during the period of rapid industrialization under consecutive military regimes (1961–1987).

The Korean state as a major agent of industrialization since the early 1960s has tried to utilize nationalism as a way to legitimize repression and exploitation of the populace throughout the process. Industrialization as a national project gained priority in the postwar period of economic development. The reality of the Cold War has also shaped nationalist rhetoric, which touts "the building of a prosperous and strong Korean nation." Specifically, the issue of national defense has become crucial to state nationalism in Korea, due to the unique experience of the Korean War and the continuing military confrontation between North and South. The effectiveness of state nationalism depends upon the collective memory of Japanese colonization and the Korean war, as well as on popular recognition of neo-colonial aspects of the American military and strategic dominance in Korea and Korea's technological and economic dependence upon the United States and Japan.

However, the state's attempt to conjure up the image of a timeless Korean nation through representations of its history and tradition is highly contradictory because this very discursive practice masks the marginalization of women and their exclusion from the putatively homogeneous and egalitarian community. This inconsistency is exemplified in the androcentric subtext of the official discourse of national history and tradition.

This essay is divided into three parts. First, I will situate the discursive form of official nationalism dealing with Korean history and tradition in the larger historical and social context of Korean nationalism and Third World nationalism. Second, I will analyze its androcentric subtext by focusing on books and articles produced by President Park Chung Hee (the main architect of official nationalism), the Ministry of Education, and state-sponsored research organizations—i.e., the Association of National Ethics Education Research (*Kungmin yulli kyoyuk yŏn'guhoe*), which was inaugurated in 1972 and renamed Association of National Ethics Studies (*Kungmin yulli hakhoe*) in 1980, and the Institute of Korean Mental Culture Research (*Chŏngsin munhwa yŏnguwŏn*), which was founded in 1978. In particular, I concentrate on texts dealing with Korean history, tradition, ethics, thoughts, and culture that comprise the discourse of national history and tradition. Then I will discuss the extent to which women resist androcentric official nationalism tinted with militarism and anti-democratic traditionalism. For this purpose, I will focus on women's movements organized around the issues of family law reform and exploitation in factories, which challenge the ideas behind official nationalism. Finally, I will argue that it is important to examine the discursive form of official nationalism, because it reveals the androcentric view of a nation that military regimes have tried to build through the ideology of economic development. The nation envisioned in official nationalism is a patrilineal community of men, the order of which is rooted in essentialized differences between women and men. These differences are ultimately hierarchical, as images of men and women represented and implied in the nationalist discourse illustrate. Official nationalism, which constructs the Korean nation as a community of men in which women exist merely as its precondition, has serious implications for gender relations in contemporary Korea. Although some women have resisted the androcentric order of Korean society, economic development pursued with such a view of nation cannot bring about any substantial change in a persisting gender hierarchy.

Historical and Social Context of State Nationalism Under Authoritarian Military Rule

With the establishment of the Republic of Korea (1948), the postcolonial state adopted nationalism as an ideology of political legitimation. All postcolonial regimes in Korea have tried to exploit popular nationalist sentiments in order to legitimize their authoritarian rule. During the First Republic (1948–1960), Rhee Syngman's regime tried to countervail its tenuous legitimacy with nationalist rhetoric based on anti-Communism and anti-Japanism. Park Chung Hee, who led the 1961 military coup d'état, which was followed by three decades of authoritarian military rule, attempted to justify the overthrow of the democratically elected Second Republic (1960–1961) in the name of "national reconstruction."

Apart from varying degrees of criticism and praise, Park was unquestionably a central figure who laid the groundwork not only for the modern South Korean economy but also for the discursive form of official nationalism. During the junta period (1961–1963) Park, as the Chairman of the Supreme Council for National Reconstruction, launched the ideology of official nationalism with the themes of "self-reliant economy," "self-reliant defense" based on fierce anti-Communism, and "national character." Since then, the postcolonial state has adopted the triple goal of modernizing the nation through capitalist industrialization, defending it against the Communist North, and establishing a national identity in the midst of the rapid socio-economic change. This issue of national identity has been crucial to the state because that is what the nation-state is supposed to represent. The discursive form of official nationalism that I will analyze exemplifies the ways in which the state imagines the nation by invoking Korean history and tradition.

Park's nationalist themes as the mainstay of official nationalism share certain elements with earlier forms of nationalism of the colonial period as well as at the turn of the century. First of all, there is a common nationalist interest in "restoring" history and tradition as the essence of the nation. In the 1920s and 1930s, such folklorists as Ch'oe Nam-sŏn, Yi Nŭng-hwa, and Son Chin-t'ae attempted to reclaim Korean history and tradition from the Japanese interpretation of them.[3] Second, Park seems to have borrowed rhetoric and ideas from earlier forms of nationalism. Thus he utilized the themes of "reconstruction" and "self-reliance," first made current by the Protestant nationalist intellectuals such as Yun Ch'i-ho and An Ch'ang-ho.[4] As I will show later, Park also employed the idea of *tongdo sogi* (morality of the East and technology of the West), which was the hallmark of the elite nationalism that emphasized social reforms toward the end of the Chosŏn Dynasty (1392–1910).[5]

The themes of "self-reliant economy" and "national character" are not unique to Korean official nationalism. They have become nationalist concerns shared by Third World elites, which were often used to appeal to populaces in the period of decolonization after the end of World War II. What is crucial to the nationalist link between the two themes is the emergence of the ideology of development, which views economic growth as a formulaic achievement based on capital, technology, and the market system of the West. In this hegemonic framework, economic development inevitably involves Westernization, which is at the same time perceived to be a threat to national identity. In this situation, Third World elites consider the issues of economic development and national identity as a dilemma. Consequently, the project of modernization (*choguk kŭndaehwa*) concomitant with the increasing adoption of Western institutions and practices, can engender fertile grounds for traditionalism.

Park tried to resolve this dilemma by resorting to the turn-of-the-century nationalist principle of *tongdo sŏgi*.[6] Although he subscribed to the idea of "modernization" to "build a prosperous and strong Korean nation," he was suspicious of such Western values as liberal democracy and individualism.[7] From his junta period (1961–1963) on, he articulated as his goal the building of Korean-style democracy—i.e., "administrative democracy." Like many nationalist elites, he tended to believe that the unchecked influx of Western values and the indiscreet imitation of Western institutions during the First Republic (1948–1960) and the Second Republic (1960–1961) led to not only social disorder but also the weakening of Korean national consciousness. Therefore, from the beginning of his regime Park was conscious of counteracting Western liberalism in the midst of rapid modernization.[8]

However, the theme of "self-reliant defense" emerged as a result of the unique Korean experience of the Cold War. Koreans have lived through the national division, which resulted in the separation of ten million family members. The Korean War generated two million casualties. Military tensions between North and South have persisted for decades. Anti-Communist sentiments among the populace have been quite strong because of the bloody civil war triggered by the Communist North's invasion and because of the perceived threat of an impending war. Although not explicitly reflected in the official discourse of national history and tradition, anti-Communism plays a significant role in producing an official nationalism that contains a strong militaristic strand and therefore implications for gender hierarchy in Korean society.

Predictably, the military regimes saw education as a means to foster national consciousness, which they equated with "Korean tradition" and anti-Communism in the historical context of developmentalism and the Cold War. Park Chung Hee argued that Korean education should be able to produce not just an educated person but a "Korean." This view was well illustrated by the state's extensive control over the production and distribution of primary and secondary school textbooks. Under both Park's rule and later Chun Doo-hwan's, the state either published the textbooks or approved them before their distribution. These regimes also implemented a series of educational reforms in 1963, 1973, 1981, and 1987 in order to incorporate anti-Communism and authoritarian traditionalism into textbooks, particularly for such subjects as Anti-Communist Morality (*pankong todŏk*), Right Living (*parŭn saenghwal*), National Ethics (*kun'gmin yulli*), National History (*kuksa*), and National Language (*kugŏ*).[9]

The state's effort to build national consciousness through education was not limited to young students. In 1968 Park proclaimed the Charter of National Education, which began with the sentence, "we were born into this land with a historical mission for national restoration." The Charter was printed on the first page of every textbook and government publication. It was displayed with the picture of President Park and the Korean national flag in every public building. Similarly, in 1981 Chun's regime launched the "national mentality education" (*kungmin chŏngsin kyoyuk*) campaign into which issues of "unification and national security," "national ethics," "national economy," and "social purification" were integrated.[10]

Yet it was not until the Fourth Republic (1972–1979) that the state elaborated its nationalist discourse with growing attention to Korean tradition, especially thought and ethics. This escalating traditionalism took place in the context of the political change marked by the end of popular election under the *Yusin* Constitution. This signified the hardening of authoritarian rule during the Third Republic, which stirred up popular protests. This situation necessitated the escalation of the state's ideological control of citizens, especially (male) university students, who played a significant role in challenging authoritarian politics since the overthrow of the First Republic in 1960. In this milieu, the Association of National Ethics Education Research (*Kungmin yulli kyoyuk yŏn'guhoe*) was created in 1972 to conduct research on national ethics education at the university level. The inauguration of the Association of National Ethics Education Research was immediately followed, in 1973, by another educational reform that emphasized national security and Korean tradition. The subject of national ethics was initially created for high school curricula at the beginning of the Third Republic, through 1963 educational reform measures.[11] Since then, national ethics had become a central issue in the official nationalist discourse.[12] The Association was composed of pro-government professors, whom I call "state intellectuals." Although it did not have any official status, it functioned as a state research center, fully funded by the Ministry of Education. In 1980, during the political transition to the Fifth Republic, it was renamed Association of National Ethics Studies (*Kungmin yulli hakhoe*).[13]

The foundation of the Institute of Korean Mental Culture Research in 1978 also illustrates the state's growing interests in Korean tradition, especially ethics and thinking. Park was a key figure in the establishment of this institute. He articulated the need for a specialized center for studying Korean culture in a 1976 presidential decree. His rationale was that it was time to pay sufficient attention to Korean tradition and culture, which had been pushed aside by the exigencies of economic growth.[14] A group of professors was recruited for this research institute. They soon formulated a plan to establish a graduate school of Korean Studies, which was approved by the state in 1979. Equipped with state-sponsored finances and sophisticated intellectuals, this institute made a major contribution to the production of official nationalist discourse in the 1980s, until the formal end of the military rule in 1987.

In the following section, I will analyze the androcentric subtext of the official nationalism authored by President Park, the Ministry of Education, and the state intellectuals working in or affiliated with the aforementioned state-sponsored research organizations. Authors of official nationalism consciously or unwittingly select various elements concerning Korean history, traditional thinking, and ethics, as well as images of a "desirable" (*paramjikhan*) Korean from the complex of Korea's past. By combining those elements, they construct antiquity and the uniqueness of the Korean nation. Their representation of Korean history and tradition sometimes makes questionable links among those selected elements. I am not primarily concerned here with verifying narrative constructs, although I try to discuss them in endnotes.

Korean Nation of Men and by Men

Pivotal androcentric themes emerging from official nationalist Korean histories are the Tan'gun myth and various national crises caused by foreign invasion and patriotic struggle. The importance of the Tan'gun myth lies in its explanation of the origin of the Korean nation.[15] During the colonial period, nationalist folklorists such as Ch'oe Nam-sŏn, Yi Nŭng-hwa, and Son Chin-t'ae also paid special attention to this myth of national foundation. Their investigation into the national origin had a special meaning under the colonial policy of acculturation that tried to Japanize the Koreans. Hence, it was an effort to resist the colonial policy of eliminating Korean identity. Contemporary authors of official nationalism picked up the Tan'gun myth that had gained hegemony due to its significance to colonial nationalism. As a result, it has become the basis of the national calendar and a national holiday. Despite its historical ambiguity, 2333 B.C., the reputed year of the foundation of the oldest Korean state by Tan'gun, is accepted as an historical fact. Since national independence from Japan, the Tan'gun's year (*tangi*) which adds 2333 to the dominical year, has been used along with the latter. In addition, October 3rd has become a national holiday (*kaech'ŏnjŏl*) commemorating the foundation of Korea by Tan'gun.[16]

According to Tan'gun myth, Korean history started with Tan'gun wang'gŏm, the legendary founder of the Korean nation, roughly five millennia ago.[17] He was the son of Hwanung, an illegitimate son of Hwanin, the heavenly lord, and Wungnyŏ (which literally means a "bear-woman"). The story relates that illegitimate Hwanung (literally meaning "heavenly male") was interested in ruling the human world, and his father allowed him to descend on earth with his entourage and magical power. One day, a bear and a tiger anxious to become humans asked Hwanung to fulfill their wish. He ordered them to stay in a cave without sunlight and to eat garlic for one hundred days. While the tiger failed to observe this command, the bear patiently followed it and became a woman. Then Hwanung married the bear-woman and begot Tan'gun.[18] The representation of gender is noteworthy in this narrative. In the myth, the woman is depicted merely as the bearer of the heir, thereby suggesting that woman's only contribution to the creation of the Korean nation was the provision of a proto-nationalist womb. In other words, it implies that the Korean nation is ultimately the community of men, created by an extraordinary man, in which women exist only as its precondition.[19]

This nationalist view of women, more precisely of women's bodies, is pervasive in state-sponsored family planning, which has been official-ly incorporated in the Five-Year Economic Development Plans. Male state bureaucrats who implement family planning policy tend to use the rationale that women are expected to accept birth control because unchecked population growth will jeopardize the economic growth of the nation.[20] In other words, women's patriotism means submitting to the state anti-natal policy for controlling their nationalist wombs.

The heavenly man, Hwanung, and the bear-woman symbolize the essentialized difference between men and women and gender hierarchy as the very foundation of the Korean nationhood. While the man comes from heaven, his female counterpart is not only a mere earthling but is also of sub-human origins.[21] Her animal roots place her close to nature, whereas his celestial roots distance him from it. She stands for women who produce sons for the nation as the community of men. In addition, the transformation of a bear into a woman carries the deep social meaning of womanhood epitomized by patience to endure suf-fering and ordeal.

Furthermore, the narrative depicts Hwanung as an illegitimate son.[22] The issue of "illegitimacy" reflects a set of patriarchal social relations in which women are subordinated to men in the institutions of marriage and patrilineal kinship. It also indicates a hierarchy among women based on their marital status and sexual relations with men—e.g., mar-ried and legitimate wives, married but illegitimate concubines, and unmarried and illegitimate mistresses. This kind of division among women reveals a patriarchal strategy to control women—i.e., divide and rule. An implicit but powerful message in the Tan'gun myth is that patriarchy existed from the beginning of Korean history and even before, and is a "natural" part of Korean culture. It is also implied that change would reduce Korean-ness or even dissolve the order of the Korean nation. In fact, as I will show later, this kind of fear was expressed by self-proclaimed Confucianists whenever reform of family laws was discussed.

The nationalist discourse on history tends to highlight numerous invasions of Korea and patriotic struggles. This approach to Korean history represents the nation created by Tan'gun being defended by men, especially by "righteous warriors." The discourse emphasizes the following events of foreign invasions and patriotic defenses that have become familiar to Koreans through formal schooling and mass media.[23] This line of history starts with Wu-ti, the Emperor of the Han Dynasty, who invaded Kochosŏn, the oldest Korean state, and established Chinese commanderies at the sites of his conquest. However, they were reclaimed by the kingdom of Kogŭryŏ (?–A.D. 668). In the seventh century, Kogŭryŏ also fought with the Sui and the T'ang dynasties of China. General Uljimundŏk saved the nation by defeating Yangti, the Sui Emperor who invaded Kogŭryŏ with 1,130,000 troops, near the Salsu river. Park and some state intellectuals praise Kogŭryŏ for its courageous, strong and martial spirit and its role as a bulwark of the Korean nation in history. They represent it as the glorious and independent past of the Korean nation, which is to be revived.[24]

The nationalist discourse cites the invasion by the T'ang dynasty around the time of the "national unification" of the Three Kingdoms by Silla (?–A.D. 668) in the mid-seventh century.[25] Collaborating with Silla for the conquest of the two other kingdoms, Kogŭryŏ and Paekche (?–A.D. 660), T'ang attempted to annex the conquered territory to its own empire. Silla successfully drove out T'ang from the Korean Peninsula and unified Korea. According to the discourse, this unification by Silla, which developed later than the two kingdoms and was isolated by its geography, is attributable to the patriotic spirit of a *hwarang* (flower boy) and *hwarangdo* (the code of the elite youth corps).[26] I will return to the idea of *hwarangdo* later in the discussion of the construction of Korean tradition.

The nationalist discourse points out the Mongol invasion of the Koryŏ Dynasty (A.D. 918–1392) in the early thirteenth century in order to provide evidence of the strong spirit of national defense. Despite the devastating war and forty years of Mongol rule (1231–1270), the Korean nation survived. A text published by the Research Center for Peace and Unification suggests that *sambyŏlch'o*, a special capital defense unit during the Koryŏ Dynasty, fought to the last man without surrendering to the Mongol invaders.[27]

Another national crisis was the Japanese invasion of 1592–1599, during which the Korean nation was defended by Admiral Yi and *ŭibyŏng*, which literally means "righteous soldiers." They are called righteous because they volunteered for patriotic sacrifice. In the post-1961 period, Admiral Yi was elevated to the position of a "sacred hero" who saved the nation from total destruction and inspired many young men who inherited the spirit of *hwarang* to join *ŭibyŏng*. These warriors were not professional men of the sword who were duty-bound to fight for the nation, but Confucian scholars, Buddhist monks, and peasants who were all, of course, male. They collaborated to save the nation, regardless of their religious and economic differences. A text published by the Research Center for Peace and Unification mentions the battle of Haengju Castle, in which General Kwŏn Yul, who was a civil official prior to the invasion, and Cho Yŏng, a Buddhist monk, went into battle together.[28]

According to the nationalist discourse, foreign invasions and the patriotic defenses by *ŭibyŏng* reached their peak in the late nineteenth and the early twentieth centuries, especially during the period between the annexation of Korea to Japan (1905) and its colonization (1910).[29] Moreover, the patriotic spirit of righteous fighters did not die out after the colonization of Korea. It underlay militant nationalist struggles in the Korean Peninsula and abroad until the end of colonial rule.

This specific representation of Korean history, which is quite familiar to the general public, reveals the androcentric and often militaristic nature of official nationalism. The continuous necessity to defend the Korean nation masculinizes it by linking citizenship to soldiering. This also exposes the discrepancy between seemingly egalitarian membership in a nation and its gendered nature by pointing to the reality that some Koreans are more legitimate than others; men, especially able-bodied young ones who can be warriors, are more legitimate than women.

The militaristic tint in constructing a male warrior as the legitimate subject of Korean history appears to have been stronger during the 1970s when military authoritarian rule became more rigid. For example, the first book published for the National Ethics Series by a state-sponsored research association in 1979 was *Korean Soldiers' Spirit*. A drift toward militaristic expansionism in official nationalism sometimes appears quite explicitly. For example, *Investigation of the Image of a Korean* (1974), published by Korean Education Development Institute, mentions that the "national spirit" runs through the Kingdom of Kogŭryŏ, which conquered Manchuria; the Kingdom of Paekche, which attempted to conquer the Shan Tung peninsula in China; and the Unified Silla, which attempted to be the tributary center in East Asia.

Despite its anachronistic nature, this ethos of militaristic expansionism is well institutionalized in the Korean Military Academy established by President Rhee (1948–1960) in the midst of the Korean War. Modeled after West Point, this four-year military academy started as a key instrument to realize Rhee's official policy of "marching-to-the-north" unification. Since its opening in 1951 *"pukchin t'ongil, kot'o hoebok"* (unification by marching to the north, recovery of old territories) has become a central slogan embedded in the daily routine of salute practices as well as elementary military training for new cadets. This motto was also inscribed on the academy's buildings until 1988 when Korea held the Summer Olympics in Seoul. Its elimination was probably motivated by an official concern with Korea's image during that international event. Yet, the practice of shouting the motto at the time of salute and during elementary training continues.[30]

Androcentrism tinted with militarism is best articulated by President Park himself. As one of his initial speeches after the coup illustrates, he conceives of the Korean nation as a community of men. His junta spoke to its "beloved brethren" of the "inevitability" of military "revolution" and the necessity of supporting it.[31] His initial calls for patriotism contain a strong desire to build a fully masculine Korea. Park was ambitious

44

to reconstruct the Korean nation by "recovering" ancient histories, "especially those concerning the knighthood of Kogŭryŏ and *hwarang*."[32] He argued that the long history of vassalage to succeeding Chinese empires since the Koryŏ Dynasty undermined the spirit of Korean independence and ultimately Korean masculinity. He wrote:

> The Korean tragedy is basically different from the tragedy of Western Europe. The West European tragedy fights fate and dies gloriously . . . We do not have any of the manly tragic consciousness of the West. We want sentimental sympathy. This weak and frail desire for maudlin sympathy cannot foster true human courage among the populace nor engender a genuine pioneering spirit in life . . . [Confucian formalism] was so obsessed with ceremonies, rites, and manners that it did not achieve any beneficial social result . . . [Consequently] "honor" (in the sense of Western European chivalry) did not develop . . . The real national image of the great man was not that of a weak pedant but rather of a patriotic fighter who would readily die on the battlefield in defense of his country. [33]

As I pointed out earlier, this strand of militarism in official nationalism reflects the reality of national division, the bloody civil war, and military confrontation between North and South that has lasted for decades. The Korean Peninsula has become one of the most militarized regions in the world. In this unique milieu, militarism, which values male soldiery, has underlain such ruling ideologies as national security and anti-Communism. These ideologies in turn enabled the military regimes to manage to stay in power until the late 1980s. To be sure, they have been challenged by participants in the dissident movement, especially radical students, religious leaders, intellectuals, and politicians opposed to the military dictatorship. Yet the general public has accepted the dominant ideologies.

Constructing Korean Tradition

The nationalist history of Korea, represented in terms of foreign invasions and defense by patriotic warriors, conjures up the antiquity of the Korean nation. Yet this is not sufficient to establish its unique identity in a period of rapid modernization. The increasing influx of "Western" values and attitudes in the process of aggressive industrialization, accompanied by rapid integration into the global market, has led to a popular concern for Korean identity.[34] The military regimes have recognized this issue and exploited it in order to secure their rule.

A text published by the Research Center for Peace and Unification defines Korean tradition as "what Korean people thought and think" and "what contributes to the development of Korean thoughts."[35] Reflecting the earlier nationalist strategy of *tongdo sŏgi*, an underlying rationale here is that the modernization or transformation of Korea into a strong and wealthy nation does not mean becoming like Westerners. Although Koreans change their appearance, their real identity lies deep in their thinking or spirit, which is not to be affected by the Westernization of material life.[36]

The nationalist discourse produced by Park, the Ministry of Education, and the state intellectuals portrays the spirit of Tan'gun, the spirit of *hwarang*, "state-protecting Buddhism," and Confucianism as the principal elements of Korean tradition. As we will see, all these components of Korean tradition are interpreted in such a way as to articulate the interests of male ruling elites.[37] A critical content analysis of textbooks on national history (*kuksa*) and national language (*kukŏ*) taught in primary and secondary schools since the late 1950s also reveals a similar bias in the construction of Korean tradition.[38]

In line with his privileged position as the founder of the Korean nation, Tan'gun's spirit occupies a special place in the officially represented Korean tradition. According to the nationalist discourse, Tan'gun's spirit constitutes indigenous Korean religion, thoughts, and ethics as opposed to Buddhism and Confucianism, which were imported and Koreanized. The ideas of *kyŏngch'ŏn aein* (worshipping Heaven, loving human beings) and *hongik ingan* (widely benefiting human beings) epitomize Tan'gun's spirit. The idea of *hongik ingan* is said to be Tan'gun's spirit of national foundation (*kŏnkuk inyŏm*). Officially, it has been adopted as a philosophical tenet of formal education since the establishment of the Republic of Korea (1948). Han Sŭng-jo, a leading state intellectual, argues that these ideas of *kyŏngch'ŏn aein* and *hongik ingan* later developed into the Korean brand of humanism. This tradition that values human life and promotes collective welfare runs through Korean history.[39]

Han also argues that in association with Tan'gun's humanism, the Confucian notion of *minbon juŭi* provides the traditional basis for Korean democracy. *Minbon juŭi* refers to the belief that the basis of ruling or polity is the people, that is, the ruled. The notion of Heaven is central to this belief, as is Tan'gun's humanism. Both the spirit of Tan'gun and Confucianism draw the basis of political authority from Heaven. Confucianism as a philosophy of rulers relies upon the moral concept of the Heaven's Mandate (*ch'ŏn myŏng*) in order to legitimize otherwise naked power. Given the unity of Heaven, earth, and human beings, Heaven as the source of legitimacy means that ruling is based on those who are ruled. Ruling in harmony with the Heaven's Mandate means, in principle, ruling for the people. In other words, politics is about taking care of the ruled and this politics for the people is represented as the Korean tradition of democracy.[40]

Aside from the paternalistic and moralistic characteristics of this definition of democracy, there are conceptual limits to the notion of *minbon juŭi* . First of all, it does not address who decides what kind of needs are to be taken care of and how. This silence is conducive to administrative dictatorship in the Tocquevillean sense. When there is little room for grassroots participation in political processes, people will at best be depoliticized by the mere satisfaction of immediate material needs. In addition, the Confucian idea does not discuss what people can do when politics fails to respond to their needs. This absence is not conducive to democratic politics based on equality among individuals.[41]

Some state intellectuals try to vindicate the absence of the notion of individual equality in Korean "humanism" (*inbon juŭi*) with the emphasized presence of Korean "community consciousness" (*kongdongch'e ŭisik*). This refers to a priority of the collective over individuals. Lee Tong-jun and Han Sŭng-jo argue that the Korean people have maintained their oneness since the foundation of the nation by Tan'gun. *Paedal minjok*, the self-referential term for the Koreans, constructs their oneness.[42] Moreover, millennia-old agrarian life has generated a strong sense of belonging to one's community. One sees oneself not as an individual but as a member of one's community. They affirm this "commu-

47

nity consciousness" as an essence of Korean identity in contradistinction to the "Western identity" based on individualism. Furthermore, the nationalist discourse represents "Western individualism" in relation to pursuits of selfish interests and praises the Korean collective orientation grounded primarily in Confucian social relations as well as Buddhist transcendence and selflessness.[43]

As core values of the "community consciousness" (as opposed to Western individualism), the nationalist discourse emphasizes loyalty to the state (ch'ung), which is equated with the nation, and filial piety to the parents (hyo). It represents these "Korean values" as being derived from Confucianism. This conservative tendency to revive the ideas of ch'ung and hyo was especially strong during the 1970s, when the state launched the ch'ung hyo education campaign in schools at all levels. The following excerpt illustrates the focus on individual duty to presumably natural units of collective life—i.e., the family and the state—without safeguarding the rights of the individual.

> According to Nature's laws, the earth sprouts seeds, produces flowers and fruits. And old leaves fall, are decomposed, and become fertilizer for new lives. Ancestors infer the ethics of human relations from this and live accordingly. Parents love their children, and the children feel grateful to their parents and perform filial piety. A husband loves his wife, and she respects him. All of them consider one another constituting one body which cannot survive without the roles that they play. Therefore, antagonism makes survival impossible. It is not an issue at home whether parents come first, children come first, the husband comes first, or the wife comes first. All of them are masters by playing their roles.[44]

What is noticeable in this emphasis on Korean collective orientation is that it tries to legitimize the lack of civic freedom under military rules in terms of Korean tradition. In other words, anti-democratic tradition becomes useful to the ruling elite when they perceive political participation of grassroots and decentralization as counter-productive and destabilizing. The state has to mobilize the populace to achieve economic growth but at the same time keep the grassroots politically obedient and loyal to it. One way to cope with this challenge of democracy is to invent Korean tradition. This makes not only the Korean nation distinct from other nations, but it also can be used to legitimize problems of democracy in terms of a "Korean style" of modernization rooted in Korean tradition.

In addition, the idea of collective orientation feminizes the grassroots in relation to the masculine nation-state by demanding their selfless sacrifice. The masculinity of national identity represented in official nationalism can be seen quite explicitly in the discussion of *hwarang* (flower boy, or the "flower of male youth"). Interestingly, this appears to be the single most frequently discussed subject in the nationalist discourse on history and tradition. A *hwarang* was originally a youth from an aristocratic family in the ancient Kingdom of Silla, who became a member of an occult religious group. Following the priestly class of Sŏn'gyo (mountain-spirit religion), a Korean version of Siberian shamanism that was characterized by worshipping a mountain spirit as the supreme manifestation of the heavenly spirit on earth, the elite youth cultivated themselves by practicing ancestor worship, nature worship, poetry writing, and martial arts. They purified themselves by bathing, wearing white clothes, facing the east where the sun rises, and carrying out pilgrimages to high mountains.[45]

Later, during the reign of King Chinhŭng (A.D. 540–576), the *hwarang* were transformed into a band of elite warriors. Each of them, like a military officer, led a group of subordinates called *nangdo*. This change reflects the Silla state's need to supply well-trained soldiers at the time of its expansion during the period between the sixth and seventh centuries. A text published by the Center for Peace and Unification states ironically, "these young people [*hwarang*] were organized into warrior groups and this organization became a source of supply of warriors in the year of King Chinhung, the Elite Youth Corps was under state control, and the state trained them."[46]

According to the nationalist discourse on tradition, *hwarang's* religious practices originate in Tan'gun's religion. *The Identity of the Korean People* represents the institution of *hwarang* as a splendid synthesis of Korean thought—Sŏn'gyo, Buddhism, Confucianism, and even Taoism.[47] It uses the *hwarang sesok ogye* (five secular injunctions of *hwarang*) as evidence of the synthesis. The five injunctions were made by Wŏnkwang, a highly regarded sixth-century Silla Buddhist. The rules are: 1) loyalty to one's king, 2) filial piety to one's parents, 3) no retreat

49

in battle, 4) fraternity with fellow *hwarang*, and 5) mercy in taking lives. The first and second injunctions reflect Confucian concepts of *ch'ung* and *hyo*, which emphasize the obligation of subordinates to pertinent authorities. Since this version of Confucianism as a philosophy of rulers presents hierarchical differences as the order of things, the ruled are at the mercy of a ruler's good will, which is paternalistic at best. The fifth injunction mirrors a modified Buddhist precept against killing. Yet, this version of Buddhism as a state ideology, like Confucianism, serves rulers' interests in safeguarding their state. It is not clear how Sŏn'gyo plays a part in these injunctions except that *hwarang* were originally followers of Sŏn'gyo priests. What is noteworthy here is that the nationalist discourse equates Korean tradition with that of male ruling elites by conflating their interest with the nationalist spirit of protecting the nation.

President Park (1961–1979), who came from the military, idealized the *hwarang* as the paragon of a Korean—i.e., a young, patriotic, male warrior. According to him, a *hwarang* is, first of all, a warrior who will not retreat in battle. He is a public man who will sacrifice himself for the sake of honor and national welfare, a humanist who can restrain himself from killing in battle, and a man of nature who can enjoy leisure time being in and appreciating nature.[48] Although tinted with Buddhist and romantic values, these virtues still reflect militarism and Confucian hierarchy. The idealized representation of *hwarang* can be understood as the expression of a militaristic undercurrent of androcentrism constitutive of official nationalism. Consequently, Park sees the nation as a community of fellow men, who are ideally young, courageous, and patriotic warriors.[49]

This militaristic selfhood of the "desirable Korean" Park constructs in his emphasis on *hwarang* may have been resisted by state intellectuals, who seem to pay more attention to *sŏnbi*, a generic term for Confucian scholars of the Yi Dynasty, as another desired type of a Korean.[50] Yet, this image of a Korean is not necessarily incongruent with that of the righteous warrior, because a *sŏnbi* would turn himself into a patriotic fighter in times of national crisis, as the narratives on national history maintain. State intellectuals sometimes display militaristic tendencies by echoing the idea that national independence is ultimately guaranteed by military superiority because national history

50

is characterized by foreign invasion and patriotic defense. For example, Min Tong-kŭn deplores the loss of Korean sovereignty at the end of Chosŏn Dynasty (1392–1910), and attributes that loss to the lack of military might.[51]

In discussing "Korean values" rooted in tradition, official nationalism constructs another version of the selfhood of a Korean—the male head of the family. For example, an educational text, *For Ordinary People of Our Time* (1986/1988), which was published presumably for all adult Koreans, is filled with gender stereotypes. It represents women as passive, meek, gullible, and talkative housewives. Similarly, *Investigation of the Image of a Korean* (1974) is replete with both Confucian and contemporary values and attitudes that a "desirable" Korean should internalize. Yet, the text explicitly states that although social service is important, it is absurd for a woman who cannot raise her child and respect her husband and the elderly (at home) to participate in social activities. Women's exemption from social service due to domestic duties illustrates the extent to which women are marginalized in the community of male citizens.

Mapping Women's Resistance to Androcentric Nationalism

The discussion of official nationalism containing androcentrism, militarism, and anti-democratic traditionalism so far raises a crucial question about the existence of women's resistance to it. It is not easy to identify a direct counterdiscourse to it for the following reasons. First, the repressive politics based on surveillance and vengeful punishment did not allow the explicit articulation of counterdiscourses. Second, the nationalist discourse of history and tradition was produced largely in isolation from the public. Under the military authoritarian rule from 1961 to 1987, state activities were marked by their technocratic and anti-democratic orientation. Citizens were reduced to objects of manipulation and followers of ready-made decisions, although this has never been completely successful, as is shown by the continuous presence of grassroots movements.[52] In this milieu, the production of knowledge about national history and tradition was the exclusive domain of professional experts who were pro-government scholars in this case. Third, despite the exclusive nature of the production of the nationalist discourse proper, its salient elements were internalized by many Koreans through mass media as well as textbooks for such subjects as Morality, National History, and National Ethics. Consequently, the Tan'gun myth, the history of foreign invasion and patriotic defense, the Tan'gun spirit, Confucianism, and Buddhism became widely accepted by the populace as basic ingredients of Korean culture. The hegemonic nature of the nationalist discourse reduces the possibility of an explicit counterdiscourse.

However, it is valid to focus on the women's movement in contemporary Korea as indirect resistance to official nationalism, which constructs the nation as the community of men and defended by men, in which women exist merely as a precondition. Androcentric discourse tinted with militarism delegitimizes women as citizens who are excluded from soldiering, constructing them instead as carriers of nationalist wombs to deliver heirs and potential warriors who can defend the nation. This implicit message goes hand in hand with official nationalism's emphasis on collective orientation as opposed to Western individualism. In other words, Koreans are to sacrifice themselves for the nation, and women do so by performing their domestic duties. Women's movements organized around issues of family law reform and exploitation in export-oriented factories illustrates the extent to which women have been challenging androcentric official nationalism.

The women's movement to revise family law has aimed at eliminating discrimination against women in marriage, family, and kinship, as shaped by the Neo-Confucian principle of patrilineage.[53] Family law, which refers to Part Four and Part Five of the Civil Code of the Republic of Korea regulating kinship and the inheritance of property, respectively, has been a target of public debate since its enactment in 1948. Sharply contradicting formal gender equality guaranteed by the constitution, the family law enforced between 1948 and 1990 protected men's dominance over women in patrilocal marriage, patriarchal family, and patrilineage in kinship and the inheritance of property.

A core element of family law that supports the modern patriarchal family based on the Neo-Confucian principle of patrilineage is the institution of the household head (*hoju jedo*). Reflecting the principle of primogeniture, the legal order of succession of household headship moves down from the first son, to the first son's first son, to the second son. When there is no male heir, the first daughter can assume the domestic authority of the household head, but only on a temporary basis, until she marries. When there is no daughter at all, the wife, the mother, the daughter-in-law, and the granddaughter-in-law can inherit the domestic authority in descending order. The pre-1991 version of family law granted the husband as the provider of his family a series of rights over family members—i.e., the right to accept or refuse one's entry into the family register, the right to expel a family member from it, the right to decide a place of residence, and the right to exercise primary custody over children in case of divorce. With this state-delegated domestic authority, the husband was even entitled to admit an "illegitimate" child he begot with another woman into his family register without his wife's consent! The mandatory succession of the household head's authority primarily revolves around men, which has been an essential means to marginalize women. Thus, women's subordinate position as breeders in the patrilineal order concretely reflects official nationalism in family law.[54]

Patrilineal family law was enforced for more than four decades without any major change until the 1989 revision was put into effect in January 1991. Yet the revised family law still prohibits marriage between persons with the same family name and ancestral seat (*tongsŏng tongbon pulhon*) and the formal succession of household head ship(*hoju sŭnggye*). The marriage prohibition is an extreme manifestation of exogamy based on patrilineage. An assumption behind this legalized taboo is that one's identity is determined by her/his father's blood, which is presumably identifiable by his surname and ancestral seat, or the putative place of his clan's origin. The formality of the succession of the household head persists even after most mandatory rights and obligations between the *hoju* and his family members are eliminated. Both of these elements strongly reflect the Neo-Confucian principle of patrilineage that reduced women to mere breeders to continue the agnatic family lines.[55]

Coalitions of women's organizations have pursued the revision of family law since the early 1970s. There were three organized efforts to reform family law in 1974, 1984, and 1987 before the women's movement achieved substantial changes in family law in 1989. Each time, a number of women's organizations formed a coalition group and forwarded the reform proposal to the National Assembly. The coalition's reform attempts were always met by hostile reactions from self-proclaimed Confucianists and lukewarm responses from the legislature. Both Park's and Chun's regime responded reluctantly, with a piecemeal reform in 1977 and by brushing aside proposals in 1984 and 1987.[56]

The presence of the self-proclaimed Confucianists as a significant force in the politics of family law reform is very interesting because, although an obscure and anachronistic group, they seem to represent the widespread conservatism facing the reform attempts among the general public. As early as 1972, "Confucian representatives" protested against the idea of revising family law in the name of "five million Confucianists." By 1975, the conservative forces assembled a national federation to impede the revision and collected signatures from one million people.[57] In 1984, the Confucianists criticized women's attempts at family law reform for allegedly "[shaking] the roots of the nation itself."[58] Again in 1987, 5,000 Confucianists protested against the reform proposal, which suggested modification of the marriage prohibition, and was forwarded to the National Assembly by the coalition of eighty women's organizations. The state, which has responded militantly to student protests and dissident movements in general, largely condoned Confucianists' vociferous demonstrations.[59]

The women's movement to revise family law challenges official nationalism by undermining the patrilineal family as the basic unit of the nation.[60] As I showed earlier, official nationalism constructs the nation as a community of men in which women are marginalized as domestic reproducers of heirs and potential warriors. This patrilineal gender hierarchy is institutionalized in family law, which the women's movements have attempted to change. Moreover, the nationalist discourse uses this particular form of the family as an ultimate metaphor for paternalistic "harmony," which underlies such elements of Korean tradition as community consciousness and collective orientation. In other words, the Korean nation is essentially a familial community in which members have collective orientation as opposed to "Western individualism." Hence, the egalitarian family that women's movements advocate disrupts the established order, not only in the family but also in the nation. Interestingly, the Confucianists express this fear by arguing that family law reform would shake the roots of the nation itself.

State intellectuals producing the androcentric discourse about Korean history and tradition seem to be aware of the emergence of women's voices demanding family law reform. The following excerpts from texts published by the state illustrate this point.

> These days there are prolific debates about equality between men and women. But as far as the relationship between husband and wife is concerned, the discussion of equality itself results from a misunderstanding. The conjugal relationship is based not on the conflict of interests but on harmony and love.[61]

> A wife takes care of her husband and children without sleeping at night not because she is a coward or a fool but because she feels responsible for performing the traditional duty, and she does it with pride . . . [P]ubu yubyŏl (differences between husband and wife) does not intend to discriminate against women but it means that [men and women] have different roles to play.[62]

The first part reflects a strategy to obscure inequality in the name of "harmony." This strategy underlies the nationalist discourse on Korean tradition. It is ultimately a conservative response with a modern twist to the rise of women's voices demanding equality. It argues that women's domesticity is not about equality and discrimination but about functional differences between the sexes that *pubu yubyŏl,* one of the five Neo-Confucian principles guiding human relationships, teaches.

Another strand of the women's movement that challenged official nationalism was labor union activities of young women workers in export-oriented industries during the 1970s and the 1980s. To be sure, not just female workers but also male workers have suffered from subminimum wages, long working hours, and hazardous working conditions. However, women workers were made even more vulnerable to exploitation due to stereotypes of female docility and of the male as provider. Presumably, women would not engage in militant protests against exploitation and their income would be mere supplements to men's (and therefore women would accept lower pay). Moreover, young women workers were subject to varying degrees of sexual violence by male supervisors. Indeed, women workers were paid barely half of men's wages throughout the 1970s and the 1980s even though they worked longer hours than their male counterparts.[63]

However, even under the extremely repressive labor control by the state as well as management, female factory workers refused to remain "cheap" and "docile."[64] The women workers' movement began spontaneously in response to extreme exploitation that threatened the women's day-to-day survival. Although confronting violent assaults and threats from the police and company-hired thugs, women workers organized democratic unions outside the company-sponsored ones.[65] Initially, their demands were directed toward wage raises and the return of unpaid wages, but they expanded toward the end of the 1970s to encompass women's right to work after marriage, pregnancy, and childbirth. For example, women workers in Pfeizer and Control Data requested the abolition of the not-so-subtle practice of forced retirement at the time of marriage or pregnancy. Women workers in Samsung Pharmaceutical Company obtained paid time for feeding their babies.[66]

By the early 1980s, the female workers' movement shrank because of at least two factors. First, the state, again taken over by the military junta led by Chun Doo Hwan in 1980, launched an undeclared offensive against grassroots movements, including democratic labor unions, which had been activated by the political vacuum created by the sudden assassination of Park Chung Hee in 1979. Second, the economy moved its focus from light industry to heavy and chemical ones by the end of the 1970s. As textile and garment industries that hired young female workers on a massive scale declined, the majority of women workers left factories and returned to their homes in the countryside or got married. Then the women's labor movement was eclipsed by a rapidly growing number of male workers in steel, shipbuilding, and automobile industries in the 1980s.

The women workers' movement to organize democratic unions and their struggle to gain the right to work after marriage sharply contrast with the image of domestic and reproductive women constructed by official nationalism. As I discussed earlier, the military regimes promoted economic development in the name of national modernization. Under the official export promotion strategy, young women were massively incorporated into export-processing zones. They were treated as raw materials to be used to build the national economy. The women workers' movement challenges official nationalism, subverting the masculine nation by refusing a marginal place for women as the nation's mere precondition. Their movement also undermines anti-democratic traditionalism, which emphasizes loyalty and sacrifice in the name of "community consciousness" (*kongdonch'e ŭisik*) or collective orientation.

The Implications of Official Nationalism for Gender Relations

The analysis of the nationalist discourse on Korean history and tradition strongly suggests that industrialization as a way to build a "prosperous and strong" Korea is a highly gendered process of societal transformation in and by which women are assigned subordinate positions in the nation. Official nationalism also implies that the order of the nation is firmly rooted in essential and hierarchical differences between woman and man. While men are the founders of the nation with heavenly origins, righteous warriors or patriotic soldiers, and heads of households, women have sub-human origins and are the bearers of sons who will inherit the nation and defend it. In other words, men are creative actors and legitimate citizens, whereas women are reproductive and domestic beings who cannot be full members of the nation since as a part of nature they can only contribute their bodies as a precondition for building or developing the masculine nation.

The deep-rooted view of women as a part of nature producing for the community of men implies that economic growth in Korea relies upon women's identity as primarily reproductive and domestic beings, which prevents them from being full citizens who participate in all aspects of a democratic society. As a result, the incorporation of women workers into the process of industrialization as "cheap" labor cannot transform their primary identity. Rather, this would be used as an excuse to marginalize women workers in the expanding national economy.

Women's subordinate positions as represented in official nationalism are not simply a discursive construction isolated from the process of economic growth and the reality of military confrontation with the Communist North. In contrast, the military regimes as producers of the nationalist discourse on Korean history and tradition have exploited women's dubious citizenship. As I discussed earlier, patrilineal family law has persisted throughout the process of industrialization. Women have been forced to carry a reproductive and domestic identity that pre-empts their full membership in the national community. In fact, the state's insistence upon patrilineal family law as the nuclear family grows indicates that it has viewed the neo-patriarchal family based on the gendered division of labor between the husband-provider and the reproductive housewife as a basic unit of the Korean nation.

This feminine identity as a breeder in the patrilineal order goes hand in hand with the exclusion of women from soldiering, as implied in the discursive construction of the masculine selfhood of a Korean citizen. Delegitimized as citizens, women are bodies carrying wombs and labor power. The integration of women in the economy as "cheap" factory workers illustrates the actual manifestation of the androcentric view of woman as the bodily precondition for building and developing the nation.

Although some women have challenged the androcentric ideas behind official nationalism, their organized power is still weak *vis-à-vis* the state and hegemonic androcentrism pervasive in the society. The central implication of official nationalism for gender relations in contemporary Korea is that industrialization cannot bring about substantial change in hierarchical gender relations. Indeed, gender hierarchy has been recomposed in modern forms.[67] As a result, more and more women face the contradiction that they carry the *socially ascribed* status of female gender in industrializing Korea which espouses, in principle, individual equality and achievement. To be sure this does not automatically lead to the explosion of women's movement, but it prepares a fertile ground for it.

NOTES

I would like to thank Chungmoo Choi and Farzin Vahdat for their helpful comments and information.

1. Throughout the 1980s, studies vindicating Confucianism as the cultural ethos behind East Asian economic development were produced. A conference on "Confucianism and Economic Development in East Asia" was held at the Chung-Hua Institution for Economic Research in Taipei, Taiwan from May 29 to 31, 1989. See also Ronald P. Dore, "Confucianism, Economic Growth, and Social Development," in *In Search of an East Asian Development Model*, eds. Peter L. Berger and Hsin-Huang Michael Hsiao (New Brunswick, N.J.: Transaction Books, 1988); Ronald P. Dore, *Taking Japan Seriously: A Confucian Perspective on Leading Economic Issues* (Stanford: Stanford University Press, 1987); Michio Morishima, *Why Has Japan 'Succeeded'?: Western Technology and the Japanese Ethos* (New York: Cambridge University Press, 1982). In addition, studies on economic development in South Korea tend to discuss nationalism as a crucial factor. See Roger L. Janelli with Dawnhee Yim, *Making Capitalism: The Social and Cultural Construction of a South Korean Conglomerate* (Stanford: Stanford University Press, 1993); Carter J. Eckert, "The South Korean Bourgeoisie: A Class in Search of Hegemony," in *State and Society in Contemporary Korea*, ed. Hagen Koo (Ithaca: Cornell University Press, 1993).

2. "Official nationalism" was coined by Seton-Watson in his historiography of nationalism. See Hugh Seton-Watson, *Nations and States: An Inquiry into the Origins of Nations and the Politics of Nationalism* (Boulder: Westview, 1977).

3. See Roger L. Janelli, "The Origins of Korean Folklore Scholarship," *Journal of American Folklore* 99 (1986): 24–49.

4. See Kenneth M. Wells, *New God, New Nation: Protestant and Self-Reconstruction Nationalism in Korea, 1896–1937* (Honolulu: University of Hawaii Press, 1990).

5. See Jae-Hyeon Choe, "Strategic Groups of Nationalism in Nineteenth-Century Korea," *Journal of Contemporary Asia* 16 (1986): 223–36.

6. A similar nationalist strategy was used by Bengali elite in colonial India during the nineteenth century. See Partha Chatterjee, "The Nation and Its Women," in *The Nation and Its Fragments: Colonial and Postcolonial Histories* (Princeton, N.J.: Princeton University Press, 1993).

7. There are many anecdotes illustrating how deeply Park was "Korean" in terms of his life style, taste, and attitudes. Coming from a poor peasant family, he despised urbanites with refined Western manners and tastes—e.g., who drank cocktails and ate Western foods.

8. Park Chung Hee, *Minjok chunghŭngŭi gil* (A Way to National Prosperity), Seoul: Kwangmyŏng, 1978 (there is an English translation of this book, *Korea Reborn: A Model for Development*, Englewood Cliffs, N.J.: Prentice-Hall, 1979); *Our Nation's Path: Ideology of Social Reconstruction*, Seoul: Dong-A Publishing Co., 1962; Cabinet Planning

and Regulating Room, ed. *Minjokui tungbul* (Beacon of the Nation), Seoul, 1971.

9. Kim Chin-gyun and Hong Sŭng-hui, "Hanguk sahoeŭi kyoyukkwa jibae ideologi" (Education and Ruling Ideology in Korean Society), in *Hanguk sahoewa jibae ideologi* (Korean Society and Ruling Ideologies) (Seoul: Noktu, 1991).

10. See note 9.

11. Hong Ŭng-sŏn, "Kungmin yulli kyoyukŭi naeyong" (The Content of National Ethics Education), *Kungmin yulli yŏngu* (Aug. 1976); 303–15.

12. For explicit emphases on national ethics see Ch'oe Ŭi-t'ae, "Hyŏndae kungmin yulli kyoyukŭi ponjilgwa gŭ kinŭng" (The Nature and Function of Contemporary National Ethics Education), *Kungmin yulli yŏngu* 13 (April 1982): 199–209; Han Sŭng-jo, "Kungmin jŏngsin kyoyukŭi inyŏmgwa yŏnsu kyoyukŭi gwaje" (The Ideology of National Mentality Education and Issues for the In-Service Training Education), *Kungmin yulli yŏngu* 13 (April 1982): 227–252; Ku Hŏn-hoe, "Kungmin jŏngsin kyoyuk kangjwaŭi bŏmwiwa naeyong" (The Range and Content of National Mental Education Class), *Kungmin yulli yŏngu* 13 (April 1983): 263–270; Yi Ch'ang-wu, "Kungmin yulli kyoyuk mokchŏkŭi jŏngnip" (Establishing the Goals of National Ethics Education), *Kungmin yulli yŏngu* 10 (November 1980): 159–167; Yu Dal-yŏng, "'Kungmin jŏngsinŭi gibon banghyang' seminae jūūmhayo" (On the Seminar "A Basic Direction of National Mentality"), *Kungmin yulli yŏngu* 5 (August 1976): 245–255.

13. This brief history of the Research Association of National Ethics Education is based on my review of its journal, *Kungmin yulli yongu* (National Ethics Studies), from 1973 to 1982, and especially on the prefaces to various issues.

14. See Yi Sung-nyŏng, "Hanguk jŏngsinmunhwa yŏnguwŏn sosa" (A Brief History of the Institute of Korean Mental Culture Research), *Chŏngsin munhwa* 4 (1981): 21–28. Singapore, which has also undergone a rapid socio-economic change, shows a parallel case. The Singaporean state has tried to reconstitute the national identity based on Chinese Confucian culture in that multi-ethnic society. See the special section on Singapore in *Far Eastern Economic Review* (9 Feb. 1989): 30–41.

15. The Tan'gun myth was recorded in *Samguk yusa* by Ilyŏn, a Buddhist monk, in the eleventh century. He extracted the myth from the *Wei Shu*, which is a primary source of Chinese history completed around A.D. 554. See James H. Grayson, *Korea: A Religious History* (Oxford: Clarendon, 1989), p. 282. However, some ardent state intellectuals oppose calling the story of Tan'gun a myth despite its mythical details. For example, Chi Kyo-hŏn, a professor of the Institute of Korean Mental Culture Research, argues that the foundation story is documented in various ancient history books, and therefore, calling it a myth implies that one does not acknowledge the historical facts. See his "Chŏngt'ong yulliŭi hyŏndaejŏk ŭiŭiwa gŭ sahoejŏk kinŭng" (Contemporary Significance of Traditional Ethics and Its Social Function), in *Chŏngt'ong yulliŭi hyŏndaejŏk jomyŏng* (Contemporary Perspectives of Traditional Ethics) (Seoul: Institute of Korean Mental Culture Research, 1989); Association of National Ethics Studies, ed. *Hangugŭi jŏngt'ong sasang* (Traditional Thoughts in Korea) (Seoul, 1983).

16. For European and Indian examples of such inventions of national traditions and rit-

uals, see Eric Hobsbawm and Terence Ranger, eds., *The Invention of Tradition* (Cambridge: Cambridge University Press, 1983).

17. Both Korean and foreign scholars of Korean history argue that the tribal state of Kochoson was founded in the fifth or fourth century B.C. See Carter Eckert, et al. *Korea Old and New: A History* (Seoul: Ilchokak/Cambridge: Harvard University Press, 1990); James H. Grayson, *Korea: A Religious History* (Oxford: Clarendon, 1989). Yet, all state intellectuals tend to insist on the longer history. See Han Sŭng-jo, "Hanguk minjujuŭiŭi kukkaronjŏk kijo" (The Theoretical Basis of the Korean State and Korean Democracy), in *Hanguk kukkaŭi gibon sŏnggyŏkkwa gwaje* (The Basic Nature of the Korean State and Its Problems) (Songnam, Korea: Institute of Korean Mental Culture Research, 1988); *Kungmin jŏngsin gyoyuk ch'ujin wiwŏnhoe* (Council for Furthering National Mental Education), ed. *Uri sidaeŭi bot'ong saram dŭrulwihayŏ* (For Ordinary People of Our Times) (Seoul: Koryowon, 1988); *Minjok munhwa ch'ujinhoe* (Association for Proceeding National Culture), *Chont'ong yulli gyobom jaryojip I: Samguk—Koryŏ* (A Collection for Teaching Traditional Ethics I: The Three Kingdoms Period—Koryŏ) (Seoul, 1986); Research Center for Peace and Unification, *The Identity of the Korean People: A History of Legitimacy on the Korean Peninsula* (Seoul, 1983); Institute of Korean Mental Culture Research, *Hanguk sasangkwa yulli* (Korean Thoughts and Ethics) (Songnam, Korea, 1980); *Chollanamdo gyoyuk yŏnguwŏn* (South Cholla Province Center for Education Research), *Uri gojangŭi ch'ung hyo yŏl* (Loyalty, Filial Piety, and Chastity in Our Community) (Kwangju, Korea, 1978); Park Chung Hee, *Minjok junghŭngŭi gil*; *Our Nation's Path*; Ch'oe Ch'ang-kyu, "Hanminjokŭi juch'esŏng" (Subjectivity of Korean People), *Kungmin yulli yŏngu* 1 (October 1973): 131–142.

18. Some official nationalists argue that the mythical transformation of a bear into a woman might signify an exogamy between Hwanung, a leader of a ruling clan, and a woman from a clan whose totem was a bear. See Research Center for Peace and Unification, *The Identity of the Korean People*.

19. This kind of androcentrism is not unique to Korean official nationalism. For example, between the 1870s and the 1930s, the construction of German national identity relied upon bourgeois German masculinity as the core of German national identity. See George Mosse, *Nationalism and Sexuality: Respectability and Abnormal Sexuality in Modern Europe* (New York: Howard Fertig, 1985).

20. Elsewhere I discuss family planning policy as an element of gender politics that contributes to the recomposition of gender hierarchy in South Korea during the period of rapid industrialization. See Seungsook Moon, "Economic Development and Gender Politics in South Korea, 1963–1992" (Ph.D. diss., Brandeis University, 1994).

21. Metaphors that convey this kind of ontological difference between woman and man are constitutive of various myths and especially foundation myths of nations. See the appendix in Grayson's *Korea: A Religious History* for foundation myths of other tribal states in the Korean Peninsula. For cross-cultural evidence of these deep-rooted metaphors see Joseph Campbell, *The Hero with a Thousand Faces* (Princeton: Princeton University Press, 1972). In his analysis of myths from various cultures, Campbell discovers a universal theme that protagonists in all mythic narratives are heroes, while

women are designated as symbols of what the heroes should overcome or achieve. In other words, a woman is depicted as either a temptress with a subhuman origin or a celestial queen (or a heavenly beauty) that symbolizes a hero's successful adventure. This is interestingly similar to the Christian representation of a woman as whore/Madonna. De Beauvoir uses an essentialized gender dichotomy in her representation of man and woman who signify transcendence and nature respectively, in her explanation of women's oppression. See Simone De Beauvoir, *The Second Sex* (Harmondsworth, N.Y.: Penguin, 1972). For a critical examination of the dichotomy of women-nature and men-culture see Sherry Ortner, "Is Female to Male as Nature is to Culture?" in *Women, Culture, and Society*, eds. Michelle Z. Rosaldo and Louise Lamphere (Stanford, CA: Stanford University Press, 1974).

22. This information does not appear in Grayson's *Korea: A Religious History*.

23. Sometimes an exact frequency of invasion—931 times—is used. It appears that official nationalists quote the frequency as a way to make "true" their claim that national defense overrides any other issue. For example, see Council for Proceeding National Mental Education, *Uri sidaeŭi botong saramdŭrŭl wihayŏ*, pp. 13–15; Research Center for Peace and Unification, *The Identity of the Korean People*, p. 16, p. 25, p. 26.

24. See, for example, Institute of Korean Mental Culture Research, *Hanguk Yulli Sasangsa* (A History of Korean Ethical Thoughts) (Songnam, Korea, 1987); Association of National Ethics Studies, *Hangugŭi jŏntong sasang* (Traditional Thoughts in Korea (Seoul, 1983); Association of Mental Education Research, *Kungmin yulli I: Hangugui gunin jongsin* (National Ethics I: Korean Soldiers' Spirit); Korean Education Development Institute, *Hangugin sangui t'amgu* (An Investigation of the Image of a Korean); Park Chung Hee, *Our Nation's Path*.

25. In contrast to the nationalist claim, the Korean Peninsula was not unified by Silla. The Unified Silla (A.D. 668–936) coexisted with the kingdom of Parhae (A.D. 713–926) which was founded by Tae Cho-Yŏng, a General of the extinct Kingdom of Koguryo. Parhae occupied Manchuria and the northern part of the Korean Peninsula above the Taedong River.

26. Research Center for Peace and Unification, *The Identity of the Korean People*, p. 143; Han Sung-jo, "Chŏnt'ongjŏk kach'ikwangwa hyŏndae minjujŭŭi," p. 74; Association of Mental Education Research, *Kungmin Yulli I*; Park Chung Hee, *Minjok jonghungui gil*, p. 22; *Our Nation's Path*, pp. 39–40.

27. Research Center for Peace and Unification, *The Identity of the Korean People*, p. 18; Park Chung Hee, *Minjok junghungŭi gil*, pp. 13–14.

28. Research Center for Peace and Unification, *The Identity of the Korean People*, pp. 19–20.

29. In the end of Yi Dynasty, *ŭibyŏng* from Confucian scholars protested not so much in favor of national independence as against the undermining of the Confucian social order that was ultimately centered around the imperial order of the Chinese Kingdom. Ironically, the nationalist narratives document that the Confucian *ŭibyŏng* rose up fervently after the royal decree of hair-cutting in the first decade of the twentieth century.

See Min Dong-gŭn, "Hangukŭi chont'ongjŏk yulli sasangŭi balgyŏn" (Discovery of Korean Traditional Ethical Thoughts) in *Hanguginŭi Yulligwan II* (Korean People's Perspective on Ethics) (Songnam, Korea: Institute of Korean Mental Culture Research, 1984), p. 62. The removal of a hair top-knot was perceived by the Confucian scholars as a symbolic violation of the Confucian order. This kind of insistence on a certain appearance as the core of a challenged identity has been observed in many Third World countries since the late nineteenth century. See Haleh Afshar, "Behind the Veil: The Public and Private Faces of Khomeini's Policies on Iranian Women," in *Structures of Patriarchy: State, Community and Household in Modernizing Asia*, ed. Bina Agarwal (London: Zed Press, 1988); Emelie A. Olson, "Muslim Identity and Secularism in Contemporary Turkey: 'The Headscarf' Dispute," *Anthropological Quarterly* 58 (1985): 161–69.

30. Kim Nam-guk, *Kungminŭi kŭndae, kŭdŭrŭi kŭndae* (People's Army, Their Army) (Seoul: P'ulbit 1995), pp. 57–58.

31. These phrases are from the announcement made by the junta government immediately after its takeover of the state. See Sejin Kim, *The Politics of Military Revolution in Korea* (Chapel Hill, N.C.: University of North Carolina Press, 1971), pp. 93–94.

32. Park, *Our Nation's Path*, p. 40.

33. Ibid., p. 75, p. 80, and p. 92 (my translation and emphases).

34. The growing public interest in something Korean is illustrated by the proliferation of popular publication in the forms of fictions and essays on Korean culture, history, and identity since the mid-1970s.

35. Peace and Unification, *The Identity of the Korean People*, pp. 129–130.

36. Ch'oe Ŭi-t'ae, "Hyŏndae kungmin yulli kyoyukŭi ponjilkwa kŭ kinŭng"; Han Sŭng-jo, "Kungmin chŏngsin kyoyukŭi inyŏmkwa yŏnsu gyoyukŭi gwaje," "Sae chŏngsin munhwaŭi inyŏmjŏk kijo"; Kim Kwe-gon, "Hanguk chŏngsin munhwaŭi kijo"; Hwang Du-hwan, "Kungmin yulli kyoyukŭi kyoyuk kwajŏng punsŏk" (An Analysis of the Curriculum for National Ethics Education), *Kungmin Yulli Yŏngu* 12 (Dec. 1981): 351–374; Yi Ch'ang-wu, "Kungmin yulli kyoyuk mokjŏkŭi jŏngnip" (Establishing the Goals of National Ethics Education), *Kungmin yulli yŏngu* 10 (Nov. 1980): 159–67.

37. This kind of problematic construction of national tradition is also found in Indian nationalist discourse. Indian male nationalists in the late nineteenth century equated Indian tradition with the Hindu Scriptures, i.e., the tradition of the male Indian elites. See Lata Mani, "Contentious Traditions: The Debates on SATI in Colonial India," *Cultural Critique* (Fall, 1987): 119–56 and Uma Chakravarti, "What Happened to the Vedic Dasi?: Orientalism, Nationalism, and a Script for the Past," in *Recasting Women: Essays in Colonial History*, eds. Kumkum Sangari and Sudesh Vaid (New Dehli: Kali for Women, 1989).

38. See Yi Sun-kwŏn, "Yŏksa kyoyukkwa minjokjuŭi" (History, Education, and Nationalism), in *Hanguk minjokjuŭi ron II* (Theories of Korean Nationalism II), eds. Song Kŏn-ho and Kang Man-gil (Seoul: Changjakgwa bipyong, 1983) and Kim

Jin-kyun and Hong Sŭng-hui, "Hanguk sahoeŭi kyoyukgwa chibae ideologi" (Education and Dominant Ideology in Korean Society).

39. Han Sung-jo, "Hanguk minjujuŭiŭi kukkaronjŏk kijo" (A State Theory of Korean Democracy) in *Hanguk Kukkaŭi gibon sŏnggyŏkgwa gwaje* (The Basic Nature of the Korean State and Its Problems) (Songnam, Korea: Institute of Korean Mental Culture Research, 1988), p. 10, p. 50; Han Sŭng-jo, "Chŏnt'ongjŏk kach'igwangwa hyŏndae minjujuŭi" (Traditional Values and Contemporary Democracy) in *Chŏnt'ongjŏk gach'ikwangwa sae gach'ikwanŭi jongnip* (The Establishment of Traditional Values and New Values) (Songnam, Korea: Institute of Korean Mental Culture Research, 1980), p. 86; Park Chung Hee, *Minjok junghŭngŭi gil* (A Way to National Prosperity) (Seoul: Kwangmyong, 1978), pp. 23–24.

40. See note 38.

41. Unlike the Judeo-Christian God, the Heaven's Mandate speaks neither to the ruler nor to the ruled. It does not demand specific responsibility from a ruler in relation to the ruled. It supposedly manifests itself through natural disasters—e.g., drought, famine, flood, etc.—when it is violated. See William T. De Bary, *The Trouble with Confucianism* (Cambridge: Harvard University Press, 1991) for an excellent discussion of the problems of the notion of Heaven's Mandate.

42. *Pakdal* comes from the name of a tree in the Tan'gun myth. According to the myth, Tan'gun founded the Korean nation under the *pakdal* tree.

43. Yi Tong-jun, "Chŏnt'ongjŏk kach'igwanŭi hyŏndaejŏk sŏngch'al," pp. 13–15; Han, Chŏnt'ongjŏk kach'igwankwä hyŏndae minjujuŭi," p. 86; Park, *Minjok Chunghungui Kil*, pp. 13–15, 17–19, 68, 74, 140.

44. *Investigation of the Image of a Korean*, p. 77.

45. See Grayson, *Korea: A Religious History*.

46. Peace and Unification, *The Identity of the Korean People*, p. 147.

47. Some official nationalist intellectuals indicated Taoism as an element of *hwarangdo* instead of Son'gyo. For example, see Lee Tong-jun, "Chŏngt'ongjŏk kach'igwanŭi hyŏndaejŏk sŏngch'al." However, Taoist influence in Korea was very much limited and Taoism never formed any school in Korean religious history. See Grayson, *Korea: A Religious History*.

48. Park, *Minjok junghŭngŭi gil*, p. 21.

49. This kind of exclusive male camaraderie is often haunted by homophobia. George Mosse explores this issue in relation to German nationalism. See his *Nationalism and Sexuality*. Some argue that the institution of *hwarang* is an example of a homoerotic military elite which has its parallels in Japanese Samurai and the Ottoman Janissaries. See Stephen O. Murrary, "The Hwarang of Ancient Korea," in *Oceanic Homosexualities*, Stephen O. Murrary, ed. (New York: Garland Publishing, 1992).

50. Chi, "Chŏngt'ong yulliŭi hyŏndaejok ŭiŭiwa gŭ sahoejŏk kinŭng"; Association of National Ethics Studies, *Hangugŭi jŏnt'ong sasang*; Kim Kwe-gon, "Hanguk chŏngsin

munhwaŭi gijo"; Son, "Hanguginŭi chŏnt'ongjŏk kyoyuk ŭisikgwa hyŏndae gyoyukŭi che munje."

51. Min, "Hangugŭi chŏngt'ongjŏk yulli sasangŭi balgyŏn"; Association of National Ethics Studies, *Hangugŭi jŏnt'ong sasang.*

52. Grassroots movements under military rule involved factory workers, students, dissident intellectuals, and politicians. See Cho Hwa-Soon, *Let the Weak Be Strong: A Women's Struggle for Justice* (Bloomington, Indiana: Meyerstone Books, 1988); Carter Eckert, et al. *Korea Old and New: A History*, chapter 19; George E. Ogle, *South Korea: Dissent within the Economic Miracle* (London: Zed Books, 1990).

53. Elsewhere I deal with the women's movement for family law reform more extensively as a crucial dimension of gender politics which the Korean state is involved in the process of economic development. See Seungsook Moon, "Modernization of Gender Hierarchy in South Korea: Politics of Family Law Reform," *The Journal of Modern Korean Studies* (Summer 1996), forthcoming.

54. Kim Chu-su, "Kaejŏng gajokpŏpŭi gaejŏng gyŏngwiwa gwaje" (Issues in the Revision of the Family Laws), in *Kaejŏng gajokpop kwa hanguk sahoe* (Seoul: Korea Women's Development Institute/Korean Family Laws Studies Association, 1990); Kim Chu-su, "Hyŏnhaeng gajokpŏp sangŭi namnyŏ ch'abyŏl" (Sexual Discrimination in the Current Family Laws), *Yŏsŏng* 91 (May 1973): 5–10; Kim Sŏng-suk, "Kaejŏng gajokpŏbŭi naeyonggwa munjejŏm" (The Content and Problems of the Revised Family Laws), *Yŏsŏng Yŏngu* 26 (3): 119–148; Pak Pyŏng-ho, "Kaejŏng ch'injŏk kwangyeŭi je munje" (Problems of the Revised Kinship Relations), in *Kaejŏng gajokpŏp kwa hanguk sahoe*; "Minbŏp sange natanan namnyŏ ch'abyŏl" (Sexual Discrimination in the Civil Law), *Yŏsŏng* 91 (1973): 16–17.

55. See note 52.

56. Yi Hyo-jae, *Hanguk yŏsŏng undongsa* (A History of the Women's Movement in Korea) (Seoul: Jongwusa, 1989); Yi Sang-uk, "Yŏsŏng ŭi pŏpjŏk jiwi wa gajokbŏp gaejŏng non" (Legal Status of Women and an Argument for the Revision of the Family Laws), *Yŏsŏng munje yŏngu* 13 (1985): 343–359.

57. Yi Hyo-jae, *Hanguk yŏsŏng undongsa*, p. 226, pp. 247–49.

58. Ok-Za Yoo, "Korean Women in the Home and Work Place: Their Status Since 1945," *Korea and World Affairs* 9 (Winter, 1985): 820–872. See p. 830.

59. John McBeth, "A Family Feud for Confucians and Women," *Far Eastern Economic Review* (26 Feb., 1987): 38–41. See p. 38 and p. 40.

60. This particular movement is an example of gendered activism. I am aware of the paradoxical ability of this kind of women's movement to reproduce the essentialized link between women and domesticity. Although in their reform attempts women step outside the domestic sphere, they are still involved in family issues. Yet, the distinction between domestic and public is already undermined in official nationalism, which deploys "family" as a primary metaphor for a Korean nation rooted in "collective orientation."

61. *Hangukin sangŭi t'amgu* (Investigation of the Image of the Korean) 1974, p. 196: my translation.

62. Ministry of Culture and Information, *Hangukui chont'onggwa kwansup* (Korean Tradition and Custom) 1982, p. 13 and p. 21: my translation.

63. Korean Women's Development Institute, *Yŏsŏng goyong ch'okjin bŏpche'e gwanhan yŏngu* (A Study of Legal Promotion of Women's Employment) (Seoul, 1985), p. 4.

64. It appears that the state was quite aware of the possibility of labor disputes in factories hiring a large number of young women workers in the early 1970s. The Bureau of Labor undertook studies of the working conditions of factory women. See Bureau of Labor, *Yŏsŏng kŭlloja silt'ae josa gyŏlkwa bokosŏ: kongdan jiyŏkkwa ch'ongkye p'ibok sangga jiyŏgŭl jungsimŭro* (Report on the Working Conditions of Women Workers in Industrial Estates and Ch'ŏnggye clothing shops), 1974, *Kullo yŏsŏngŭi hyŏnhwang* (The Working Conditions of Women), *report*, 1974, *Yŏsŏng kŭlloja silt'ae josa bogosŏ: chejoŏpch'e, unsuŏpch'e jungsimŭro* (Report on the Working Conditions of Women Workers in Manufacturing and Transportation Companies), 1973.

65. There were quite a few reported incidents of labor control in which male managers either alone or in collaboration with company-hired thugs manipulated sexual stereotypes. They attempted to discourage women workers from organizing by deploying culturally constructed male sexual aggression—i.e., they confronted defiant female workers, mostly young and unmarried, with their naked male bodies or made gestures as if to assault them sexually. In some cases male supervisors used rape as a means to control female workers. See Cho Sun-kyŏng, Yŏ Nan-yŏng, and Yi Sŏk-jin, "Yŏsŏng nodonggwa sŏngjŏk t'ongje" (Women's Labor and Sexual Control), *Hankuk yŏsŏnghak* 5 (1989): 164–185; Sin Illyŏng, *Yŏsŏng, nodong, pŏp* (Women, Labor, and Law) (Seoul: P'ulbit, 1988), pp. 294–297.

66. Ewha Womans University, "Minjok minju undonggwa yŏsŏng haebang undong" (National Democratic Movement and Feminist Movement), *Ewha* 46 (1991): 247–270, see p. 258; Pak Ŭn-sik, "Hangugŭi yŏsŏng nodong undong: 5. 15 putŏ yusinsijŏl kkaji" (Women's Labor Movement in Korea: From May 16th to the Yusin Period), *Yosong* 275 (Sept., 1990): 24–27, (Aug. 1990): 20–23, (June, 1990): 32–35; Pak Sŏk-bun, "Ch'abyŏlŭi sasŭrŭl ttulk'o jŏngjinhanŭn yŏsŏng nodongja undong" (The Process of the Women Workers' Movement Breaking the Chains of Discrimination), in *Yŏsŏng* 3 (Seoul: Ch'angjakkwa bip'yongsa, 1989).

67. By modernization of gender hierarchy I refer to the fact that although women have increasingly more access to formal education, are more often employed outside the home and have fewer children, they continue to be subordinated to men in the economy, politics, culture—i.e., the production of arts, meanings, and knowledge—sexuality, and within marriage/family/kinship.

4

ELAINE H. KIM

Men's Talk:
A Korean American View of South Korean Constructions of Women, Gender, and Masculinity

***T*his paper** *is based on interviews conducted mostly between 1987 and 1988, during a crucial moment in recent South Korean history—between the massive protests for democratic reforms that ushered in a new civilian government and the opening ceremonies of the Seoul Olympics. The paper looks at how men from various walks of life in Seoul in the late 1980s talked about women and about themselves as men, with some attention to how a man's social status informed and was implicated in the views he expressed. It also provides a glimpse into how women from various backgrounds adhered to and rebelled against patriarchal attitudes and practices, and how these attitudes and practices influenced their relationships with and their views of one another.*

Originally, I had planned to interview only women, but I understood that research for women does not have to always be about women. Masculinity is not exclusively about men; as Eve Kosofsky Sedgwick points out, women as well as men are consumers, producers, and performers of masculinities.[2] Men's political struggles and economic activities dominate official discourse, while their sexuality, though always tied to power, remains in the shadows. At the same time, female sexuality is represented by men. Examinations of the relations of power must include examinations of emotional, spiritual, intellectual, and economic relations of men as men to the rest of society. Research for women can explore the masculine discourse about women, gender, sex, and sexuality in relation to the construction of masculinity and femininity and the maintenance of gender inequality. Bringing the constructed male subjectivity of Korean men into focus in relation to the issue of gender could reveal tools useful to the task of dismantling attitudes and practices that objectify and dehumanize both women and men.

It should go without saying that I am in no way disinterested or "neutral."[3] Korean cultural constructions of masculinity and femininity have shaped Korean American men's and women's experiences, which include the subordination of women in political, economic, social, and cultural domains. Certainly analyzing the ways Asians have been represented in the popular imagination in the U.S. has been important to the Asian American struggle for racial justice. By analyzing white racist thinking about Asians, many Asian Americans have been able to "kill the white man within them" and free themselves from internalized feelings of racial inferiority. Likewise, feminist education in the West often begins with reading about patriarchal attitudes and practices over the centuries. If Korean and Korean American women are imprisoned by patriarchal attitudes and practices, understanding the prison and those who guard it might aid in the escape attempt, although it is important to recall that ending the prison system requires understanding the power relations that produce it, since interventions are possible only when the larger picture is understood and kept in mind.

I wish, then, to offer whatever I learned to South Korean women, as well as to other Korean American women, in the hopes that it might contribute to the ongoing efforts of women to challenge attitudes and practices that debilitate and disempower them.

During a visit to Seoul in 1986, I was astonished by the proliferation of multiple forms of disguised prostitution for which there was a huge South Korean market.[3] The burgeoning "entertainment trade" included not only the "room salon" and the *yojŏng* (places vaguely reminiscent of the traditional *kisaeng* [geisha] houses of pre-industrial times and featuring drinking and western and Korean food, with hostesses arrayed in dressy western attire or fancy Korean clothing, respectively), but also thousands of other places where men were served by female sexual service workers, including cafes, tea rooms and *ch'atjip* (tea shops where female servers keep company with their customers), *yangjujip* (western liquor shops with female companions), *tallanjujŏm* (liquor houses where customers sing and fraternize with hostesses), certain Japanese restaurants, barber shops, massage parlors, and different classes of prostitution houses.

After seizing power in 1981, Chun Doo Hwan ended what had been the world's longest-lasting curfew, and the *sul munhwa* (lit. liquor culture; "cafe culture") that had once been enjoyed primarily by foreigners and South Korean men in the uppermost echelons of business and government spread as South Korean business expanded through the 1980s.[4] Few arenas of society remained untouched by the *sul munhwa*, and certainly not gender relations.[5] While there were reportedly still some young women trapped or even kidnapped into sex work by unscrupulous procurers, by the mid-1980s, many female sex service workers seemed to view what they did as just another form of work in the unofficial, informal economy in which so many South Korean women take part.[6] Instead of being used to attract foreign capital, Korean women's bodies, whether as "office girls," prostitutes, or housewives, were now being mobilized primarily to help maintain Korean men's effective participation in the South Korean labor force. Like modern-day "comfort women" for an army of civilian men, wives were to comfort and care for their hard-working husbands; female office workers were to stimulate male co-workers to better work performance through their supportive manner and good looks; and sex service workers were to help working men "release their stress."

Between September 1987 and August 1988, as well as in October 1989 and July 1990, Yonsei University Women's Studies instructor

Ch'u Aeju and I[7] conducted in-depth interviews in Seoul of 54 married men between the ages of 24 and 69.[8] Although we did not try to replicate their proportions in society, we tried to make sure we interviewed enough men in each of three rough socioeconomic categories that we had constructed. For us, "upper-class men" meant men whose earnings were more than three million wŏn,[9] or about $4000–4500, monthly. We thought of the men who had not completed high school as "lower-class men." The remaining men we generally classified as "middle-class men." Our interviewees ranged from business tycoons, politicians, and upper-and middle-level managers to construction workers, bus washers, building guards, and street cleaners. We found our male subjects wherever we could—by asking everyone we knew to introduce us to men who would be willing to be interviewed about their lives and their relationships with women, including their mothers, wives, sisters, daughters, co-workers, and lovers. Ms. Ch'u enlisted a man she met in a parking lot and a taxi driver she met when traveling across the city. I convinced the proprietors of stores I frequented, such as the dry-cleaning shop and the film developing shop, to be interviewed.

Our interviews were unstructured, although we asked certain questions at every interview, such as "What female in Korean legend, history, or contemporary life do you admire?" We also asked each man about his first sexual experience and about his mother's relationship with his wife. Usually, when we asked men to talk about their own relationships with their mothers, they told us their life stories. What was astonishing was that many men seemed to think that an interview about gender or women meant a discussion of sex.

We usually arranged to meet our interviewees at a cafe or restaurant, where we hosted them in the most pleasant and relaxed atmosphere we could arrange. Generally, we met wealthy men in expensive restaurants and coffee shops that they suggested; middle-class men in downtown or South River area cafes that were close to public transportation stops; and poor men in tea rooms near where they lived. In Seoul, people who were not related often socialized at food and drink places where no one hurried them to relinquish their table. Most interviewees seemed to enjoy their interviews; in most cases, it was difficult for us to call an end to the meeting. For example, we had scheduled a two and a half hour interview with a well-known television actor, and after six hours he was still talking. Many men wanted to meet again and again, and some of them introduced us to their friends. Their willingness, even eagerness, to be interviewed might have stemmed from the fact that they considered the topic of gender and women inconsequential and could not imagine that any harm would come to them as a result of the discussion.[10] Indeed, many of them seemed titillated at the prospect of talking about sex and gender with middle-class, middle-aged women academics.[11] They may have found the experience novel.[12] They seemed exhilarated to be speaking about themselves before a rapt *female*—that is, what they thought of as a non-judgmental, appreciative, maternal, nurturing—audience.[13]

The men's willingness to be interviewed for long hours may also have stemmed in part from the fact that I was from America. I found that many South Koreans liked to "teach" Korean Americans about "Korean culture," such as their interpretations of Confucian proprieties.[14] At the same time, the fact that I was an outsider whom they assumed had no connections with their social networks made me safe to talk to because they thought their stories would not reach any mutual acquaintances. They could be frank with a female American stranger. Thus, in a certain sense, my marginality was an asset. Sometimes, because we wanted to take advantage of the sense of ease interviewees felt about talking to a stranger from another culture, Ms. Ch'u would stay in the background in the role of research assistant to a professor from Berkeley. At other times, when they were disconcerted with my "foreignness" and clumsy use of the Korean language, we could direct them back toward Ms. Ch'u, a sympathetic native Korean.

There were some significant differences in the openness of the poor and of the rich men that may be traced to us as interviewers. The poor men were less comfortable talking about themselves to us than the rich men, many of whom could barely conceal their excitement. I wondered whether some of the poor men felt ashamed of their lives and apologetic towards their wives and families, whether they were cowed by us because of our social status, or whether I was imagining their reticence according to my own expectations. I can only conjecture about how they viewed me, but I did notice that poor men interviewed by me and Ms. Ch'u were more reticent than those I interviewed with another colleague. Seoulites, at least those over 25, seem able to quickly assess the quality and price of others' clothing and accessories as part of their attempt to pinpoint social status. Ms. Ch'u's expensive jewelry and clothing, together with her strong Taegu accent, seemed to put a distance between her and the poor men we interviewed, almost all of whom were from the Chŏlla provinces.[15]

Creating and Managing Women's Otherness

The overtly misogynistic attitudes expressed by so many of the men we interviewed could be taken as evidence of the strength and resilience of Korean patriarchy in contemporary times. At the same time, they might also be viewed as part of the practice of constructing and reiterating a masculinity that needs continuous reinforcement precisely because it is something men could lose. Indeed, the men's sense of the ultimate fragility and instability of patriarchal ideology may be what made them so eager to argue for what are supposed to be universally shared notions of masculinity and femininity.

Most of the men we interviewed alluded frequently to a fixed notion of hierarchical opposition between men and women. Perhaps fear of the potential power of women was at the root of the men's disdain for what they considered the female, as opposed to male mentality. Dr. C., a gynecologist, asserted that men had little to learn from women, who are unable to carry on "deep conversation," while Mr. K., a business magnate who boasted about his countless sexual encounters with women from many backgrounds, told us that he hated women's conversations, which he said were invariably about silly, small things because women are by nature petty and prone to jealousy. The problem, according to Mr. K., was that "there are certain things missing from women's world that men have, like ŭiri (loyalty/steadfastness), forgiveness, broad-mindedness, and generosity."

During our interviews, supposed "natural" and "biological" differences between the sexes were frequently invoked to explain social inequities.[16] One man suggested to us that men were more intelligent than women because their brains are larger, which made men more able to do creative and conceptual work. More than one man believed that women are passive and better suited for staying at home with the family because their genitals are "inside" their bodies, while men are outgoing and active and better suited for working for society because their genitals are on the "outside."[17] Even men we interviewed in medical and scientific institutions upheld biologistic notions of female difference and social inferiority. Dr. Y., the director of a huge cancer hospital in Seoul, said:

> It is genetically ordained that men should win over women. Think about it: can a dog give birth to a rabbit or a rabbit have a puppy? Men and women are physiologically different. If you don't agree with my opinion now, you will in the future. God made it this way; that's why He made two sexes. I am on the outside, and my wife is on the inside. Is that system not efficient? Of course, if I were a woman, I might not like it, but I am a man.

Dr. Y.'s comment is particularly ironic in light of the South Korean medical profession's complicity in "genetic engineering" efforts during recent years to "make" more males than females: so many female fetuses were aborted after amniocentesis in the 1980s that the ratio of primary school boys to girls is now abnormally—and quite astonishingly—high.[18]

Despite the fact that women work as much outside the home as men in most societies, and despite females' longer life span and lower infant mortality rates except when they are given less food and less medical attention than males, Mr. P., a high-income executive, insisted that "women are like ceramics that break easily when they go outside." Many men expressed the belief that men are "logical," while women are "emotional." This view helped them rationalize differences in socially sanctioned sexual practices. The majority of rich and middle-class men we interviewed believed that it was "natural" for men to seek variety and for women to love only one man. "A woman can't get pleasure from a hundred men the way a man can get pleasure from a hundred women," one 48-year-old magnate said. Unlike men, he insisted, women are so "emotional" that they easily transfer their affections from one man to another and are thus more likely to "endanger their families" if they engaged in extramarital activities. On the other hand, because they are "logical," men are able to keep their married lives separate from their "play." Mr. P., a 40-year-old taxi driver, put it this way:

> Of course I have had lots and lots of women since I got married. I usually meet them while working, like I met you. There are all kinds, married and unmarried, it doesn't matter. I have never fallen in love with any of them. I make sure it never happens (*sarang haji antorok handa*). I set things up that way; usually, I see a woman only once or twice. That way I never give them a chance to fall in love with me. They just get together with me because they want sex. It's just for fun.

Most of the men we interviewed seemed unaware of the contradiction between their belief that "by nature" a woman can only have one man and their insistence that *chigŏp yŏsŏng* (career women or working women; a term used by some men to refer to sex service workers) engage in the sex trade because they enjoy it. They blamed both wives and *chigŏp yŏsŏng* for men's promiscuity. According to Professor S.:

> It's a mistake to blame men; women are the ones becoming prostitutes and tempting men . . . they do it because they enjoy that kind of work. Also, I think women should try harder to please their husbands sexually. Then perhaps they could prevent them from fooling around with other women.

That irresponsible male behavior is generally blamed on women can also be seen in popular clichés about mothers creating the problems by spoiling their sons. Indeed, in our interviews men blamed women for a number of other contemporary social problems, such as real estate inflation, socially destructive familism, and social corruption, including bribery of teachers, and luxurious consumption habits. Housewives were sometimes sneeringly referred to as "real estate aunties" who were having affairs on the side with "real estate uncles." A number of men, while admitting that their own behavior might be viewed as sexually promiscuous, insisted that housewives were contributing to the disintegration of "Korean culture" by frequenting cabarets in search of lovers or paying masseurs in beauty salons for sex.

Our interviewees' notions of female biological inferiority were not simple extensions of traditional Confucian precepts. Rather, they were reformulations of those precepts for deployment in a modern state that defends and supports women as preservers of male dominance and as facilitators of men in the public sphere. Thus, notions of biological determinism concerning masculinity and femininity go hand in hand with the socially constructed definitions of "masculine" and "feminine" to which almost all of our interviewees, no matter what their age or social status, ascribed. They measured "manliness" according to social status "outside," particularly earning ability, while they judged women by their ability to maintain strong households and take good care of children "inside."

Thus, the *chigŏp yŏsŏng*, no matter how physically attractive or skilled at pleasing men, remained permanently below the wife.[19] Likewise, it was never sexual attractiveness or prowess that made a man "masculine," but the implication of wealth (and thus, earning ability) that accompanied his ability to attract sexual partners and to pay for female entertainment, which at the highest levels is enormously expensive, involving generous tips to the women as well as payment for food and drinks. When rich men bragged to us about their sexual exploits, then, they were also boasting about their earning ability, or their socially constructed "masculinity." Social power was indistinguishable from "masculinity," and since women were excluded "by nature" from masculinity, their proximity to social power was determined by their relationships with powerful men.[20]

Most of the extramarital sexual relations the men described could only have been indulged in by a man who could well afford them. One 69-year-old corporation executive bragged about the young college women he had his employees procure for him. What this man viewed as a reciprocal relationship was in fact a reiteration of gender and class inequalities. The best candidate, he said, was a girl who needed money to attend the university. The relationships lasted between two months and two years, he said; he always ended them, but he was certain that the girls had no regrets, since during the courting, he would buy them expensive gifts, give them cash, pay their tuition fees, and even pay their housing expenses. When the affair was over, he would present them with large cash gifts. "It's a mutually beneficial arrangement," he said proudly. "I get what I need, and the girl gets what she needs."[21]

Male Bonding

The traditional Confucian virtue of loyalty between male friends seems to have been reformulated for the modernization of South Korea, which has been built on interlocking relations between the military, government, and industry—all hierarchies run by networks of tightly bonded men. No matter what their age, the middle-class and wealthy men we interviewed particularly emphasized the importance of male friendship, by which they also meant male networks and connections that were concomitant with the debasement of women.

Male bonding incorporates, even appropriates, traditional notions of filial piety. For the most part, the middle-aged men we interviewed could not speak without tears forming over the memories of their mothers,[22] who lived through the Japanese colonization, World War II, the partition of the nation, and the Korean War. Often the women of this generation had little formal education and devoted themselves to their sons; after all, for centuries the only viable way for a woman to command respect in Korean society was to be the mother of a son. Although the men agreed that their mothers were worthy of their sentimental attachment, their reverence for one woman was connected to the derogation of another, since they commonly compared their wives unfavorably to their mothers. At the same time, these same men repeated anecdotes about the importance of male solidarity, even when it meant that they had to be part of a group who victimized their own mothers. Mr. L. spoke about his stepfather:

> He had a concubine in every town, with one or two children by each woman, like a *chigekkun* (a day laborer who carries loads on an A-frame) with a *p'ojangmach'a ajumma* (a woman who cooks and serves food at a roadside or sidewalk stall)—there are always women for a man. When I was younger, I felt sorry for my mother, but now I understand that what he did was natural.

76

According to Professor S.:

My father was famous for his affairs with the ladies. My mother was sick about it, but I understood him. If a man is wealthy and capable of managing several women, it's all right because it won't destroy the family. My mother was very upset, but I just laughed. I said, "Be glad he is healthy." My sisters didn't agree, but my brothers understood.

For most of the men we interviewed, the *sul munhwha* or cafe culture and the *chigŏp yŏsŏng* were simply part of their camaraderie with other men, whether co-workers or friends, in critical business dealings or in stress-relieving pleasure.[23] The *sul munhwa* was an essential element for men's work and role in the public sphere. As Mr. P., a young company middle manager explained,

There's a saying, work plus liquor plus women equals business. To do well, you have to go along with this. It's not like you say, "Hey! Let's have sex with hostesses tonight." That just happens, depending on the atmosphere and how you feel.

To create the desirable atmosphere of male comfort while bonding with one another for business, we were told, a hostess must be cheerful, pleasing, and fun. Hostesses have to laugh at the men's jokes, dance with them, and avoid talking about heavy or serious matters. Instead, they tell sex jokes, make small talk, and sing songs. Since the women facilitated good relationships among the men, the pleasure was *for* business, but business and pleasure are not mixed. The business was for the men, as was the pleasure, which the women provided.[24] Of course the women should be attractive and well dressed, with beautiful clothes and sparkling accessories; the more expensive the room salon the more important her clothing and makeup, which are after all part of the atmosphere being created. But a woman's skill at facilitating the "fun" was deemed more important than her looks *per se*.

To many of the men we spoke with, it was important that women not come between male colleagues and friends. When groups of men visited cafes, bars, and room salons, it would be extremely awkward if one of the men became attached to one of the women, for then he would no longer be primarily part of the male group. Ascribing to the popular belief that only a fool brags about his own wife or allows himself to be seen as henpecked, the men were anxious not to be seen as overly concerned about women, whether they be wives, mistresses, lovers, or hostesses. In fact, male feelings of solidarity with other men were in direct proportion to their disdain for women. As industrialist Mr. P. said, "With women, I get hot and cool down fast; with men, my relationships go on for years and years." His close friend, gynecologist and clinic director Dr. C., asserted that he despised women, whom he considered as petty and ignorant. "I like men as human beings much better," he told us, "they are more active, more interesting, more exciting, and challenged by their work." Many of our interviewees, in particular the wealthy ones, described South Korea as a "paradise for men," perhaps envied by the West as a place where men's "natural instincts" could be fully indulged. As Mr. P. said:

> There are many snakes on the mountain. If you take a pitchfork and stab it anywhere, you will get one. You just jab back and forth until you get a response . . . My attitudes are common among men over 40 in the middle class and above. I know for a fact that when western men come to Korea, they are 99 percent like us. If they had the chance, they would live the same way we do all the time.

As Mr. K, a wealthy businessman, said: "You don't want the same food all the time; you can't eat *sŏllŏngt'ang* every day. Women are like property; you always want more." Many of our interviewees thought of the *chigŏp yŏsŏng* as objects, repeatedly associating them with food, sport, toys, flowers, decorations, atmosphere, or a temporarily invigorating bath at the *mogyokt'ang* (public bath house). Variety was an important factor; Mr. P., a 50-year-old company president, described "having different women" as being like "hitting a ball in tennis or golf: every play is different, and every woman is different. It's just fun." None of the interviewees who frequented cafes and room salons had ever given the hostesses much thought. According to a 32-year-old taxi driver, "Let's face it: a woman [whom you pay for sex] is like a nice meal. It's part of having fun. You pay for the meal, partake of some, and leave the rest. You forget about it; you don't *respect* it." Men talked about these women as diversions and as rechargers of their "low batteries" drained by work pressures or boredom with their wives.

When I was living in Seoul in the 1960s, I was continually struck by how everyone and everything seemed to have its widely understood appropriate place and function, separated by differences in social class, age, place of origin, and, of course, gender, and situated within a hierarchy of values that always made it clear what belonged above and what below. Professors were expected to behave "like professors." Women were supposed to behave "like women." Poor people were supposed to be treated differently from rich people. People who studied literature were not supposed to comment on politics. An *ajumma* (older woman) was not supposed to wear her hair like an *agassi* (young unmarried woman).[25] In the 1980s, the speedy transformation of South Korean society into a capitalist culture made some aspects of people's daily lives and relationships wildly contradictory. Styles and trends turned over in rapid succession. Still, I detected rather general agreement on the suitability of various kinds of social behavior. For the most part, the men we interviewed felt comfortable with marriage, love, and sex being kept separate and believed that clear distinctions had to be drawn between wives and lovers.

"A Lover Can't Become a Wife"

A 50-year-old high school director told us, "If the lover tried to invade the *anpang* (inner room), I'd end it right there. She would be trespassing the proper boundaries." While hostesses were equated with inanimate objects, wives, who preserved a man's social status and reputation, were granted human dimensions. The men we interviewed drew a clear distinction between marriage and sex, just as wives who bore men's children were distinguished from the educated and decorative *kisaeng* who were romanced in earlier centuries.[26] For many of the wealthy and middle class men we interviewed, "decent" meant "middle-class," and both were associated with wives and mothers, while "indecent" and "working class" was associated with the *chigŏp yŏsŏng*.[27] It was important to segregate the two kinds of women. As Professor S., a 48-year-old teacher of statistics at a major university, told us:

I have affairs with hostesses, but never married women....What's important is not to wreck . . . [any man's] family [meaning in part, deprive a man's children of their birth mother].[28] It would be indecent to do it with a student, a virgin, or a married woman. To me, a wife is a wife and a hostesses is a hostess.

Virtually all of the men who said they frequented room salons and cafes said that they would never divorce their wives for other women. As Mr. L., a 39-year-old attorney specializing in international trade law and employed by the most prestigious law firm in Seoul, said:

It would be a disaster and a mistake to get seriously involved with some [service] woman. It could damage a man's career, family, parents, and children. It could affect everyone, almost his entire life. I never want that kind of disaster.

As a rule, the men we interviewed had their first sexual experience when in their youth with a prostitute, almost ritualistically—usually after drinking heavily with friends. Even when asked, no one could remember anything about the prostitute. The men we interviewed did not consider sexual encounters with women in exchange for money to be "extra-marital affairs." Rather, they are merely "entertainment," like sports. Mr. P., a 50-year-old company president, said, "Sex should be like sports—fun. You have to be able to do it laughing, without being possessive or jealous, and without feeling guilt or regret. A man's relationship with his wife is totally different: that is not a game."

Some men, far from viewing their extramarital activities as harmful to their wives, said that they engaged in activities with *chigŏp yŏsŏng* precisely to preserve Korea's most sacred institution, the family. A well-known television actor in his mid-40s, Mr. L., asserted that prostitution, which provides men a way to satisfy their "desires" and "curiosity," was necessary to protect wives and daughters. This view reflects the logic behind the public prostitution system in Japan: to maintain the integrity of the household as the base unit of the state. Indeed, the "good wife, wise mother" ideal—promulgated in Japan in the first decade of this century as a way to interpolate women into the service of the state during a period of intense industrialization, foreign expansionism, and militarism—was adopted by Japanese colonial and native Korean political leadership as well and continues to shape social constructions of gender in contemporary South Korea.

Especially among the men old enough to have been deeply touched by the ideologies of the colonial period, a "good wife, wise mother" was not associated with sex. A wife should not be sexy; like the man's sacred mother, she should be wise, virtuous, and proper. She should shore up her husband's reputation in society and raise his children to be successful citizens.

But while they were spoken of as binary opposites, wives and *chigŏp yŏsŏng* also seemed inextricably bound, both holding up albeit in different ways the patriarchal household as a sacrosanct bulwark and base unit of the modern state. And despite their insistence on their ability to preserve the boundaries between the *chigŏp yŏsŏng* and their wives, men sometimes blurred the distinction, objectifying both hostess and wife. Some men asserted that seeing the same wife every night was "boring" to them: in the words of 38-year-old Mr. K, a *kwajang* (office manager), "My wife is like one of my belongings. She's just there beside me all the time. New things look so nice to me." Another 32-year-old *kwajang* asserted, "Most men have affairs. You look at your wife and think, *kŭ ŏlguli kŭ ŏlguligo, kŭ momi kŭmomigo* (that face is that face, that body is that body), and you want a new face, a new body. I have had about twenty or thirty affairs. I didn't love any of them, and I don't really remember them either. Believe me, everyone does what I do. They are lying if they say otherwise." As Mr. S., the 48-year-old college professor, put it, "Sometimes [the wife] is better and sometimes [the hostess] is better . . . it's like playing the piano and the guitar; each instrument has a different response."

Paradoxically, while the men tried to rationalize and justify their extramarital activities as helpful to the preservation of the family system and the sanctity of their wives within that system, they also blamed their wives for their infidelities and suggested that the wives needed to be flexible and tolerant "to protect and preserve the family." Mr. L., a 50-year-old dentist, asserted that at least half of the responsibility for husbands fooling around with other women belongs with the wives. "I would never have done it myself if my wife had been ideal," he asserted. Television star Mr. L. also warned that wives should persevere, adding that if the wife was not "nice," her husband might start comparing her with the many other available women.

Class Matters

Although our focus here is gender, the imbrication of gender in class relations is evident: as we look at gender, we find we must look at class. Nowhere is the interpolation of masculinity and femininity into the service of the modernizing state clearer than when the male discourse on women is viewed through the lens of class. While the captains of industry might think of the *chigŏp yŏsŏng* as a new toy or a snack between meals, tasted and quickly forgotten, and of the wife as a status-preserving accouterment, the unemployed manual laborer is likely to identify the cafe hostess as a fellow worker struggling to make a living and the wife as an indispensable economic partner. Because the richest men benefited the most from existing hierarchies, they were invested in the preservation of distinctions among women that were all but meaningless for the poorest men.

Our interviews revealed that very wealthy men were the most unabashedly patriarchal, in part because they believed that their wealth and power gave them license to do whatever they wished. In general, among the men we interviewed, rich men wanted wives who were obedient and who could successfully manage whatever their husbands required, whether this was relations with their husbands' kin, supervision of the children, or making themselves into a suitable adornment for their husbands. The wife should not nag, complain, or insist that her husband mediate disputes between herself and his mother.

Of course, a wife's talents and resources would have to be directly harnessed to the husband's family. Dr. H., a 36-year-old oncologist, said that he was the tenth eldest son in ten generations of his family. Since both his grandfathers had graduated from Kyŏnggi High School and Seoul National University and were physicians, and since his family was very wealthy from land speculation, he was considered superior husband material. Dr. H. told us that he had had about one hundred *mat sŏn* (introductions), and these were only a tiny percentage of the requests for introductions, since his mother would choose only two or three from among thirty requests per month. Dr. H. was looking for an obedient woman.

> Women are best at home; a wife must serve others, not herself. Men are better than women in terms of having ideas. Women who work quit or go home early. They tire easily. There is only one administrator at our hospital, and she is the chief of the nurses. She had to be a woman because all the nurses are female.

Dr. H. married a pediatrician who refused to obey his order to quit her job.[29] He pointed out to us that she brought very little to the marriage: her parents supplied the couple with only one small apartment.[31] To punish her and pressure his wife to obey him, Dr. H. said he withheld sex and then beat her. Although she did not quit her job, he bragged that she was only disobedient 10 percent of the time now instead of 60 or 70 percent like before: "She changed because she knows I like obedience." When we asked him what complaints she might have about him, he replied, "There is nothing to complain about; I am very generous."

Seoul in the late 1980s was a bustling place, imbued with a spirit of intense competition. The high level of stress from which South Korean men were popularly thought to suffer seemed a condition of the middle-class men who struggled fiercely for a foothold in the rapidly fluctuating market culture. Teaching English conversation to young *sawŏn* (managerial trainees) of the D. Group, I learned that only two of the eight or ten trainees would be promoted to *kwajang*, the next level. Thus, although they had to spend all day in each other's company five and a half days each week, and although South Korean male culture is still infused with the importance of male friendship and bonding against a common enemy (such as a rival corporation), an undercurrent of fearful rivalry characterized their relationships. In the end, capitalist culture limited the possibility of real trust and intimacy among these men, and male bonding seemed most clearly efficacious for the already powerful.

The quality of human relationships within the family was tainted for the young *sawŏn* as well; they frequently complained to me that when they arrived home after long hours at the office (they could not leave the offices until their bosses did), they were too tired and stressed to talk to their wives. Besides, according to one young husband,

> We don't like to talk about work with our wives. We already experienced the stress; why should we relive it? We just want a peaceful quiet evening. But our wives and children make additional demands on us.

This view was reiterated by Mr. H., a 35-year-old middle manager:

> I want free time more than anything else. Right now I have none. Besides working, I have to spend my extra time shopping with my wife, attending holiday activities with the family, and so forth. To me, all this is just more burden.

Pre-capitalist and capitalist patriarchal practices combined to lock middle-class men into holding in their stress at home as well as at work. The men at D. Group explained that most South Korean husbands don't talk to their wives about their work problems because of the customary segregation of the men's and women's arenas both inside and outside the home and because talking about difficulties and apprehensions might weaken the wife (and children's) respect and confidence for the husband/father.

Far from critiquing the disciplinary systems that determined their social relations, overworked office men looked to those very systems for relief. They wanted their wives to understand them and comfort them like mothers. Indeed, middle-class men were at times ambivalent about what they expected from women. Often, they wanted both what rich men wanted and what poor men looked for: wives who were both pliable and resourceful—skillful in household management and taking care of the children, prepared to serve their in-laws and to make sure that relationships were smooth in the extended family, and talented at maintaining or advancing the household economy. In addition, they wanted wives to provide a restful, peaceful environment in which they could recover from the stress of their work. They often commented that they considered their wives' lives simple and easy compared to theirs because they saw society, where they worked, as being much more complicated than the household, where their wives worked. Almost every man we interviewed thought that a "good husband" works hard to make his family comfortable, while communicating and spending time with wives and children was not considered critically important. When we asked men if they listened to their wives' problems, they often said, "She has no problems."

Middle-class men often insisted that Korean women have enormous power at home, since wage-earning husbands often turn their entire paychecks over to their wives and since women have almost the sole responsibility for shaping the children. Yet the middle-income and wealthy husbands we interviewed saw themselves as making the major decisions, while their wives took care of the details. "I decide on the basics," one husband explained, "such as whether we should switch our investments from real estate to stocks; she takes care of the details, like selecting the broker, the buyer, and the price. I don't have time for that sort of thing." This thinking was totally consistent with the popular belief that women are best suited for detail work, while men think broadly and widely. Moreover, several men, when asked if they would return to the next life as a woman, said they would never want to be women because then they would have to take care of babies. Delegating small and irksome everyday tasks to wives, they said, leaves room for creative and conceptual work on the part of husbands.

Many men asserted that wives should "sacrifice for their families" by staying at home waiting patiently for their husbands. Love, they said, means sacrifice, and sacrifice develops character. Besides, a woman's patience is usually rewarded.[31] If they are frustrated by their husbands' promiscuity, instead of nagging or trying to take revenge by being promiscuous themselves,[32] they should go to church or get involved in sports. In fact, they should be grateful that their husbands are energetic and virile enough to engage in extramarital activities, since energy and virility are equated with economic success. A man's promiscuous behavior was thus recast as beneficial sacrifice for his wife and family, displacing the female's sacrifice with that of the male. Thus, his "outside activities" for the sake of relieving his work stress and being a better breadwinner might be interpreted as part of his sacrifice for his wife. At the same time, women's sacrifice was deemed inconsequential because it is necessary: men are meant to be in society and women are meant to be at home.[33]

Out of the Loop

If "masculinity" in contemporary South Korea is measured by earning ability, poor men are by definition not "masculine," and their women do not have to be "feminine." Lacking money, poor men have little access to *chigŏp yŏsŏng*. When asked what they looked for in a wife, poor men valued resilience and resourcefulness, or *saenghwalyŏk* (power to survive, livelihood power). *Saengwhalyŏk* was particularly important because in poor families, the wife often contributed importantly to the family's economic survival. Few wives in the poor families we were introduced to did much in terms of serving their husbands' families. The families did not expect much because of their lack of resources; besides, the parents-in-law were often still living far away, in the countryside.[34]

None of the statements about sexual activities and about South Korea as a "paradise for men" were made by poor men. When asked questions about sexuality and sexual practices, Mr. B., an unemployed factory worker and collections agent in his late forties, replied, "When I look back, I see that because of our economic distress we never had any enjoyment. We just had to work every day. My entire youth was spent working like a dog."

Although the most strongly patriarchal and misogynist statements were made by rich men, poor men also resented women, although perhaps in surprising ways: for example, Mr. L., a handsome and young unemployed room salon waiter, told us with some bitterness:

> I have sometimes thought of how it would be to be born a woman, and I have wished I could be a woman. As a man, no matter how much ability you have, it's hard to live without specific skill. Women can just sell their bodies and live.

Likewise, a taxi driver commented ruefully that the women behind the Monmouth Hotel at Ch'ŏngnyangni earned 10,000 *wŏn* for just one trick, while he had to drive his taxi for an hour to get 5000 *wŏn.*[35]

Although many South Korean intellectuals I knew never seemed much interested in the stories told by poor men, I was deeply moved by them. Most of the men were Honam people who had migrated to Seoul from tiny hamlets in search of work as the export-oriented economy choked out agriculture. Working as unskilled construction laborers and factory workers, many of them sustained crippling injuries for which they received no private or public sector compensation and were now unemployed or only marginally employed. After twenty years of hard labor, they could barely walk or even sit up straight. In many cases, their wives worked as housemaids (*p'ach'ulbu*), factory workers, peddlers, or piece workers in small cottage industries or even at their own homes.

Although women comprise 40 percent of today's South Korean work force, most have unskilled jobs, and their average salary is only 57 percent that of a man. To their own detriment, the poor men we interviewed embraced dominant gender ideologies, such as the tenet about men earning and women keeping house. As many poor men depended on their wives' wages, they were directly harmed by the fact that women's wages were much lower than men's. Their economic oppression was exacerbated, not eased, by gender oppression, since according to dominant gender ideologies, without wealth, power, and success, they were not really men. Indeed, like women, their bodies had been placed in the service of the patriarchal state, damaged and discarded after contributing to the enrichment of other men.

One 46-year-old unemployed laborer, Mr. P., explained that he collected outhouse excrement for 300 *wŏn* a day when he arrived in Seoul in 1970. That was the only job he could find. Unlike many of his neighbors, he was not taken by the "Saudi wind" to labor in the Middle East. For many years, before he fell four stories and sustained a crippling back injury, he did construction labor in Seoul. That was during the South Korean building boom. Now he was dependent on his wife's meager earnings. Mr. P. said he sympathized with and appreciated women's problems. Like other poor men we talked to, he told us that he would not criticize a woman who left her husband because he was not properly performing his masculine role of earning a sufficient living.[36]

My wife's brother is staying with us. He has been paralyzed from the neck down for five years, after his garbage cart hit him in the neck as he was running down an icy hill pulling it behind him. He is only 36 years old. He wants to die. My wife has to turn his body over. He urinates and defecates through a tube. His wife left him three months ago with their son. I can't blame her; she is still young, and you never know when a cripple will die.

While many of the poor men we talked with expressed shame that they were unable to work and shame that they washed socks and prepared simple meals as well as lunches for their children, like Mr. P., they expressed considerable understanding of and empathy for women. With feeling, a young taxi driver told me, "Women in Korea are to be pitied. Even when they get a job, their wages are only half of men's, and companies only care about their looks. Men regard them as toys." According to Mr. P., a Yŏngdŭngp'o beer hall operator, "Women nag when their lives are hard and they can't resolve their stress." Mr. H., a young garment worker, indicated that it would be fine with him if his daughter never married, since her mother might have had a better life had she not married him. Mr. K., a taxi driver, explained that he could not be happy in a hierarchical relationship with his wife:

> I never ask my wife to bring me anything. I get it myself and ask her what she wants. I hate to have someone wait on me. She works too, selling clothes. There is no reason why she should have to work outside and inside as well. I try to share all housework and taking care of our baby. We waited seven years for our daughter, and she is very precious to us. My wife had several miscarriages. I don't feel I have to have a son. I can say I am a very happy man.

Many of the construction laborers, vegetable peddlers, male garment workers, bus washers, building guards, boiler tenders, and city gardeners we interviewed expressed sympathy for other poor people across gender lines, as well as hostility toward the rich. Mr. K., a barber, expressed his attitudes as follows:

> Rich customers are selfish and demanding . . . they think that if they

have money, they can buy anything and anyone. They make people into their servants. The rich don't know anything at all about the lives of people who are poor or hungry.

I have heard that customers sometimes complain that these days they don't get enough service and hostesses are just grabbing for tips. But why should they give service? After all, they are not doing the job for pleasure; they are trying to earn money.

Mr. J., another taxi driver, echoed the barber's sentiments:

The rich are just parasites. I would just pass by a rich woman with a flat tire by the side of the road. If it was a worker, I would spend my own money and time to help . . . the rich rule without knowing how people have to live. Taxi drivers know exactly how people have to live. You need to cry, to taste hardship, to become a human being.

In South Korean capitalism, the most marginalized men seemed to evidence the most humane attitudes towards women. At the same time, however, bias against women as a group was evident in that resentment among the poor men toward rich women seemed fiercer than toward rich men. Perhaps the expression of hostility against rich women was more permissible. In any case, some of the harshest popular criticisms of Chun Doo Hwan's regime were directed against his wife, Soonja Lee, who was seen as the epitome of illegitimacy, greed, and arrogance.[37]

Men Bond, Women Compete

It is often said that people of all classes in South Korean society ascribe to ruling ideologies and dominant values. In many cases, it seemed to us that men's anti-female attitudes were shared by women of various socioeconomic levels. According to a relatively small number of women from various social and economic backgrounds whom we were able to interview after we had completed our interviews with men, it did indeed seem that the same patriarchal attitudes and practices that bound men together in turn set women against one another.[38]

Poor women's attitudes toward the rich fluctuated between indignation and acceptance, often depending on the gender of the rich person.

Concurring with poor men's resentment of women whom they considered interlopers in the male world of wealth and status, female golf caddies said they especially hated putting the ball in front of rich women or hostesses whom rich men escorted to the golf course. Women who worked as *p'ach'ulbu* (maids who do not live at their employers' houses) admitted that they did not mind washing rich men's dirty handkerchiefs, socks, and underwear, but they felt they had sunk to the bottom when they had to wash another woman's soiled panties. They accepted the rich man's wealth as emanating from his earning ability, but they viewed the rich woman as shamefully idle, a mere parasite. One 45-year-old maid whose husband earned only 300,000 *wŏn* a month as a peddler of herb medicines mused about rich women:

> I wonder why they make others work like a slave, doing things they could do themselves. Some of the women make me wash their dirty underpants or their sheets with dried semen stuck on them. It's sickening. And these women look down on me! Sometimes, when I am slaving away, the housewife is lying down on the sofa with her clothes off. I wouldn't mind as much if she'd have me clean her room first, so that she could go in, shut the door, and lie down while I am cleaning the other rooms.

Perhaps poor women found it easier to criticize rich women than rich men because they saw the wives as being more like themselves, whereas the husbands' status was *ipso facto* unattainable. One 22-year-old room salon hostess told us that she looked down on, detested, and despised women college students because "even though they pretend to be superior, they are the same as us."[39]

Women of all classes accepted the sexual division of labor, which one woman, the 38-year-old wife of an airline executive, even described as an attractive aspect of what she thought of as "Korean traditions":

> I think sex roles are just fine the way they are. Korea has an excellent tradition. I like to see men be the pillar and women the support . . . Women should never surpass men. Anyway, the basic roles of men and women will never change.

Many of the women we interviewed believed, like the men we met, that in the ideal family, wives should be responsible for the care of the young and the elderly and should provide sympathy, encouragement, and relief for men from both the anxieties of their work and the burden of household management. They felt that wives should be "inside" people, tender and nurturing, while husbands should be assertive go-getting "outside" people. Their acceptance of this Confucian patriarchal ideal meant perpetual dissatisfaction among the wives of poor men, in whose homes the conventional roles were reversed. According to one 31-year-old wife of an unemployed sewer cleaner who cared for their children, cooked their meals, and washed the household dishes while she made accessories at home:

> Men who are too domestic can't succeed. They are too concerned about small details. My husband is not assertive or aggressive. He needs to take more responsibility for the welfare of our family. He should be more active, more positive. He's not really very manly . . . I like men who are active outside the home . . . He's a good-looking man, but I don't care if he's attractive or not, since his being attractive doesn't help me in my life.

Most of the women we talked with disapproved of women's participation in economic activities for anything other than direct support of their own families. Poor women often preferred working at home—making artificial flowers and costume jewelry or doing other kinds of piece work brought to them by manufacturers' subcontractors—over working as part-time maids, even though they made much less money. As the 36-year-old wife of an unemployed construction worker put it, "You have to wash people's dirty underwear. I wouldn't mind doing these things for my own family, but how can it be that I have to do it for other people? They don't even put away their bedding if the maid is coming. Even though I make more money, it makes me feel how low I am."

Traditional Confucian gender, age, and class hierarchies, combined with social inequalities created under Japanese colonialism, cast the mother, the wife, and the concubine, mistress, or *chigŏp yŏsŏng* against one another as they revolve perpetually around one man, all dependent upon and vying for his resources and affections. Victory for one woman generally meant defeat for the other. Nor did an older woman's negative gender experiences necessarily produce sympathy for the younger woman: one mother who had suffered a great deal when her husband carried on a protracted affair with a young secretary told her daughter-in-law that it was all right for her son to stay out late in the company of other women because "men are men."[40] Mothers also passed on patriarchal attitudes to their own daughters, sending them back to violent husbands with the admonition that they must "persevere" for their children's sake.

According to a recent Korean Women's Coalition survey, 87 percent of working women report that they have been sexually harassed, and there are increased reports of domestic violence, rape, and other violence against women. These developments go hand in hand with South Korean economic development policies, which favored the enrichment of giant business conglomerates and the development of the contemporary masculine culture, producing a society that discourages female bonding as much as it encourages male bonding.[41] Wives and *chigŏp yŏsŏng* we interviewed blamed each other for men's promiscuity. Bar hostesses valorized men's work, expressing sympathy for the men and their need to "relieve their stress," while railing against their wives for nagging and being unable or unwilling to provide a soothing and peaceful atmosphere at home. Wives criticized hostesses for tempting men into immoral behavior for money. A number of women married to wealthy men pathologized sexual labor, believing that if hostesses were more conscientious and not merely concerned with making "easy money," they would work as housemaids. According to one housewife, "'service girls' don't even deserve my hatred; they are beneath contempt." Poor women, on the other hand, rarely condemned the *chigŏp yŏsŏng*. One housemaid asserted that hostesses cannot be blamed for trying to survive: "Some married women do what hostesses do, and there are secretaries who act like hostesses. With hostesses, at least it's their job."

"I Like Men Who Are Kind and Understanding"

Though the South Korean women we interviewed shared many of the men's views about what gender roles and relationships "should be" and expected assertiveness, not tenderness, from men, many of them were deeply dissatisfied with the men in their lives. Some made passionately negative comments about Korean men as a group. This could mean that they did not believe that the men were measuring up to the patriarchal ideal; it could also mean that the women felt patriarchal attitudes and practices were in some way preventing them from feeling fulfilled. Whether or not women's expectations of marriage and men have been influenced by the Hollywood films and television programs that have proliferated in South Korea since the 1960s, many of the women we talked to, wives and *chigŏp yŏsŏng*, said that what they missed most from men was kindness, understanding, and communicativeness.

Ms. K., a 22-year-old hostess from Apkujŏngdong, looked for these things among her customers, and when she did not find them, she was almost gleeful about taking money from them in exchange for her own "kindnesses." We met Ms. K. in mid-afternoon, a few hours before she was to begin her nightly routine of keeping company with three different sets of male guests—those who arrived at 8:00 p.m., those who appeared at around 10:00 p.m., and those who came in sometime after midnight. "I guess we work here because we are lazy," Ms. K. offered. She used to earn 180,000 to 200,000 *wŏn* a month as a cashier, but now she makes between 500,000 and 600,000 *wŏn* , or three times as much. True, she had to spend much more on clothing, cosmetics, and a hairdresser and was not able to save very much money, but she was sending some money to her family. Like many other hostesses, her family did not know how she was employed. She lived in a rented room so that they would not see her returning home late every night drunk—she estimated that she drank half a bottle of whiskey each evening—and so that she could accept occasional invitations to spend the night with a customer, who might give her an extra 100,000 or 150,000 *wŏn* .

Ms. K. said that she had stopped seeing her friends from high school and from her old neighborhood because "Korean people don't understand or approve of women who work in liquor places." Ms. K. wished to see herself and her work as socially useful, perhaps even "in the national interest," because she was helping to relieve men of their stress by "kindly pouring drinks and trying to cheer men up so that they might forget their worldly cares." With the help of hostesses, she said, men are prevented from committing "terrible crimes that would throw the whole society into danger," and even though people think of hostesses as "human trash who engage in dirty sexual games," she said, "our proper role is to take our customers' disgraceful behavior with sincerity, and to prevent them from creating trouble and suffering for others." Ms. K. disliked the way the *chigŏp yŏsŏng* was portrayed on Korean television and in films—for example, as a tragic "fallen woman" who had been betrayed by a lover and was now "throwing her life away" for the sake of a younger brother's school fees. But she did seem to feel that she was somehow being "sacrificed." While she performed the needed task of helping relieve men of their stress, they would ultimately return to their wives: "We just give them good entertainment; in the end, their wives will have them." She, on the other hand, did not expect to have what she called a "normal marriage."

> I will have to accept being dumped, or marrying a guy who is older or has been married before. I'd consider marrying a foreigner, but not because I like foreigners or want to live in a foreign country. In fact, I dislike westerners, because they are so stingy. Korean customers are more generous, and at least they have the same skin. I would marry the foreigner so that I could hide my past. In our hearts, we all want a normal family life; everyone dreams about that . . . I have no hopes of marrying a decent man, because his family would never accept me.

Ms. K. believed that while many housewives are naive and self-deceptive, during the short time she had worked as a hostess, she had learned more than she wished to know about men. She deeply resented the way customers debased and dehumanized hostesses.

> Working here affects our attitude towards men. We are very disappointed by the way they act. I can't stand the ones who try to get a discount and are always trying to get us to take off our clothes. They are very crude. They say things like, "How much?" The worst ones are the professors. Everybody thinks that professors are so great, but I don't. They come in and yell, "Hey, you sluts, did you take a shower before coming here?" and things like that. They try to grab you and "play the piano" all over your body. They don't have much money and are very cheap, always trying to cut down the price. Sometimes they don't leave any tip. I don't like doctors either; they have twisted, arrogant personalities.
> People are all the same, whether they have a lot of money or not. Men all become dogs when they drink. They are slobs. They fight with each

other and try to grab us. No matter what, you can't trust them, no matter high their [social] position is. They are still animals. They use all kinds of sweet talk, but when their purpose has been achieved, they coldly turn their backs. If I saw them on the street, they wouldn't even speak to me. To them, I am just a body for the night. Since they only have sex with us, we have to aim only for their money.

Like other women we talked with, what Ms. K. seemed to long for was to be able to give and receive affection and appreciation. When asked what kind of man she preferred, Ms. K. described a customer who visited the room salon frequently, a handsome man in his forties who tipped all the hostesses generously and never tried to touch them. Ms. K. and the other hostesses enjoyed fantasizing about this man's decency, family orientation, and loyalty to his wife.

He never wants to sleep with any of the girls; he just goes home to his wife. He comes here because he wants women's company. He is lonely. His wife has been sick for a long time. I think he loves her a lot. I feel sorry for his children and have even thought that I would like to raise them. I like him because he treats us like human beings. I like men who are kind and understanding.

What hostesses like Ms. K. wanted, wives also coveted. Whether married to rich, poor, or middle-income men, the wives, like Ms. K., said they wanted warmth and kindness from their men, but did not find it. Forty-five-year-old Mi Kyŏng's mother, whose husband was a peddler and who lived in Nankokdong, a low-income neighborhood in southern Seoul, was typical:

I never really liked anything about our married life, from the very beginning. I never liked sex with him. He used to get angry that I never wanted to do it with him, but now he doesn't even care anymore. We've been together for more than ten years, but we don't really give each other our hearts. It's a kind of cold relationship. He never talks. There's no communication. All he ever says is, "Where is so-and-so?" He wants to know where I am if he can't see me. He wants to know where our children are if they are not in the room. That's all he ever says.

According to Ch'ŏl Ung's mother, a 28-year-old resident of the low-

95

income Sinlimdong area whose husband was an unemployed construction worker:

> Do I love him? A woman should love her husband. But if I were born again, I would not marry at all. I'd raise a child without a husband. I could do all the housework and also work for wages. Then I'd be free; I wouldn't have to suffer because of a husband. I often think about divorce, but I can't stand the thought of giving him my son . . . I am *hansim hae* [desperate] to the point of dying. I hate him the most when he is angry for no reason and beats or curses me for nothing. At those times, I just want to die. The old ladies in the neighborhood advise me that even if he's no good, I should just be patient and tolerate it, because then something good will happen to me.

Forty-five-year-old Esther's mother of Nangokdong, whose husband was an herb peddler and who worked as a *p'ach'ulbu,* said:

> My marriage, frankly speaking, is just a duty to me. I am not actually very happy. During the seventeen years we have been married, I never thought, "I really do love him." I stopped even trying to love him. Now I look at him and think that I never even liked him very much. He thinks only of his own pleasure, never about how I feel. He was always like that. "Let's do it." And that's it. If I'm sick, he doesn't comfort me at all. If I didn't have a daughter, maybe I could live alone. I wish I knew what it was really like to be in love. Some of my friends are really attracted to their husbands, but I don't feel anything for mine.

And in the words of Chae Uk's mother, 42, of Sadangdong, a part-time maid whose laborer husband was unemployed, "If I heard he died tonight, I'd feel bad because he's a human being, but that's about all."

Most of the poor men's wives said that they did not enjoy sex with their husbands. Almost all believed that their husbands thought sex was important: some husbands brought home books about sex or "porn" videos, and one was purportedly advised by a family counselor about how to assure his wife's pleasure. But the women insisted that they were either disgusted by or uninterested in these materials. As 31-year-old Su Yŏn's mother, a home pieceworker in Sillimdong whose husband was an occasionally employed sewer cleaner, said:

I don't like sex and never have. It's a bother. I heard that middle-aged women are supposed to like it, but I never have. I just do it as a favor to my husband. He brings home books about sex, but I never look at them. He asks me if I can feel anything, but I say no.

The "good wife, wise mother" ideal does not require women to function as exciting sex partners for their husbands. On the contrary, as suggested earlier, sexuality was viewed by many of our male and female interviewees as almost antithetical to motherhood. Men who had talked about their fathers' adultery were stunned into silence when we asked if their mothers had ever engaged in extra-marital affairs. Although most of the poor women seemed to wish to present themselves as virtuous mothers without much concern about sex, one of the poor women we interviewed, a 45-year-old peddler of rice cakes, fruit, and homemade bread at Sadang Market, started out saying that she was occasionally tempted by young men and felt curious about what sex would be like with someone other than her husband. Later on in the interview, she admitted that she had "tried it once or twice." She had an affair, she said, with another peddler about her age; they met at a shop. She said that she had never liked sex with her husband, and she didn't really like the "sex part" of her relationship with the peddler. What she did like about the affair was the conversation and the "warm feeling."

Though some of the rich women we interviewed seemed to want to make us envy them and their luxurious lifestyles, they, like the poor women, ultimately expressed profound dissatisfaction with their husbands and their marriages.[42] One 47-year-old wealthy widow, Mrs. K., described the wives of wealthy men as being trapped in gilded cages: two-thirds of the women she knew would divorce their husbands if they could support themselves, she asserted. "They are simply existing. They don't feel loved or happy." Mrs. P., 45, a wealthy attorney's wife from Apkujŏngdong, talked about how she often found lipstick on her husband's shirt collars and once even discovered a large photo of a nude woman in his pants pocket. She rationalized that since she disliked sex, perhaps "that sort of thing is the hostess' job" and determined never to ask him where he went. "I don't want to know," she told us. "I'd be happy if I just don't get VD." Despite her suggestion that "rich women can play golf and buy expensive clothing if they are unhappy with their husbands," near the end of the interview, Mrs. P. said, "I don't know why I sometimes feel so sad . . . My husband doesn't know when I'm sad. If he knew, he'd ignore it or try to minimize it."

Mrs. C., a 43-year-old widow introduced to us by one of the wealthy men we interviewed, presented herself at first as a "liberated woman" who enjoyed sexual relations with various lovers. She claimed to have a strong sex drive, so that men in their fifties could not "keep up with me." "We all want young men," she said coyly. "When my friends and I want to enjoy ourselves, we say, 'Let's go smell some men.'" Eventually, however, Mrs. C. admitted that older wealthy women were sometimes taken advantage of and tricked by *chebijok* (young gigolos), who later blackmailed the women by threatening to reveal their adultery to their husbands. Still, she suggested that married women take lovers because what women want is love, not "just sex or money." By the end of the interview, her bravado had lapsed into a kind of pensive sadness:

I've never been fully satisfied by men. Not that I expect anything much. Men can't express their feelings. They just pay the bill. It's kind of sad; they are like stones. I feel sorry for them. Eighty percent of Korean men just stick it in. They say women are frigid, but they have no skill. University professors are the worst. They want dominant sex to bolster their pathetic egos. What is sex if you aren't sensitive to the other person's feelings? You can't get turned on unless the other person is turned on. But most Korean men don't know anything about this. My friends all want communication. Korean men can't communicate. They can only talk about themselves. It's so boring.

Mrs. K., 47, another widow, concurred:

What Korean women want is a real relationship. But Korean men are interested in drink, duty, and success. They get impotent at an early age. Rich men prepare for sex as if they were getting ready to participate in some sport. They usually abstain for several days, go to a sauna, eat, and sleep well before they have sex . . . Korean men are cruel and uncivilized. They just want to oppress and use women.

The reaction of women from various economic backgrounds to Ms. Ch'u and me was revealing. Poor women were the most forthcoming, perhaps because they had the least to lose by being frank. Due to their spouses' economic weakness in the relationship, poor women enjoy positions of relative strength within their marriages, compared to women of other backgrounds. The least frank interviewees were middle-income men's wives who did not work outside the home. Their revelations could jeopardize their marriages and their social positions by divulging too much, but I also sensed that they felt competitive with me and Ms. Ch'u, who are both mothers and career women. These women occasionally criticized, if obliquely, women whose work kept them from devoting themselves to their children and their homes. They suggested that women with too much formal education are often unable to succeed in marriage because they are too self-centered and individualistic to be willing to sacrifice themselves for the sake of their families.

Mrs. S., 38, of Ich'ondong, boasted that her marriage was "perfect" and "ideal." She noted that the role of mother was much more important than the role of wife and that men want most for their wives to be good mothers. Being a good mother, she explained, means devoting oneself to the children's success in school. Indeed, even the poorest Seoul parents believed that one of the surest paths to a secure and comfortable life was graduation from one of the nation's top universities. Each year, however, only about 3 percent of 800,000 South Korean high school seniors were able to gain admission to these schools. A child who successfully entered Seoul National, Yonsei, Korea, or Ewha Womans University was viewed as proof positive of her/his mother's good parenting and her/his parents' good genes. Thus, Mrs. S. told us proudly, "I do everything for my children's education. I think about their food, match my schedule to their assignments and exams." Mrs. S. insisted that she and her husband enjoyed both excellent communication and "great sex." But she added that she was happiest when her children were doing well.

> My happiest moments are when Daddy teaches our oldest daughter math. I worry so much about my daughter's exams that I've lost interest in sex, but I know my husband is very satisfied. Sometimes he's very tired from work, so he's stopped being interested in sex himself anyway.

Chewing Old Meat

Mrs. S. asserted that relationships between Korean men and women had been changing radically every day. She believed that gender equality had been achieved in Korea, stressing that "these days, men try hard to please their wives." Many of our male interviewees also enjoyed talking about the "dramatic changes" in gender roles and relations they had been witnessing and experiencing. Many of these "changes" might be viewed as matters of form rather than content. One small business owner pointed out that while men of the past kept concubines and supported extra households and babies, modern Korean men socialize with hostesses for a night in exchange for money, which allows them a "clean break." Several men lamented that neither hostesses nor wives were as giving and as self-sacrificing as women of the past, and they took this as a bad sign for the society as a whole. Several male interviewees complained that even being in cafes and room salons was becoming stressful for them because hostesses were coldly mechanical and too obviously mercenary instead of warm and welcoming as in the past. Mr. B., a corporation executive in his late 40s, recalled his mother wiping grease from the soy sauce bottle and making sure that bottle lids were screwed on tight. "She was very fastidious and conscientious compared with my wife," he explained.

> My wife sets out socks with holes in them. Even if my mother were sick and didn't get enough sleep, she would still get up in the morning to make our lunches. But my wife just gives the kids money to buy their lunches that day. I know that my wife is more self-sacrificing than my friends' wives, but I can't help thinking that my children are not getting the kind of treatment I enjoyed when I was a child. The world has changed a lot.

Mr. P., a 32-year-old middle income company *kwajang*, congratulated himself on being less demanding than his father, who used to wake his mother up in the middle of the night to demand a glass of water. But he mourned the loss of what he remembered as "oriental women's behavior" at the workplace, which he found beautiful and appealing:

In the old days, everything was set up for the men and the women just endured it. Things have changed, but I think it's getting out of hand. In the old days, office girls were innocent and obedient. Today, they go dancing at bars and have sex relations freely. They are not polite and respectful as in the past. They are just concerned about their rights, not their responsibilities. If I say, "Ya! Bring some juice for our visitors," they say, "We don't have any," or "Mr. P. *soni ŏpsŏyŏ* (don't you have any hands)?" This really makes me mad. I think men should have their work and women theirs. Women are the ones who should serve the coffee. It looks so good seeing them do it (*pogi chot'a*).

While some men had apparently turned away from hostesses, this seemed due less to a change in gender relations or to the elevation of women's status than to an increase in the recreation possibilities for men. As Mr. P., a wealthy 50-year-old businessman and graduate of a prestigious university who considered himself part of the vanguard of Korean men who express enlightened attitudes towards sexuality, put it:

I have always enjoyed women a lot. When I was young I met women almost every day and had sex with them. These were hostesses and other *chigŏp yŏsŏng*. I've had gonorrhea 21 times. You never remember anything about these women. You just get excited after drinking with a group of friends, and each of us would have one woman. We never had sex with the same one twice. None of them loved me, and I didn't love them either. It was just entertainment, to go along with drinking. If I really liked a girl, I wouldn't sleep with her.

After 40, I went for housewives, widows, and divorcees I met at my health club or at cabarets and discos. I don't need to give them money, and they don't give me any either . . . Very young women are not to my taste. It's a matter of cycles not matching: like a radio, you have to hit the station exactly for it to come out clearly. *Nŭlgŭn mari k'ongŭl mani mŏngnŭnda* (the old horse eats a lot of corn). Chewing tough meat can be delicious.

Mr. P.'s equation of women with radio stations, animals, and meat suggests that while distinctions between female professional entertainers and wives may be fading, the subordination of women as a group may not be.

*　　　*　　　*

Eight years have elapsed since these interviews were conducted. The year of the research is now described by many as a watershed year in South Korea. In 1987, massive citizen protests resulted in the first free elections in Korean history. Weary of prolonged sacrifice and privation "for the nation," South Korean workers demanded a share of the wealth they produced, spawning spectacular labor movement activities that rocked the country all year long. The South Korean government heralded the 1988 Olympics as the symbol of the nation's emergence as a *sŏnjinguk* ("developed country") and exhorted the citizens to "be cosmopolitan."

During the past eight years, many old notions have been challenged: for the first time in history, ordinary South Korean citizens were permitted to travel abroad freely. People with at least some money can now learn first-hand about countries other than Japan and the U.S. The break-up of the Soviet Union and the demise of the socialist bloc undermined the Cold War stance of South Korean officialdom, while throwing the South Korean Marxist or Marxist-oriented social movement into disarray. Many people say that everything about gender roles and relations has completely changed in Seoul. The nuclear family is increasingly important as a social unit. Business in room salons and cafes has diminished to almost nothing on weekends, because young men are spending their weekends with their wives and children. The male culture is diversifying rapidly. Today, when the office boss invites his young male employees to go drinking after work, some young men dare to leave early, saying, "Sorry, but my wife is waiting for me at home."[43] Some middle-class young men have even begun to wash dishes and help their wives with the cooking; many believe that to do so means that they are modern and enlightened. In modern Seoul, much of what is understood to be "western" has come to stand erroneously for gender equality. Nowadays there is a popular series of jokes about "husbands with guts" who dare to ask their wives for breakfast or who want to know where their wives are going when they leave the house. Current films feature career women and "decent" women engaging in sexual activities. Sexuality is even being discussed on television talk shows. Sex education is now offered in primary schools. Recently, a symposium was held on a university campus about "campus sex."

But the advent of new, "softer" masculinities or indeed the decline of patriarchy may not necessarily be precursors to the emancipation and empowerment of South Korean women. They certainly have not been in the U.S. In her study of changing representations of masculinity in U.S. popular culture, Abigail Solomon-Godeau argues that new representations of eroticized, androgynous, "soft" masculinity "do not necessarily transgress—and indeed, may affirm—the patriarchal privileges of masculinity, however inflected."[44] What Barbara Ehrenreich sees as the end of patriarchy in the U.S. has by no means been the same thing as women's liberation. Particular groups of women are protected by patriarchal practices, although usually at the expense of another group. According to Ehrenreich, the decline of patriarchy in the U.S. has spelled not empowerment for women but "new forms of exploitation and degradation," since it has been accompanied by a convenient (for men) sense that even middle-class white women do not need protection, which results in, among other things, more women-headed households and declining male interest in children, as well as more male anger against women in general as displacers or indeed "oppressors" of men.[45]

I suspect that it is not yet time to relegate the opinions and attitudes I heard expressed in Seoul eight years ago to the dustbin of history.[46] At this moment, it seems to me, gender relations in class-inflected South Korean commodity culture are a complex, contradictory tangle of the residual and the emergent. There seems to be an element of extremism. Today's rich old businessmen prefer intellectual young women, whom they gift with laptop computers instead of jewelry and expensive handbags. While it is true that "love hotels" have sprung up around college campuses in recent years, it is also true that surgeries to restore the hymen are very popular. The smart young upper-class or upper-middle-class woman of today, I am told, has three boyfriends: a rich old one, a sexy young one, and the one from a good family and good earning potential whom she will marry. Young women walk the streets of Seoul in mini-skirts and halter tops, their navels completely exposed. And eating disorders have spread rapidly among young South Korean women in the past decade.

While today's South Korean youth may be free not to reproduce certain kinds of hierarchies with long histories of brutality, the brutality of class differences has not yet been destroyed and will undoubtedly remain as long as capitalism thrives in South Korea. Working-class women remain at the bottom of the socioeconomic scale and are still disproportionately victimized by various forms of violence and sexual harassment. Moreover, increases in South Korean women's status may be less related to increases in gender equality than to the influx of female service workers, including sex service workers, from the Third World. Like patriarchy, capitalism favors some at the expense of others.

In modern South Korean life, attempts to commodify and capitalize on men's and women's desire for human warmth and sympathy threaten to disfigure and and limit gender relations. If the only "real men" are the *chaebol* (conglomerate magnates) and women of all classes are privatized for masculine needs, women must be mercenary and gender relations are reduced to financial transactions. For the building of modern South Korean patriarchal capitalism, a certain kind of male subject has been called for, over and against female labor and sexuality. Masculinity requires loyalty and obedience to hierarchy, as well as a sexuality articulated through intensely homosocial activities. For South Korean men, the price of this masculinity has been high—not only in terms of stress and anxiety but also loss of affective qualities and perhaps even early death. If male formation in South Korea divides feelings from sexuality, women can only be debased as sexual objects (hostesses) or deprived of emotional connections (wives), so that they must struggle to be and do everything, even though they will never be good enough.[47] While there is no doubt that the contemporary family and thus the state would disintegrate without them, women continue to be widely viewed in South Korean society as secondary and insignificant compared to men.

As long as South Korean masculinity is based on disdain for women and on the creation and management of female otherness, women cannot realistically hope to receive from men the warmth, kindness, and understanding they long for. In the meantime, men, seeking instant, if ephemeral, relief from the stresses of their exploitation in the service of the state and of the expectations of wives who measure their worth by their earning ability, will turn to the *sul munhwa* for male bonding and a brief opportunity to talk with women who, knowing that they have but one way to benefit, exchange their sympathetic smiles for cash.

104

It is clear that efforts to bring about gender equality must involve not an indictment of male subjects but of a state that requires gender to be practiced in this way.

Although no concrete solutions emerge to the many problems suggested by what people say about gender constructions and relations, we can detect a certain precariousness about contemporary South Korean patriarchal ideology, cross-cut as it is by class, fraught with differences of all sorts, and underscored by an insistent desire for human warmth and compassion. Patriarchal attitudes and practices in contemporary South Korean society may appear a thick, seamless, and unruffled surface, but a closer look reveals cracks and fissures, openings through which women might maneuver and that might make change possible.

A Stake in the Outcome

The invincibility of Korean patriarchal practices has been challenged throughout the history of Korean women in the U.S. Despite the attempts of village elders, community leaders, and Korean Association presidents from Honolulu to New York City to maintain male dominance by equating patriarchy with patriotism and "Korean culture," the untenability of Korean patriarchal practices in this social environment is instantiated in many ways. For example, many immigrant parents, wanting the best for both sons and daughters, educate the boys to expect pampering and subordination from women, while at the same time encouraging the girls to excel in the public domain. Apparently, they are comfortable with the contradiction of telling their sons that males should not enter the kitchen and pressuring their daughters to earn high grades and enter prestigious careers. Inevitable clashes between male and female expectations of marriage were averted somewhat until the mid-1980s as young Korean American men traveled to South Korea to find wives. But the rise in South Korean living standards, among other things, has made such marriages less and less attractive to Korean American women in recent years. As a result, the male dream of female pampering and subordination may have to end.

Korean American women share a long legacy of female insubordination, from the first Bible women and "picture brides" who sailed for Hawaii at the turn of the century, to the women who put down an anchor for their extended families when they married U.S. servicemen, to the thousands of other women who left Korea and stayed away because they could not or would not conform to the expected gender roles—women who did not want to marry, women who wanted careers, divorcees, single mothers, childless women, survivors of scandals, artists, intellectuals, eccentrics. Sometimes leaving South Korea for the U.S. or elsewhere in the world gave women more ways to be female, not because gender equality exists in these other places but because the women could recreate themselves in new social environments, distanced from the discipline of the militarized masculine state and the social mechanisms that maintain it.

Lisa Rofel warns us that the production of knowledge about Asia is "far from a matter of neutral or objective description." Rather, she suggests, it is "infused with and implicated by the long history of European and American colonialism."[48] Caught amid intersecting dominations, the Korean American feminist, while mindful of these infusions and implications, traverses the boundaries between feminist and cultural nationalist concerns and might offer another view. Like their counterparts in Korea, Korean American feminists must struggle with cultural nationalists who place all other political progress over gender equality and cling fiercely to sentimentalized notions of Korean women as symbols of some traditional essence, as martyrs of colonial domination, as the sacred mothers of male leaders and warriors, and as repositories of the Korean past. After all, Korean American feminists walk a tightrope similar to the one on which South Korean feminists are precariously balanced. At the same time, for the Korean American feminist who needs a vocabulary for her identity, a language to make sense of her own experiences, an understanding of South Korean gender issues is helpful in clarifying the importance of both class and gender in the formation of cultural identities. This realization is particularly useful because the racialization that plays such a major role in shaping Korean American, as opposed to South Korean, experiences often obscures class and gender oppressions. Of course the sexism in the U.S. is very often racist sexism. Thus, for the Korean American woman, relinquishing her identification with "Korea," however patriarchal, means abandonment to other oppressions, such as the West's eager embrace of her victimization by Asian patriarchy as a concrete demonstration of western cultural superiority.

Clearly, patriarchal attitudes and practices, as well as other hierarchies of oppression, can only be ended if people work together to destroy them. Though fiercely courageous as individuals, Korean American women, like their sisters in South Korea, need to create more opportunities to work collectively toward common goals. Perhaps Korean and Korean American women may recognize each other in some intellectually and psychologically safe space so that they might work together as sisters across the waves, with love and compassion, to dismantle the structures that deform and dehumanize both women and men. Collectively, they could refuse to participate in the production of state-sanctioned masculinity. Perhaps gender and sexuality can function as one of the key sites where rage against various kinds of repression and erasure and desire for a new politics can be worked out. Hopefully, disappointment with and resentment of men can be transformed into energy to struggle not against individual men but against the state that originates, sanctions, and reinforces certain kinds of masculinity and requires gender to be thus practiced. Likewise, the goal of this struggle would have to be so much more than men's affection and attention; it would have to be an ultimately better world for both women and men— a world in which exploitative hierarchy and the exclusion and commodification of women are but memories of a long-forgotten past.

NOTES

I wish to thank Professor Cho Hyŏng of Ewha Womans University for introducing me to my research associate, Ch'u Aeju. I am also grateful to Jung-In Kang, Candice Kim, and Ann Park for assisting with various interviews, and Nancy Abelmann, Lauren Bryant, Chungmoo Choi, Kyonghee Choi, Eungie Joo, Suk-man Kim, Susan K. Lee, Lisa Lowe, Eithne Luibheid, Albert Rhee, Lisa Rofel, Moira Roth, and Lilia Villanueva for generously reading and commenting on various versions of this essay.

1. Growing up Korean American in Maryland in the 1950s (my father came to the U.S. as a foreign student in 1926 and my mother was either born in Hawaii or arrived there with her plantation worker mother when she was an infant), I felt the sting of race discrimination almost every day of my life, while Korean and American patriarchal practices struck only an occasional contrapuntal chord. My brother and I were often treated like creatures from an alien planet. Although we were continually asked where we were "really from," since it was a given that we could not possibly be "from" America, almost no one who asked had ever heard of Korea.

Living among people who continually reminded us that we did not belong made it all the more important to us to be *from* somewhere. My brother and I believed that Korea, that always comforting thought, was our "home." Our father regaled us with stories about Korea, describing people and events that could never be found in our school textbooks. Our parents, believing in encyclopedias as the key to progress, modernity, and the West itself, had three sets. Our father's stories were often punctuated with a validating gesture toward a well-thumbed entry on "Korea," to which the "K" volume always fell open. That way, he tried to prove to us that Korea did not exist only in his imagination. Since our mother hadn't lived in Korea, she saw it through his eyes just as we did. His stories, however, did not prepare me for what I was to experience in Korea as a female and as a Korean American when, armed with an Ivy League education and a burning desire to become "Korean," I signed up to teach at Ewha Womans University between 1966 and 1967.

The Korean society I encountered was far from the comforting "home" I had expected. Eighteen months later, I returned feeling no more "Korean" than I had been allowed to feel "American," with my sense of gendered identity profoundly shaken. All year, I had been given instructions by everyone on how to walk, talk, and think properly. I soon realized that these instructions were aimed at crafting me into a suitable wife and mother. I hadn't known that since I was twenty-five by "Korean age," I was already "over the hill." At the time, most young women in Seoul who were my age were already married. My relatives and their friends looked on me with a sense of urgency, as when a vegetable begins to wilt and has to be tossed out if it can't be sold. Relatives, acquaintances, and even strangers sighed sympathetically and commented that it would not be easy for someone like me to find a husband, without whom I would not be able to fulfill my destiny. I had *toduknombal*, or feet like a thief (only men's shoes fit my size 7 1/2 feet). I could not speak Korean well. Everyone agreed that even a permanent wave and more attractive clothing would not really help.

What made things almost impossible was that I was born in the year of the horse, an excellent year for men but a terrible year for women. No parents want their sons to marry horse women because, I was told, horses are known for wandering away from hearth and home. The year I arrived in Seoul was 1966, the year of the fire horse, which comes once every sixty years. South Korea was still a poor country then, and many families worried that they would be unable to marry off daughters born that year, for it was said that husbands of women born in the year of the fire horse die young. I noticed that there was not a single wedding for four months at the church next door to where I lived, ostensibly to prevent the birth of a baby girl until the following year. During semester break in late 1966, I volunteered at an orphanage. Girl babies were deposited on the steps of the building every day. I understood that there were many more babies brought to the orphanage than usual. Whether from simple son preference or from wishing to avoid fire horse girls, only one of the perhaps one hundred babies brought to us was a boy, and he was adopted within a few weeks. Not one girl was claimed.

More than twenty years later, I decided to spend another year in Seoul on a Fulbright grant, teaching and conducting a research project so that I could try to understand that encounter with a powerful set of patriarchal practices that had so overwhelmed me two decades earlier, and from which I have even now not yet completely recovered. This project was conducted during the year 1987–1988.

2. Eve Kosofsky Sedgwick, "'Gosh, Boy George, You Must Be Awfully Secure in Your Masculinity,'" in *Constructing Masculinity,* ed. Maurice Berger, Brian Wallis, and Simon Watson, New York: Routledge, 1995.

3. In the 1970s, Korean church women and others conducted a campaign against sex tourism in South Korea. Most of the "tourists" were from Japan. By the late 1980s, I learned from bar hostesses, customers from Japan continued to be important, but many of them were Korean Japanese, and South Koreans vastly outnumbered men from Japan.

4. During the long decades of military rule in South Korea, beginning with the 1961 military *coup d'état* and extending to the end of the 1970s, when Park Chung Hee was assassinated, I heard many stories of women tricked or lured into working as prostitutes and "service girls" to support families in the countryside or to send younger brothers through school. Indeed, I myself was accosted at Seoul Railway Station by a man furtively whispering something about a job and a place to stay, probably because I was wearing a long braid and *komushin* (rubber shoes) and looked confused as I tried to make out Korean writing on the boards. During that period, everyone, including women, was mobilized into the service of the South Korean government's export-oriented economic development plan based on attracting foreign capital for the development of South Korean conglomerates, with skilled, productive, cheap South Korean labor kept docile under harsh military rule. Thousands of women were drawn from the countryside into low-wage factory work in Seoul and other cities (in 1960, two out of three South Korean workers were farmers; according to the latest South Korean census, by 1990, only 18 percent of the labor force remained in agriculture, fishing, and forestry). But Korean women were drawn into serving the cause of "modernization" with their bodies in more ways than one. During the 1970s, the South Korean government even encouraged what came to be known as "*kisaeng* tourism," or the provision of female sexual services for mostly Japanese tourists, issuing identification cards to Korean hostesses and even publicly praising the women for earning much-needed foreign exchange through their "hard work" for the nation.

By the end of the 1980s, a huge number of South Korean women were engaged in sex service work: according to a 1989 National Assembly report, fully one in four women workers were engaged in "sex businesses," including room salons, nightclubs, massage parlors, and barbershops. South Korean feminist groups attributed this phenomenon to the commodification of women and sex in South Korean society, but the other crucial factor that cannot be ignored has been the paucity of other attractive job opportunities for women, including not only rural and working-class women but also growing numbers of middle-class, educated women. At the same time, the South Korean economy's meteoric growth during the 1980s heralded an increase in personal wealth and consumption of leisure activities among South Korean citizens. As the service sector grew, the gap between the wages women could earn there as opposed to in production labor widened.

5. Some of the Koreans I talked to suggested that the "cafe culture" was allowed to flourish as a kind of anesthetic that would keep citizens from rebelling against military rule and the continuing postponement of political reforms in the name of economic development. Others insisted that the government obtained "underground money" for slush funds through bribes from entertainment industry operators. Still others believed that the *sul munhwa* is rooted in Japanese and Korean military culture, and a few thought it came from the West. But all agreed that it had become pervasive by the mid-1980s. According to one high school principal, whom I later interviewed:

> Sex [for men] is available everywhere—at restaurants, in tea rooms, on golf courses, everywhere. Sometimes even we men say, "What a society!" If you go to Yongdong [a cafe district in the South Han River area], you will see a barbershop [that provides masturbation, fellatio, and full sex as well as shave, haircut, and massage] on the first floor, a massage parlor that provides sex on the second floor, and a church on the third floor. It's like hell, earth, and heaven in three layers. It's like Sodom and Gomorrah in the Old Testament. Even the ministers go to saunas and massage parlors . . . I think it would be better to legalize prostitution formally. What if there were barbers for haircuts, massage parlors for massage, and sex places for sex? Wouldn't that make more sense?

6. For example, one woman said that she had put down *chŏnse ton* (key money) for a "shop" in which she offered massages, masturbation, oral sex, and full sex. She also sold cigarettes, beer, and soft drinks to her customers at a profit. She said that after accumulating enough funds, she planned to get back her *chonse ton* and start a different "small business," this time selling sports shoes on the street. Although she might have cursed the fate that necessitated a life of struggle and hard work, clearly she did not regard herself as a victim of male exploitation but as an independent entrepreneur taking advantage of a particular market; nor did she view selling sexual services as being significantly different from selling other kinds of services or goods. And indeed, although the social status of masseuses who provide sex services was not high, street vendors were not especially respected or well-regarded either. Thus, she could view herself as exploited by the social system as a whole rather than by men in particular.

7. Ms. Ch'u and I each conducted several interviews alone. Sometimes I was assisted by

bilingual Korean American students from Berkeley who were visiting or working temporarily in Seoul.

8. We also designed and implemented a 47-item survey questionnaire, which we administered to more than 650 men. We asked one company executive to allocate 45 minutes to a large group of office employees, and we were able to get another company executive to allow his staff to administer hundreds of questionnaires to a group of construction workers. Two hundred ninety-nine of the surveys were usable because they were complete. The tabulated data corroborated quite well what was said in our interviews.

Although Ms. Ch'u and I discussed the possibility of presenting our research findings somehow, we were unable to continue these discussions after I returned to my work in the U.S. for various reasons, including the loss of my house and many research materials during the 1991 Oakland firestorm. In the end, conducting the interviews was a profoundly invaluable learning experience for both of us, especially since the men and women we listened to were people of various social and economic backgrounds whom we might otherwise never have met.

9. In 1988, one U.S. dollar was worth about 790 *wŏn*.

10. This is in marked contrast to the 47 women between the ages of 22 and 59 whom we interviewed after we had completed our interviews with men. In a society that still places a high premium on female virginity and chastity and in which social acceptance and economic viability are difficult for divorced or single women to attain, it is much riskier for women than men to divulge certain kinds of information about their sexual practices than it is for men to do so.

11. Formal education and college professors, once highly revered in Korean society, seemed to be still respected, particularly among most of the middle-aged and older men. Whether they meant it or not, some of the poor and middle-class women we interviewed told us that they admired female professors most among women, although hostesses made it a point to tell us that male professors were the clients they disliked the most, ostensibly because their behavior in bars and cafes is *not* respectable and they are thus merely posturing moral hypocrites.

12. Traditional sex segregation practices gave men relatively few opportunities to talk with women about any serious subject, including sex and gender.

13. To my knowledge, little or no research involving many in-depth interviews of Korean men about gender, women, sexuality, and masculinity has been conducted to date, whether by Koreans, Korean Americans, or other Americans, male or female.

14. As a Korean American woman, I was sometimes reified and misread by our interviewees, multiply interpolated as a performer in their fantasies about the West. In some cases, a man might wish to present what he believed would be the most positive picture of Korean life, measured against what he understood were American cultural values. In other cases, he might wish to lay the blame on America for what he thought was corruption of traditional Korean values.

15. South Korean presidents Park, Chun, and Roh appointed primarily persons from their own Kyŏngsang province to positions of power and influence while systematically

excluding most people from the Chŏlla provinces. Throughout the regimes of these three presidents, people from the Chŏlla provinces have experienced persistent discrimination in many walks of life; even television dramas routinely featured protagonists with Yŏngnam (Kyŏngsang province) accents and servants or criminals with Honam (Chŏlla province) accents.

16. In keeping with the traditional Korean view that women's labor outside the home degrades the family and in keeping with the social practice that assures women's social mobility through marriage rather than through career, many of the wealthy and middle-income men we spoke with were strongly opposed to careers outside the home for women. Mr. I., an engineer, said he would not want to see a woman getting a high salary because that would mean that she was not paying enough attention to her children. But the men we interviewed also invoked naturalized gender differences to explain and justify social inequities in the workplace. For example, the popular belief that men are better able than women to do "difficult work," that is, to make decisions and to handle emergencies, helps explain why a hospital director we spoke with was uninterested in hiring women as managers. Male company workers commented that women coworkers cannot be legitimate members of the work team. When we asked a family court judge why there were so few female judges, he replied that the bar examination is "too difficult" for women, adding again that women cannot participate as equals in the workplace because of competing demands from their families. One young architect told us that women have no *jŏng* (compassionate feelings), not acknowledging that *chŏng* (compassionate feelings) among employees is built up through drinking together after work. He concluded that women are petty and selfish, interested only in their own assignments and not in the well-being of the group. Thus, their presence spoils the work climate for the men unless, of course, they are merely "office flowers."

Social equality for women has not received much institutional support in South Korea. A former congressmen we interviewed, Mr. H., told us that he believed that the best social system is with men outside and women in the house. He said he lamented the fact that men were such philanderers but said that the "desire for variety" is natural. He also told us that he wanted to work for the economic development of the country and therefore had no time to think about "side issues," like women's issues. "You can't force changes," he said confidently, "Our lifestyle is already westernized. The status of women will change by itself automatically."

The legal arena was no more sympathetic to women than the political and educational arenas. Family Court Justice K. of Kajŏng Pŏbwŏn (Family Court) also ascribed to the popular belief that women should take care of households. He complained that women in the workplace make excuses for themselves, demand special treatment, and suffer from a "victim mentality." If they want reform, he admonished, they should stay away from controversial issues that offend people and start instead with issues that no one opposes. Furthermore, Judge K. did not believe that wife rape was possible and blamed women for their own rapes, asserting that in the vast majority of cases, the assault could have been avoided if the woman had been more careful.

17. The female body was considered inferior to the male body as well, as part of the general social preference for males over females. In the 1960s, I saw many large color por-

traits in photography shop windows, showing boy babies naked below the waist so as to announce the fact that they were male, but I never saw girl babies' photographs in the windows, let alone any proud indication of their gender. I also recall being surprised at how often women I knew referred to women's genitals as being "dirty." The female body excited both lust and disdain from some male interviewees. One man told us that his mother showed him the housemaid's used sanitary napkin when he was a young boy to impress upon him how sickening female sexuality is, and he had remained disgusted by the thought of women's bodies.

18. Elizabeth Choi, "Status of the Family and Motherhood for Korean Women," in *Women of Japan and Korea: Continuity and Change,* ed. Joyce Gelb and Marian Lief Palley, Philadelphia: Temple University Press, 1994, p. 194; also, see Park Chai Bin, "Preference for Sons, Family Size, and Sex Ratio: An Empirical Study in Korea," *Demography* 20 (August, 1983): 333–352.

19. A young widow or divorcee would also be looked upon as a "failed woman."

20. Similarly, racism excludes men of color from social power on the grounds that they are intellectually inferior or, in the case of Asian American men, morally and physically/sexually inferior.

21. For the rich older men we interviewed, having sexual relations with women for money was a way of testing their virility. Mr. C., the 69-year-old corporate executive, felt that his activities proved his health and vigor, despite his age. Unlike many men in the U.S., he did not think that having had a vasectomy made him any less "manly." On the contrary, he said, "If one of these girls turns out to be a *kkotpaem* (flower snake, or young woman after a man's money) and pretends to be pregnant, she won't be fooling me. This way I can be more free sexually."

22. According to all prevalent notions of filial piety and propriety, it was completely permissible for men to express sentimental feelings about their mothers, while displaying sentiment about one's wife was regarded as foolish. At the same time, since male formation necessitated the cleaving of the affective from sexuality, the men's emotions were invested in their mothers.

23. Almost every man we spoke with had had his first sexual experience with a prostitute when drunk with his male friends. No one could remember anything about the woman. "She had eyes, a nose, and a mouth," one man said, "that's all I know."

24. Fifty-year-old independent businessman Mr. K. related a very extreme example of male bonding in a room salon during the late 1970s, a wild time in the so-called "cafe culture." The men, who were all paired up with hostesses, decided that the man who ejaculated last would pay the main bill, and that the man who ejaculated the least would pay the tip. Afterward, they all traded soggy underwear. Although Mr. K. recalled the incident as evidence of how much hostesses enjoy their work, it seemed to be a vivid example of male bonding behavior.

> The room was so small that there were ten legs on the wall. If one guy turned left, we all had to turn left . . . It was very funny. Some guys could not ejaculate. Their partners tried everything, saying, "Come on, come on!" because they

didn't want their men to have to pay the bill. I think that these girls enjoyed it as much as we did. We were all drunk.

25. The obliteration of formerly clear-cut boundaries in recent years is not an index of women's liberation any more than it spells an end to the brutality of class differences. Cho Haejoang suggests that in South Korea today, women's domain is shrinking in size and importance; as they continue to be excluded from the male world, they must use all possible resources as they compete for scraps of affection and safety. Thus, while today's hostess is expected to look and act like a college co-ed, the typical housewife is now expected to be everything: the "good wife, wise mother," the income earner, and the sexy "date" for her husband ("Living With Conflicting Femininity: Mother, Motherly Wife and Sexy Women," paper presented at the Workshop on Gender and Social Change in Late Twentieth Century Korea, Columbia University, March 1995).

26. During the course of conducting our research, we often heard men lament that the days of courtly romance with entertainment women were long gone, and that modernity had replaced the talented *kisaeng* of yore first with pretty prostitutes who could not sing, dance, or play instruments, and now with smart young women for whom entertainment means a businesslike cash transaction.

27. The division into two kinds of women does not directly parallel the western madonna/whore dyad, since it emerges from different historical traditions. It seems rather to be rooted in traditional concubinage, according to which first wives were differentiated from concubines, and the female entertainment trade, which featured educated *kisaeng* who often wrote poetry, sang, danced, and played classical musical instruments for male guests. Although the status of the wife was higher than that of the concubine or *kisaeng*, she could not be considered morally superior in the western sense; hierarchies among women involve a number of factors, but women as a group are subordinated to men within Korean patriarchal structures.

28. Until very recently, men were automatically awarded custody of their children in South Korean divorce cases.

29. Dr. H. may have chosen a pediatrician because men who are considered good marriage prospects often choose educated brides, expecting them to use their education to raise successful children. Moreover, Dr. H. (and his mother) undoubtedly expected his wife's knowledge of medicine to be used to benefit only his children.

30. In the mid-1980s, people often joked that anyone who wanted a physician son-in-law would have to be ready to provide a dowry of three keys: the key to a house, the key to an office, and the key to a car. I understand that now, the key to a vacation home is also *de rigueur.*

31. I often heard it said that profligate husbands usually return, old and sick, to their wives in the end, since their mistresses refuse to care for them in bad times. At these moments, the wife can exact her revenge, relegating the old man to the *yogang* (chamber pot) corner.

32. As Hyungsook Yoon points out (in "Gender and Personhood and the Domestic Cycle in Korean Society [I] in *Korea Journal* 30, no. 3 [March 1990]: 4–15), men's mis-

conduct is seen as personal weakness or individual lapse rather than disastrous to the collectivity because they are considered autonomous individuals. A woman's misconduct, however, is not seen as separate from the collective identity of the household, which she must "represent."

33. In fact, as Moon Okpyo points out, middle class women are far from *ansaramtul* (inside persons): they conduct a plethora of activities outside the home, such as investment and other income producing activities. They engage in *ch'imabaram* and otherwise participate in their children's schooling. They also participate in networks of kin, neighborhood groups, classmate associations, and credit clubs. They prepare feasts for their husband's work networks and gather information on child care, education, investment, and consumer bargains from various informal sources. The activities outside the home of middle class housewives are particularly significant in light of the absence of government support of public education and social services.

34. Tensions between mothers-in-law and daughters-in-law abound in South Korean lore. Poor men complained much less than middle class or rich men about conflicts between their wives and mothers, no doubt because neither the couple nor the mother had much money to fight about. One man did say that his mother, who had doted on her son and felt sorry when he married at 36, slept between him and his wife for the first year of their marriage.

35. According to a journalist at the progressive *Hankyŏre* newspaper, female journalists have better advancement opportunities than men because military service puts men behind for their age. Women speak *panmal* (informal Korean) to men older than they are, he complained. Further, women don't have to stay overnight for *sukjik* (overnight duty watching the office by turn) or late on Saturdays, and their superiors don't criticize them as harshly as they attack the men. Women journalists told me, however, that they are restricted to working on the "women's page," as opposed to the more respected political or economic pages.

36. Poor women, like poor men, seemed less enamored of the concept of motherly sacrifice than women and men of other classes and much more willing to accept women's desertion of their husbands and children if their husbands could not earn sufficient livelihoods: without supporting his family, a man could not be "masculine"; therefore, his wife did not have to concern herself with being "feminine." We learned of one Nankokdong man who died when his son was small and his wife was only 27. His widow simply left the baby with her in-laws and disappeared. "I think I would probably do the same thing if I were in her situation," her sister-in-law said, "even though she kind of dumped the baby. She's probably trying to earn money doing who knows what right now." In 1988, women could not seek custody of their children. Nor could working class women easily make a living wage. An ordinary widow or divorcee was usually forced to give her children to her husband or her husband's relatives. Moreover, most men in South Korea's patrilineal society would not accept the children of other men.

37. Lee was not really disliked *instead* of her husband. She was viewed as the antithesis of the feminine ideal. She did not remain modestly behind the scenes like the beloved Yook Yŏng Su, wife of the previous president, Park Chung Hee. Many of the middle

class men we interviewed expressed profound admiration for Yook, whom they saw as the ideal traditional Korean wife and mother. Some men commented on how Yook, who was frequently beaten by her husband, would appear in public with huge bruises and a haggard, tragic expression on her face. They noted that when she rode in the presidential limousine, she appeared uncomfortable and sat leaning forward, as if she did not belong in the car. They commented on how she tried to gently dissuade her husband from his exploitative, authoritarian policies, and how she did charity work for poor children and disabled people. When asked about Soonja Lee's charity work, they said that Lee was only trying to copy Yook in the hopes of winning public approval by association. What people detested most about Lee was that she seemed overly proud of herself. She took every opportunity to appear in public beside her husband. She was rumored to be the (corrupting, because female) power behind the president, especially since her politically powerful father and uncle were said to have helped her husband attain his military rank. Finally, she was said to be unseemly and even immoral because she was corresponding with Chun when he was a military academy cadet and she was only a 15-year-old high school student.

38. Although we were unable to achieve the scope and distribution that we achieved with the interviews of men, we did complete some interviews with women between the ages of 22 and 59. Our interviewees included nine women who worked as maids or who did piece work at home, four room salon or cafe hostesses, three cafe owners, an office worker, a political activist, a social worker, a middle class victim of domestic violence, three professors, a journalist, an engineer, a middle class widow, a wealthy divorcee, seven wives of middle income men, and four wives of wealthy men. We were introduced to our interviewees by various acquaintances, including an employee of a school in a poor neighborhood. A few women were referred to us by our male interviewees. We interviewed some of the wealthy women at their homes and many of the poor women in tea rooms in their neighborhoods. For the most part, we met our wealthy and middle class female interviewees at the dimly-lit Mago Cafe in the stylish Apkujŏng area.

39. Finding the placement of another woman in a superior position highly distasteful, some women said they would not like to work for female bosses. As a 28-year-old government office secretary put it, "If we were both women, I would wonder why I should be below her, just because I had less education":

> Having a female boss seems upside down, unnatural. We women call each other "older sister," so it would be hard to call a woman "boss." We never call male co-workers "older brother," so it's not hard to call them "boss."

40. It is possible that she said this because she hoped that her son would not get too close to his wife and thus necessarily move away from his mother.

41. In the late 1970s, South Korean women factory workers who attempted to organize labor unions were killed, beaten, and terrorized by working class male goons hired by management.

42. Middle-aged wives of wealthy men occupied themselves with many often costly activities: aerobics six times a week, Japanese language classes, English language classes, Bible study, alumni meetings, *maedŭp* (Korean traditional knotmaking) lessons, bowl-

ing, swimming, and golf. "These days women have it great; if you don't like cooking, you can hire a maid. Or order food from a restaurant." Unlike middle class women, who viewed work outside the home as something that poor women were forced to do, wealthy women spoke of jobs as if they were hobbies, something done out of interest rather than for money. One woman wondered if her husband would have treated her better if she had had a job:

> My husband wanted me to work because he didn't appreciate the way women spend their time. But none of my friends work. Maybe if I had worked, he would not have looked down on me and said things like, What do you know anyway? What have you done. It takes a lot to run a household, but men say, "A maid could have done *that*."

43. Drinking remains integral to good business relations, but today's ever more hurried life style requires the expensive, lightning-quick drunkenness induced by the time-saving *p'okt'anju* (the "bomb drink," a shot of whiskey in a large glass of beer or, for even faster inebriation, the "hydrogen bomb drink," a shot of beer in a glass of whiskey, or the "neutron bomb drink," a shot of *soju* [Korean liquor] in a glass of whiskey).

44. Abigail Solomon-Godeau, "Male Trouble," in *Constructing Masculinity*, ed. Maurice Berger, Brian Wallis, and Simon Watson, New York: Routledge, 1995, p. 74.

45. Barbara Ehrenreich, "The Decline of Patriarchy," in *Constructing Masculinity*, ed. Maurice Berger, Brian Wallis, and Simon Watson, New York: Routledge, 1995, p. 288.

46. In July, 1994, Dongkuk University Professor and South Korean feminist Un Cho commented that it is a good thing that Ms. Ch'u and I conducted these interviews when we did. These days, she said, it is not politically correct to say such baldly sexist things, even though below the surface, fundamental ideological positions on gender and sexual politics had not changed in just six years.

47. See Cho Haejoang, "Living With Conflicting Femininity: Mother, Motherly Wife and Sexy Women," paper presented at the Workshop on Gender and Social Change in Late Twentieth Century Korea, Columbia University, March 1995.

48. Lisa Rofel, "Liberation Nostalgia and a Yearning for Modernity," *Engendering China: Women, Culture, and the State*, ed. Christina K. Gilmartin, Gail Hershatter, Lisa Rofel, and Tyrene White, Cambridge, Massachusetts: Harvard University Press, 1994: p. 232.

5

Kindred Distance

Photo Essay

A four-part ensemble of digitally processed images of photographs taken at the Reunification Observatory. The Observatory, located in South Korea near the DMZ, stands within view of North Korea. The photos focus on displays of North Korean household items, clothing in particular.

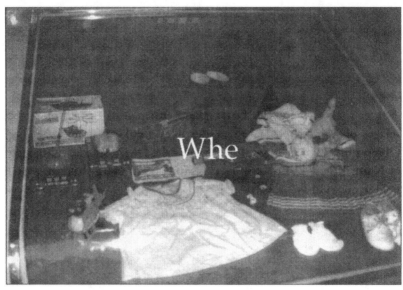

6

HYUNAH YANG

Re-membering the Korean Military Comfort Women:

Nationalism, Sexuality, and Silencing

In the late 1980s, after fifty years of profound silence, the issue of Korean Military Comfort Women[1] began to emerge. Until then, there was virtually no research, investigation, or discussion on the subject in South Korea. Korean government officials often refer to Korean colonial history as "matters of the past" (*kwagŏsa*). The term suggests that colonial history has relevance only to the past, and is unconnected to current relations between Korea and Japan. This essay calls into question the official move to freeze the history of Military Comfort Women as strictly a matter of the past. Rather events of the past can only be understood through discursive constructions, which reconstitute that past *in the present*.[2]

The main concern of this essay is to explore how the Military

123

Comfort Women issue is discursively constructed in South Korea at the present time. In particular, the essay focuses on how nationalist discourse has framed the issue of Military Comfort Women in ways that redeploy patriarchal norms of female sexuality. Through the reading of testimonies of survivors, I then discuss how the nationalist message about female sexuality has influenced former Military Comfort Women themselves. These testimonies are also important to illustrate the gap between nationalist discourses about the Military Comfort Women issue, and the women's own narratives of their experiences.

The main texts on which this essay builds are South Korean newspapers[4] and testimonies of the surviving Military Comfort Women.[5] I reviewed newspapers from September 1990 to November 1993, which was a period when important documents regarding the Military Comfort Women were discovered and public awareness was high. Though the essay questions the media's representation of the issue, I do not mean to imply that the media constitutes the leading form of social discourse in South Korea. Rather, media representations are treated as texts that reveal prevailing social sentiments. By contrast, testimonial narratives are sites where official memory, mediated by dominant discourse, can be contested. Thus, testimonies are employed as counter-discourses, even though they are also complex cultural products.[6]

History Buried in Darkness

Silence has been a condition as well as a key component of representations of the Military Comfort Women issue. Two cases illustrate the process of silencing and how the media perpetuated that silence.

In January of 1992, a Korean daily newspaper reported that an examination of student records at Pangsan Elementary School revealed that elementary school girls, aged twelve to fourteen, were drafted into *Chŏngsindae*[7] in 1944.[8] Following secret orders from the school principal, Japanese colonial teachers performed the main role in recruiting the girls. A former Japanese teacher, Ikeda Masae, confessed that she had conducted home visits after school in order to recruit *Chŏngsindae* girls. She helped draft six Korean girls from her class through persuasion, deception, and by even threatening the children's parents. She added that she was instructed to choose healthy, good-looking girls, from well-to-do families. This confession demonstrates that the Japanese colonial government was systematically involved in the recruitment of Korean women for *Chŏngsindae*, though this fact was denied by the Japanese government until July 1992.[10]

The report about Ikeda's confession evoked strong repercussions in Korea. The fact that girls as young as twelve were recruited into *Chŏngsindae* agitated Koreans. Moreover, the fact that an educational institution and teachers were in the front line of the recruitment deepened the anger. But what was startling to me about these revelations was that the student records in question had existed in Korea for half a century, without being brought to light. The newspaper printed a copy of a student record, where the drafted girl's name was still clearly visible, along with the hand-writing of "*Chŏngshindae* Recruit" and the teacher's signature underneath. Until a Japanese person, supposedly an accomplice of colonial rule, reported the story, the records were ignored. Still, the media focused only on the fact that the Japanese recruited such young girls through the elementary schools.

A day after the Japanese teacher exposed the story, a newspaper printed a short article entitled "Shameful Historical Consciousness." According to the article, the elementary school mentioned above, now renamed Yŏnghi, had exhibited various documents and pictures in front of the school entrance to proudly demonstrate the school's history. Surprisingly, at one corner of the exhibit was the record of a twelve-year-old female student, with the Japanized name Masako, which was explicitly marked in Chinese characters as a "*Chŏngsindae* Recruit." The fact that the document had not only been in the school's keeping, but even exhibited, further illustrates how the *Chŏngsindae* issue has never been brought into public debate. The article ended by saying:

> However, no one knew the meaning of this document, which has been exhibited at the entrance of the school, the most conspicuous place in the school. Neither did anyone try to inquire about it.[11]

Several days before the report about the draft of elementary school girls in the Seoul area, critical documents about the Military Comfort

Women issue were found in Tokyo by a Japanese historian, Professor Yoshimi Yoshiaki. On January 11, 1992, every major Korean daily newspaper reported that the Japanese military documents such as *t'sūchō* (military communication) and *Jinjunissi* (military daily records), had been found in the Library of the Japanese Ministry of Defense. One *t'sūchō*, dating from 1938, stated that draft of the Military Comfort Women was in such disorder that it needed to be executed by the military with cooperation of the local police.[12] In *Jinjunissi*, one account noted that "Comfort Stations" (stations for the "sexual comfort" of Japanese military personnel) were to be built as soon as possible, to prevent frequent rape of indigenous women by Japanese soldiers. The document further instructed that surveillance of the Comfort Stations should be carried out by the district military chief and by military police.[13] These were the first Japanese records to clearly demonstrate the involvement of the Japanese military in the planning, the recruitment of Military Comfort Women, and the management of the Comfort Stations.

In a television interview conducted after the military documents were found, Professor Yoshimi stated that it had taken him only two days to locate these documents. He added, "these kinds of documents are surely plentiful in the archives and can be found without any difficulty."[14] But for Koreans, especially for surviving Military Comfort Women, it took half a century to even begin illuminating the role of the Japanese military and police in organizing Military Comfort Women. Why had this issue been entirely ignored in South Korean society?

Chin Sung Chung has pointed to various reasons why the issue remained silenced. First of all, the postwar Japanese government had "classified" documents that pertained to the colonial government and the military. Second, the United States punished Japan only lightly for its World War II crimes, because the U.S. wanted to use Japan as a base from which to expand capitalism in Asia. This in turn permitted the postwar Japanese government to officially ignore the damages that Japan caused to its colonies in Asia. Third, due to shame and guilt, the victims, offenders, and witnesses remained silent about the Military Comfort Women issue. The paucity of research about the atrocities committed under the Japanese colonialism, especially those related to gender, further contributed to the "darkness" surrounding the Military Comfort Women issue.[15]

However, I think that it is important for Koreans to analyze the silence about the Military Comfort Women not just in relation to Japanese government actions and international politics, but also in relation to South Korean society itself. Professor Yoshimi indicated that finding materials about Military Comfort Women was not difficult; in fact, locating the documents in question took only two days. Although there was no concrete evidence that the Japanese had hidden the documents, the Korean newspaper report was titled "Japanese Government Has Kept the Documents Hidden." Moreover, the reporter mentioned nothing about the fact that it was a Japanese researcher who found the documents to begin with. Why would this be the case? Because if the role of the Japanese scholar were acknowledged, it would be difficult to level all criticisms against Japan. At the same time, the difficult question of why Korean scholars did nothing about this issue would be raised.

Even if many documents were intentionally destroyed or kept hidden by the Japanese imperial and post-war governments, this does not mean there has been no information available to Koreans about Military Comfort Women.[16] The elementary schoolgirls' records, showing recruitment into *Chŏngsindae*, present an example of the "un-hidden-ness" of data. Notably, the next morning after the former Japanese teacher's "confession of conscience," ninety nine other *Chŏngsindae* cases were reported by elementary schools in the Seoul area.[17] The historical data have existed in Korea, *among* Koreans. Where were the Korean teachers, who should have been aware of the draft activities that were clearly written in the school register? Where were the Koreans, who witnessed and were involved in such a massive recruitment of the Military Comfort Women? Yet the media focused only on Japanese inhumanity, rather than how and why Koreans had ignored the issue for so many years. By looking *outward* to Japan, Koreans evade questions regarding the responsibility that we have for our own colonial history.

The social atmosphere that made Military Comfort Women a non-issue cannot be understood without considering the Korean state and its policies.[18] In 1991, when the Korean Council for *Chŏngsindae* proposed to build a monument to commemorate the *Chŏngsindae* women at the site of the Independence Memorial, for example, the Korean government rejected the project by citing "the lack of sufficient land for the monument and impairment to the landscape around the Memorial Building."[19] The day after the elementary school girl's draft was revealed, the Education Council in Seoul dispatched a notice to elementary schools in the Seoul area, ordering them not to disclose school registers related to the *Chŏngsindae*. The rationale for the prohibition was that such disclosure might violate the rights of former *Chŏngsindae* women.[20] Clearly, it is not only the Japanese government that does not want Military Comfort Women to produce more issues or to further inspire memories.

What makes the silencing of the Military Comfort Women issue particularly complicated is its connection to gender and sexuality. This connection explains the intentional amnesia of the victims, as well as those who perpetrated or witnessed the events. Yet, once documents disclosed the Japanese government's involvement in the issue of Military Comfort Women, the issue was quickly framed within the pre-existing nationalist discourse.

Nationalism Encounters Sexuality

> Masking the truth, due to ignorance, neglect, and defeatism, brings shame on our people. Furthermore, that girls were recruited to *Chŏngsindae* from elementary school is a matter of our *national pride*, prior to the question of compensation. Therefore, we should disclose the truth with our own hands this time.[21]

The common phrase employed in editorials, articles, and readers' letters about the Military Comfort Women is national pride (*minjokŭi jajonsim*). This concept seems powerful enough to mobilize the feeling of unity as Koreans. What assumptions underlie this "Koreanness" or *minjok*?

Minjok refers to people who belong to a common ethnic group, such that all Koreans are assumed to constitute one homogeneous Self. Invocation of this national self affirms unified identity, based on an unchangeable essence that is transmitted through blood and homogeneous culture. At the same time, this notion consolidates the Korean nation as a geographically and culturally fixed unit. Like other forms of anti-colonial nationalism, however, unified Korean national identity was constructed to a great degree through its opposition to colonizing Others, including Japan.

The author of the article, "Japanese Government Has Kept the Documents Hidden," for example, undoubtedly recognized that it was not only the Japanese government that did not welcome the disclosure of documents related to Japanese colonialism. Rather, the article intentionally interplays with the mental structure that Koreans already hold. The main feature of the structure is the way that it dichotomizes Koreans and Japanese—us and them, victim and offender, good and bad. These categories appear exclusive and independent, yet they are mutually defined by one other. Through blaming, the existence of an enemy is made visible, and this in turn helps to confirm the collective identity of "Korean." Within this dichotomy, however, Korean identity is built only upon victimhood. This provides convenient as well as obfuscating logic through which complex issues such as the history of Military Comfort Women have been explained.

Furthermore, Korean nationalism has a strong sentimentalizing tendency, as is implied by the notion of national pride. Whenever Japanese political leaders visit South Korea, for example, one of the main concerns of the public is how much, deeply, and sincerely Japan has apologized for the damages left by colonial rule. The media analyze the depth of feeling embedded in words such as regret, repentance, apology, and sincere apology, which are used by Japanese political leaders.[22] In this sense, the politics of apology is a twin of the politics of pride (*chajonsim*).

I view this sentimentalizing tendency in terms of the outward way of looking discussed previously. When Koreans rely on Japanese documentation and Japanese interpretation of the history of Korean colonization, it is difficult for Koreans to *produce* knowledge of our own history. There is instead a tendency to recall the colonial past through sentimentalizing it as a past of *han*, or suffering and unresolved resentment and sorrow. The mood of *han* in connection with the Military Comfort Women issue can be interpreted as another aspect of silence, since silence has prevented the production of knowledge about the Military Comfort Women. Thus the sentimentalizing tendency of

Korean nationalism perpetuates rather than seeks to understand or overcome the colonial legacy.

When nationalist sentiment encounters the issue of Military Comfort Women, which has a specific dimension of sexuality, the discourse enters a more complex terrain. A letter from a male reader exemplifies the kind of popular nationalist sentiment that the issue evokes:

> This [Military Comfort Women] issue will not end with the apology of the Japanese prime minister. Nor will the issue be settled by compensation only to the old women victims. The event amounts to an act in which the Japanese throw their dirty sperm bucket into our Korean people's face.[23]

The underlying assumption here is that since our Korean women had been humiliated, so too have all Koreans been victimized by the Japanese. This is because nationalism holds that "We Koreans are one and the same body." In this logic of one-ness, however, there has always been hierarchy, boundary, and classification. When we read closely, this letter reveals a "Man's talk with a Man."[24] When the male reader wrote "the Japanese," he clearly meant Japanese men, since Japanese women could not have provided a bucketful of sperm. The sperm bucket itself offers a clue through which we can trace why the humiliation of Korean women amounts to the humiliation of Korean men, too. As implied by this "man's talk," those who are able to invade women's sexuality, and those who are obliged to protect it, are males. The reader's letter thus exemplifies how males become the only subjects involved in questions of nation and sexuality. This reveals the fictitious nature of the nationalist belief in a unified Korean body, since the body is constituted and sustained by non-homogeneity.

In the male-centered code of sexuality embedded in the nationalistic assumptions of this letter, several metaphors are at play. The nation becomes gendered, and women's sexuality becomes nationalized. Nation is equated with the male subject position, and women's sexuality is reified as property of the masculine nation.[25] In this sense, the discourse is neither *about* nor *for* the (Military Comfort) women. Women occupy a position in which they are neither subject nor even object. Rather, they are misplaced as the material or the ground for "men's talk."[26]

130

In the process, a significant shift has taken place in the construction of the issue. Through this "men's talk," nationalist discourse has shifted a key axis of *relationality,* such that the Military Comfort Women issue is no longer between Korean women and Japanese men, but between Korean men and Japanese men. Accordingly, the Military Comfort Women themselves are denied any voice with which to represent themselves. As Lydia Liu observes, it is through nationalist discourse that the man (re)constitutes himself as a national subject and is reborn. In the process, national identity becomes largely a male prerogative that allows men to preach a new gospel to their women.[27] Another reader's letter exemplifies the kind of gospel that nationalist discourse tries to convey:

> Why should we forgive the Japanese people, who abused the dignity of Korean women? Korean women regard chastity, and the shame caused by violation of it, as more important than life itself. Japan kept denying their abuse, until much evidence recently came to light. Now they are behaving in a very disingenuous manner, as if they are finding out about this abuse for the first time.[28]

This letter is one example among many in which women's chastity is presented as the most important reason of why the Japanese should apologize to and compensate former Military Comfort Women. Chastity as a notion circulates and works in powerful ways. By applying only to the women, and thus establishing a double standard of sexual conduct, the ideal of chastity plays a critical role in regulating women's sexuality. Chastity involves not virginity as such, but rather that there is always a proper place where female sexuality *belongs.* A married woman's sexuality belongs to her husband, whether he is alive or dead; an unmarried woman's sexuality belongs to her future husband; and in general, Korean women's sexuality belongs to Korean men. This notion has already alienated woman's sexuality from herself by endorsing its belongingness to man and nation.

Since the issue of the Military Comfort Women signifies the contamination of Korean women's sexuality by foreign bodies, Korean men's *chajonsim* is attacked. From the male nationalist subject position, therefore, the Military Comfort Women issue induces both engagement and embarrassment. The psychology of embarrassment includes feelings of anger, frustration, and shame. This is the point where nationalist discourse adopts the norm of chastity. By representing chastity as "more important than life itself," the male who sent the letter establishes himself as a national subject who partakes in and protects female sexuality. Female sexuality, then, becomes a matter of national concern. While the core of nationalism lies in contesting the former colonizers, this nationalist discourse, by appropriating the norm of chastity, strangely blurs the contestation and only serves the male national subject's "pride."

Now, feelings of shame, not pride, become a psychological vehicle through which women connect their sexuality with the possibility of belongingness. How has this kind of message influenced the former Military Comfort Women? A surviving Military Comfort Woman testifies:

> My brother and sisters encouraged me to register as a *Chŏngshindae*. But I felt so ashamed. In this society, people still talk behind our backs. I would feel humiliated, even if I was to receive compensation. But then, I would feel mistreated if I didn't get any compensation. Whenever I think of those years, my heart pounds and my whole body is racked with pain.[29]

The woman's feeling of shame or guilt is not only imposed from outside, but also stems from her own sense of self. Here, we find a social mechanism of shame that blames and silences victimized women who are often sexually abused.[30] Many testimonies illustrate how the shaming mechanism has worked through close relationships around those women:

> I have looked forward only to death, without telling anybody my story. My tribulations remain buried deep in my heart. Now I have reported to the Korean Council and I take part in their various activities. But I am anxious in case anyone recognizes me. I have a husband and children, so I cannot bewail my life and be so resentful in public. If, by any chance, my children's spouses and their families discover I was a comfort woman, what would become of them? . . . Who would be able to guess what inner agony I suffer with this awful story buried in my heart? My story, as hidden as it is from those around me, will follow to my grave.[31]

This testimony shows how the woman's husband, children, and children's spouses and their families have all participated in the vicious cycle of silencing.

However, another testimony demonstrates a complexity that cannot be simply reduced to norms of chastity and experiences of shame.

I discussed the matter with my other nephew in Taejon. He wept as he listened to my story and advised me not to register [with the Korean Council]. He said "It will break your son's heart. What will your step-son in the United States say when he hears this?" But I felt uneasy and couldn't sleep at all. So one day I went to a broadcasting station and told my story. They gave me the telephone number of the Korean Council. Next day, I went to the local police station, and with the help of an officer I made a report. I came home and slept soundly, making up for the troubled nights of the previous weeks. After having poured out what I had to say for so long, I felt that half of my problem was solved. I told my son about the whole thing, and he wept uncontrollably, saying "Mother, you have lived so courageously, even with such a rough past. I am proud of you." But the wife of my youngest son became despondent, and even my son is disheartened. I feel very sad and guilty when I see them.[32]

The survivor feels guilt, but she also exhibits courage and a desire to speak out about her experiences, despite of the pressure from her family to conceal her past. How can we understand that courage and desire to speak if we see the survivors only as powerless victims? She continues:

But my heart moves more and more towards the meeting at the Korean Council. I haven't missed any rallies held outside the Japanese Embassy.[30] Since I often go out, my sister from Pusan comes up and helps with the housework. Of course Japan is to blame, but I resent the Koreans who were their instruments even more than the Japanese they worked for. I have so much to say to the Korean government. The Korean government should grant us compensation as well.

Another survivor views her story not just in terms of personal experience, but also within historical context. Like the previous survivor, political agency is expressed through the woman's participation in movement activities, as well as by her resentment toward the parties responsible for the crime:

The reason I came forward to report to the Korean Council was to pour out my resentment. I have tried to write down my experiences several times, but because I had to move so often, I kept losing the notes. I am telling my life story so that nobody else will ever have to go through the same things I did. I think we must try to get what we justly deserve from Japan: a proper apology and proper compensation. There are still some who say that what we did is shameful, but they are indeed ignorant people.[34]

Testimonies of surviving Military Comfort Women have revealed how discursive practices that place chastity at the center of the issue are distant from the women themselves. A focus on chastity reduces the issue to a personalized and moralized domain. In the process, much of the historical significance has been erased. Such an approach suggests that there is no substantial difference between dealing with a rape case and dealing with the issue of Military Comfort Women. Can this crime, designed and systematically practiced by the Japanese imperial state, be equated with the violation of women's chastity? Can this crime, in which numerous young women were forced to have intercourse literally thousands of times, under the ever-present threat of violence and death, be evaluated just in terms of sexual norms? How can the dimension of sexuality, which undeniably constitutes the crime and deepens its seriousness, be taken into account without stigmatizing the women?

Clearly, we must question not just the male-centered positionality presumed by nationalist discourses, but also the framing of this enormous crime within the order of patriarchal sexuality.

In this essay, I attempted to shed light from two angles on current discourses in South Korea about the Korean Military Comfort Women issue. First, I explored how the silence surrounding the issue is conditioned not only by the Japanese government, but also by the Korean government and people. Second, I examined how nationalist logic conjoined with patriarchal codes about female sexuality to frame the issue from a masculine subject position. As a result, the Military Comfort Women issue becomes reduced to a matter of the sexualized nation, or nationalized sexuality. This representation not only marginalizes the surviving women, but it also consigns them to life-long shame, silence, and pain. The fractures that underlie a supposedly unified Korean nationalism are revealed by the very fact that framing the issue in the name of the nation (*minjok*) results in victimization of these women and reification of their sexuality. At the same time, it becomes clear that nationalist discourse has stabilized itself by appropriating the Military Comfort Women issue, rather than addressing the issue as its main concern.

In closing, it seems appropriate to quote from a testimony of a surviving Military Comfort Woman. The testimony reveals shame and frustration, hope and desire, resentment and anger, and unending pain. We still seem to be short of a language to encompass those feelings:

> I harbored a considerable grudge against the Japanese, and my whole life had been loathsome and abhorrent, largely because of them. I had been wanting to talk to someone about my past for a long time, and I told this woman that I had once been a Comfort Woman. Since then I have been called to speak in many different places, because I was the first of the Comfort Women witnesses to come forward. I find it very painful to recall my memories. Why haven't I been able to lead a normal life, free from shame, like other people? When I look at old women, I compare myself to them, thinking that I cannot be like them. I feel I could tear apart, limb by limb, those who took away my innocence and made me what I am. Yet how can I appease my bitterness? Now I don't want to disturb my memories any further. Once I am dead and gone, I wonder whether the Korean or Japanese government will pay attention to the miserable life of a woman like me.[35]

NOTES

I express thanks to Eithne Luibheid, who offered precious editorial work. I am also grateful to the staff of the East Asian Library at Columbia University for assistance in locating Korean newspapers and journals. This research was done with the support of an AAUW (Association of American University Women) International Fellowship.

1. Throughout this essay, the term "Military Comfort Women" is employed in accordance with popular usage, to denote women who were forcibly drafted by the Japanese imperial government into sexual slavery for the Japanese army, mostly between the late 1930s and 1945. Scholars agree that Korean women drafted for the military sexual comfort activities numbered 80,000 – 200,000. According to the Korean Council for Women Drafted by Japan for Sexual Slavery (hereafter, Korean Council), *Chongkunwianbu*, meaning the comfort women who followed the military, has to be translated as "military sexual slavery by Japan." For an outline of the issue of the Military Comfort Women, refer to the following: Korean Council, *Chŏngsindae Issue Resource Collection* (hereafter, *Resource Collection*), Vol 1. and 2, Seoul, 1991 and 1992; Alice Yun Chai, "Asian-Pacific Feminist Coalition Politics: The *Chŏngsindae/Juguianfu* (Comfort Women) Movement," *Korean Studies*, 17 (1993), pp. 67–91; Haesoo Shin, "*Minjokjuŭiwa peminijŭm*" (Nationalism and Feminism), *Hangu yŏsŏnghagui chŏnmanggwa gwaje* (The Prospect and Tasks of Korean Women's Studies), pp. 21–29 (Seoul: Korean Association of Women's Studies, 1994); Chin Sung Chung, "*Ilbon kunwianbu jŏngch'aekŭi bonjil*," (Nature of the Project of the Japanese Military Comfort Women), *Hanmal iljehaui sahoesasanggwa sahoeundong*, (Social Thoughts and Social Movements in the Late *Chosun* Under Japanese Colonialism), by Korean Social History Association, (Seoul: Muhakkwa jisong, 1994), Vol. 42, pp. 172–201; Yong-suk Sin and Hye-ran Cho," *Kunwianbuŭi silt'ae mit t'uksonge kwanhan yŏngu*" (A Study of the Reality and Features of the Military Comfort Women), *Ch'ongsanhaji mothan iljesigiŭi munje* (The Uncleared Issues During the Japanese Colonialism), by Korean History Association (unpublished monographs, Seoul, 1995), pp. 275–321; ICJ (International Commission of Jurists) Seminar Report, "Sexual Slavery and Slavery-like Practices in World War II" (monograph, Tokyo, 1995).

2. The accepted belief about the linear nature of the time, in which the connection between prior cause and subsequent effect is retained, has been increasingly questioned. In particular, questions about the Kantian notion of the absolute and universal dimension of time/space derive from the criticism that the notion has served as one of the bases of the "modern" project. From this viewpoint, this essay understands the past as an unsettled time-space, constructed in multiple ways. The past is the time which was present in the prior-to-the-present, and yet interacts with and is imbued with the present. For this view, refer to: Bastian C. Van Freestone, "Time in Physical and Narrative Structure," in *Chronotypes*, ed. John Bender and David E. Wellbery (Stanford: Stanford University Press, 1991); Jonathan Boyarin, "Space, Time and the Politics of Memory," in *Space, Time and the Politics of Memory*, ed. Jonathan Boyarin (Minneapolis: University of Minnesota Press, 1994).

3. By February 1993, 103 women in South Korea identified themselves as surviving for-

mer Military Comfort Women. Reportedly, 123 former Comfort Women are also alive in North Korea as well.

4. I planned to survey newspapers and monthly news magazines. However, I found that articles on the subject were sparse. Hence, I decided to focus on two newspapers, *Dong-A Ilbo*, which has dealt with the issue most frequently, and *Hangyore Sinmun*, which is known as the most progressive newspaper in society.

5. This essay will use the testimonies recorded in the book by Korean Council and Research Group of the Women Drafted for Military Sexual Slavery by Japan, which were originally published as *Kangjero kkŭllyŏgan chosŏnin kunwianbudŭl* (The Korean Comfort Women Who Were Coercively Dragged Away for the Military), trans. Keith Howard, *The True Stories of the Korean Comfort Women* (London: Cassell, 1995).

6. Maurice Halbwachs, *Collective Memory* (New York: Harper & Row, 1980); Popular Memory Group, "Popular Memory: Theory, Politics and Method," Center for Contemporary Cultural Studies, *Making Histories—Studies in History-Writing and Politics* (London: Hutchinson, 1982), pp. 205–252.

7. In Korea, the term *Chŏngsindae* is generally used to refer to the Military Comfort Women. The *Chŏngsindae*, meaning "voluntarily offered body corps," was mobilized by the Japanese Imperial Edict. *Chŏngsindae* women were generally divided into two groups, one for labor and the other for the sexual "comfort" of the Japanese soldiers. Thus, the *Chŏngsindae* in this essay could have been assigned to either group. Given the paucity of documentation, there is no way to confirm into which group the girls were drafted. Testimonies reveal that the women were transferred from the former group to the latter. The question of the degree of overlap between these two groups needs further investigation. As with Military Comfort Women, the group of women drafted as laborers have been scarcely studied. Testimonies and documents suggest the conditions of these women's lives as laborers were also miserable. They worked long hours under constant surveillance and suffered severe hunger and disease. Yet few of them received any compensation after the war. (For information about labor *Chŏngsindae*, refer to Chin-Sung Chung and Sun-ju Yŏ, "*Iljesigi yŏja kŭllochŏngsindaeŭi silsang*" [The Reality of the Women Labor *Chŏngsindae* during the Japanese Colonialism], *The Uncleared Issues*, pp. 225–273.)

8. *Dong-A Ilbo*, January, 14, 1992; *Hangyore Sinmun*, January, 14, 1992.

9. *Dong-A Ilbo*, January 15 and 16, 1992.

10. Refer to *Dong-A Ilbo*, July 7, 1992; *Hangyore Sinmun*, July 7, 1992.

11. *Dong-A Ilbo*, January 15, 1992.

12. For the document, refer to Yoshiaki Yoshimi, *Charyojip—chongkunwianbu* (Document Collection—Military Comfort Women), trans. Soonho Kim (Seoul: Sŏmundang, 1993), document 6, pp. 134-135.

13. Refer to Yoshimi, *Document Collection*, document 42 (1938) and 44 (1939), pp. 197–199 and 200–201.

14. *Dong-A Ilbo*, January 16, 1992.

15. Chung, "Nature of the Project," pp. 172–173.

16. For example, see *Dong-A Ilbo*, January 16 and 17, 1992.

17. *Dong-A Ilbo*, January 16 and 17, 1992.

18. The weak sense of colonial history in South Korea must be understood in terms of its political history since the liberation from Japan. The pro-Japanese policy of Park Chung Hee's regime (1962–1979) contributed to "un-making" colonial experiences as historical knowledge. Moreover, the U.S. occupation after liberation also hindered rigorous public discussion of the colonial period in Korea, since the U.S. occupation permitted the economic-political structure established in colonial Korea to continue.

19. Su-in Yi, "*Ilchep'ihae (Chŏngsindae) ch'ŏngwŏnsimsa jilmun*" (The Questions Concerning the Claims and Demands about the Harms Caused by Japanese Colonialism), in *Resource Collection*, vol. 2, pp. 27–32.

20. *Dong-A Ilbo*, January 19, 1992.

21. Editorial in *Dong-A Ilbo*, January 16, 1992.

22. *Dong-A Ilbo*, November 4, 1993.

23. *Dong-A Ilbo*, January 20, 1992.

24. Trinh T. Minh-ha, *Woman, Native, Other* (Indianapolis: Indiana University Press, 1989), p. 79.

25. For a discussion of how the discourse of *Minjok* appropriates and yet needs women, refer to Eunsil Kim, "*Minjokdamrongwa yŏsŏng*" (*Minjok* Discourse and Women), *The Prospect and Tasks of Korean Women's Studies*, pp. 11–20.

26. For more on this idea, see Lata Mani, "Contentious Tradition: The Debate on *Sati* in Colonial India," in *Recasting Women—Essays in Indian Colonial History*, ed. Kumkum Sangari and Sudesh Vaid (New Brunswick: Rutgers University Press, 1990), pp. 88–126.

27. Lydia Liu, "Female Body and Nationalist Discourse: The Field of Life and Death Revisited," in Inderpal Grewal and Caren Kaplan, eds., *Scattered Hegemonies—Postmodernity and Transnational Feminist Practices* (Minneapolis: University of Minnesota Press, 1994), pp. 37–62.

28. *Dong-A Ilbo*, January 20, 1992.

29. Testimony by Yi Sunok in *True Stories*, p. 123.

30. Refer to Christine Brautigan Evans, *Breaking Free of the Shame Trap* (New York: Random House, 1994), esp. pp. 251–266.

31. Testimony by Ch'oe Myŏng-sun in *True Stories*, p. 176.

32. Testimony by Kim Tŏk-chin in *True Stories*, p. 49.

33. Since January 1992, the surviving Comfort Women and their supporters have demonstrated weekly outside the Japanese Embassy in Seoul. February 1996 marked the 200th rally.

34. Testimony by Kang Tŏk-kyŏng in *True Stories*, p. 184.

35. Testimony by Kim Hak-sun in *True Stories*, p. 40.

7

KATHARINE H.S. MOON

Prostitute Bodies and Gendered States in U.S.-Korea Relations

Since the early 1980s, academics and activists have defined and analyzed military prostitution as an international system of political and economic domination, both of women and weaker nations.[1] The power disparities between nations, or governments, have been transferred onto women's bodies, namely that the women of the weaker state represent, through their prostituted bodies, the dominated and controlled position of the weaker state.

Such views, however compelling as a political metaphor, portray power relationships between governments and between men and women as static and universal. The simple fact is that the mere existence of power disparities between and among nations does not automatically translate into subordinated positions for women in a weaker country to the men of a stronger country. The U.S. is more powerful in the conventional terms of military capability, economic capacity, and political influence than Italy; but American men, whether civilian or military, are in the habit of buying Italian leather, not Italian women. Even the fact of military conquest does not automatically mean the sexual conquest—through rape, prostitution or concubinage—of the women in the defeated country. For example, the U.S. occupation force in Japan, despite its development of local military prostitution, initially enforced strict rules regarding fraternization with local Japanese women.[2] And even weaker nations have been able to manipulate existing resources and interests of the stronger state to their benefit. Saudi Arabia, during the Gulf War, is a case in point. Saudi Arabia possessed weaker military and political capability than the United States to thwart Iraqi aggression. However, because of its primary role as gatekeeper of Middle East oil supplies and strategic location in the war with Iraq, the weaker power was clearly able to prevent the U.S. military from allowing sexual fraternization with local Saudi women. Moreover, not all women of a weaker nation experience or suffer the same plight at the hands of the stronger nation's men; class, region, race, religion, and ethnicity largely determine who is abused or exploited and how.

To understand how power relationships between nations or governments are shaped, we must pay close attention to individual actors and groups who may have varying interests, norms, and goals regarding gender. That is, the "state" or the "military" or "capitalist interests" are not monolithic entities. The U.S. military, for example, does not exhibit one universal norm or practice regarding sexual interaction with local women in overseas settings.[3] Nor does it hold the same, constant view on strategic and organizational interests in different parts of the world. To continue to view different actors as conglomerates serves to politicize sexual and international affairs but takes the political process out of such interactions. Moreover, the perpetuation of a static dichotomy, in which the women of weaker nations are always oppressed and exploited by men of stronger nations, blurs our foci of analysis and activism. What exactly are we trying to explain or understand when we look at the relationship between governments and, consequently, the governments' policies toward women? With respect to U.S.-R.O.K. (Republic of

Korea) power relations and military prostitution, do we mean to explain the causes and characteristics of prostitution? Or are we aiming to assess the variations in prostitution practices among various military installations and in different time periods? Or do we focus on the kind and degree of poverty, social degradation, and "choice" confronting the individual women in the prostitution system?

The examination and understanding of military prostitution must be context-specific, grounded in an understanding of power as a dynamic and not a static zero-sum game. The challenge is to analyze the interstate context(s) that determine what Cynthia Enloe admits feminists know little about: "how bargains are struck between influential civilians in a garrison town and the local military commanders."[4] This essay seeks to strengthen and refine feminist critiques of military prostitution as a matter of international politics. The questions I am asking are how and why governments use women and gendered ideology as instruments of foreign policy; how specific uses of women's sexual labor and gendered ideology affect women's lives; and whether participation as instruments of foreign policy politicize the women involved.

Joint U.S.-R.O.K. Camptown Clean-Up Campaign

Since the very first military maneuvers, women have been instrumental to the organization and operational effectiveness of soldiering men. Through their labor as cooks, laundresses, and sex mates, women have long helped to maintain armies. From 1971 to 1976, tens of thousands of Korean military (*kijich'on*) prostitutes had the distinct "honor" of serving not only in their prescribed role as appeasers of soldiers' sexual appetites but as patriots designated and actively enlisted by their national government to help promote the U.S.-R.O.K. security alliance through their cooperation in the joint U.S. Forces, Korea (USFK)–R.O.K. "Camptown Clean-Up Campaign," or what the Korean government called the "Camptown Purification Movement." Base-community conflicts—such as racial tensions between African-American soldiers and local Koreans, high rates of venereal disease among U.S. servicemen and Korean prostitutes, unsanitary conditions in the local R&R

establishments, and black-marketing—had been brewing in the camp-towns prior to the early 1970s. But in the summer of 1971, camptown problems took a turn for the worse. Racial violence between black and white soldiers and black soldiers and local Koreans occurred more fre-quently and intensified while venereal disease (VD) rates among the troops reached what the U.S. military considered "epidemic levels."[5] (The term STDs, or sexually transmitted diseases, was not yet in use.)

The Psychological Operations unit of the Eighth U.S. Army (EUSA) in Korea made the following assessment of Korean culpability in the racial incidents:

> This [increased Korean] involvement [in racial confrontations] normally assumes three forms of progression. First, the Koreans aggravate racial problems [existing on post] by discriminatory practices. Second, they are often the injured party during black/white confrontations, suffering physical property damage. Third, they demonstrate, often violently, against U.S. troops in general and against the blacks in particular . . . Discriminatory practices by the Koreans are usually of a passive nature rather than one of violence. In the clubs, such practices include poor ser-vice, unfriendliness, and sometimes refusal to even serve black soldiers. Among business girls, such practices take on two forms. Some of the business girls refuse to associate with blacks. Some also discriminate against Koreans who do associate with blacks and consider those Koreans to be of lower status than those who go only with white soldier[s]. Polarization has developed to the point that some girls are called "black" because of their frequent association with blacks."[6]

There is no doubt that many Korean prostitutes demonstrated prej-udiced behavior toward African-American soldiers in the camptowns. In one sense, such behavior was a survival tactic. The women's social strat-ification and self-identities within the camptowns were significantly influenced by the larger racial stratification among Americans. Women who fraternized with or sold sexual services to black men were them-selves labelled "black" by Americans and Koreans, and such women faced severe social condemnation and stigmatization by others, includ-ing prostitutes who catered to white men. "Black prostitutes" and "white prostitutes" generally had to be careful not to cross the racial lines, for if a "white prostitute" fraternized with black soldiers, she might face physical abuse and/or economic boycott by white soldiers. The same fear of retribution (by black soldiers) applied to "black prostitutes" who fraternized with white men. It is important to note that U.S. military personnel have acknowledged that much of Koreans' racist behavior toward blacks was learned from white soldiers stationed in Korea. In an *Overseas Weekly* article (August 4, 1971), white soldiers interviewed in Korea admitted that "Korean locals have been subjected to the attitudes of the white majority for so long that they practice discrimination without even being aware of what they're doing."

To solve these and other camptown problems that the USFK leadership deemed threatening to the order, discipline, morale, and military preparedness of its troops, the leadership pressured the Korean government to pay attention to camptown problems and cooperate in solving them. In the late summer of 1971, the U.S.-R.O.K. Status of Forces Agreement (SOFA) Joint Committee established the Ad Hoc Subcommittee on Civil-Military Relations,[7] which then organized numerous "panels" to address camptown issues. The Korean government set up a Blue House (the residence of the Korean president) committee, the Base-Community Clean-Up Committee (BCCUC), to direct "purification" plans. Through these committees, the USFK and the Korean government developed programs to help educate local Koreans and U.S. servicemen about the evils of racism and the prevention of VD transmission. Both the USFK leadership and the Korean government pressed local Korean authorities to encourage the clubs to prevent discriminatory behavior on the part of the club employees and to maintain sanitary standards designated by the USFK.

The Korean prostitutes, in particular, became targets of such "education" and "encouragement" because of their daily intimate contact with soldiers. Since they were viewed by the USFK as a main source of black-white tensions, the Joint Committee urged club owners and managers to train and instruct club hostesses "to refrain from engaging in discriminatory practices directed against customers of any particular race in the performance on club premises of entertainment functions such as dancing or conversing."[8] For example, at the request of the Commander of the Yongsan Garrison, the 24th Psychological Operations Detachment (PSYOP) of the Eighth Army created and distributed posters, flyers, coasters (for glasses), tape-recorded English lessons, and magazine articles which were designed to inform Koreans and Americans about racial issues. Many USFK commands urged the local Korean authorities to educate Korean prostitutes about respecting the human rights of black soldiers and creating an harmonious camptown environment. Ŭijŏngbu,[9] for example, held "four meetings and five meetings respectively for regular club employees and 'business girls'" in 1972.

For the USFK, the issue was not simply dissuading Korean prostitutes from exercising racist behavior; they also saw the prostitutes' behavior as potentially damaging to the national security interests of the U.S. and R.O.K. Specifically, the USFK "educators" emphasized to the women that their discriminatory actions help fuel North Korean propaganda against the South and the U.S. military presence:[10]

> It should be noted that the North Koreans seek to exploit and exacerbate racial tensions among U.S. servicemen and conduct anti-U.S. propaganda in order to distance the U.S. and the R.O.K. from each other. This, in effect, weakens the security of our country.[11]

The USFK authorities also targeted Korean prostitutes as the main source, or "the reservoir," of venereal disease transmission among U.S. servicemen and, together with the Korean government, developed numerous programs to control the registration, VD examination, and quarantine (detention) of infected women. The Korean government's job was to enforce the registration, mandatory physical examination, and detention of *kijich'on* prostitutes in order to help reduce the spread of venereal disease to U.S. servicemen. The Korean Ministries of Health and Social Affairs (MoHSA), Foreign Affairs (MOFA), Home Affairs, Justice, and the National Police all expended considerable sums of money and energy to "clean up" these women. The Korean government allocated a total of 380 million *wŏn* in 1971–72 to improve health and sanitation in camptowns, of which 224 million *wŏn* (about $1 million and $600,000 respectively in 1971 terms) were earmarked for the prevention and treatment of VD among camptown women.[12] This money was used to build and renovate VD clinics and "educate" women about venereal disease. It also financed governmental enforcement actions such

as forced "round-ups" of women for examinations as well as "mass injec-
tions" of antibiotics to "innoculate" women against VD infection.

Throughout the Clean-Up Campaign, VD continued to be the
Achilles' heel of improving camptown life and relations between the U.S.
and Korean sides. Several USFK and Korean government officials I interviewed even noted that although the initial target of the campaign was
improving camptown race relations, control of prostitutes and reduction
of VD rates for U.S. troops consistently remained the major grievance for
the USFK and the primary focus of work for the Korean government.
One USFK Community Relations Officer commented that racial unrest
was merely the "spark" that ignited the clean-up activity and that control
of prostitution and VD constituted the crux. He also mentioned that in
his opinion, given the emphasis placed on VD control, the R.O.K.G.
should have called the clean-up campaign *"Kukka sŏngbyŏng jŏnghwa
undong"* ("National VD Purification Movement"), instead of the generic
"Camptown Purification Movement."[13] Although the Korean government did pay attention to other aspects of the base-community life, such
as paving roads, its primary aim was to control the women's sexual health
and general behavior as a way to appease U.S. servicemen. Accordingly,
curbing venereal disease was the first item on the respective comprehensive clean-up agendas of the BCCUC and the Ministries of Foreign
Affairs and Health.[14]

The Role of Prostitute Women in Foreign Policy Adoption

Social disorder, racial conflicts, violence, and crime were common problems experienced by generations of U.S. soldiers and local Korean residents. Why, then, did the U.S. military and the R.O.K. government
exert so much effort to improve camptown relations in the 1970s?

Some critics of U.S. military bases in Korea have tended to view
kijich'on prostitution primarily as a result of U.S. militarism and imperialism.[15] Without necessarily defining the meanings of these terms, such
analysts have equated the superior economic, military, and political capabilities of the U.S. with domination, and domination with militarism
and imperialism. Such views cannot explain why the Korean govern-

ment's active role in controlling prostitution in the early 1970s contrasted so starkly with its negligence and intransigence toward any U.S. requests to address camptown problems prior to 1971. USFK documents from the early 1960s reveal that VD was a serious problem and concern for the military commanders and that they tried, to no avail, to push the Korean government into cracking down on VD among *kijich'on* prostitutes. Lieutenant General T.W. Dunn, Commander of I Corps (Group), complained to the then Commanding General, Hamilton Howze, "I am convinced that we receive mostly words and bows and little practical help" regarding the "deplorable problems" related to prostitution.[16] Even three years before the Clean-Up Campaign, U.S. officials involved with camptown relations lamented the Korean authorities' lack of cooperation in controlling prostitution and prostitutes: "[T]here was a natural impatience . . . [on the American side] with a strong Korean reluctance to do anything constructive about the problems of most concern to the Americans, prostitution and venereal disease."[17]

The fact of U.S. superiority and "dominance" in economic, military, and political capabilities vis-à-vis Korea did not change from the 1950s and 1960s to the 1970s; the U.S. was still the "dominant" partner and Korea the "junior" partner in the alliance. U.S. troop presence in the 1960s, for example, stood at about 60,000 (compared to approximately 40,000 by September 1971), and the U.S. effectively had command over the Korean military through its role as head of the United Nations forces in Korea. But such power did not enable the Americans to force the Korean government to focus on problems related to prostitution or the Korean prostitutes who densely populated the areas around U.S. bases. In 1963, a USFK official admitted to the EUSA Deputy Chief of Staff that the USFK was powerless to control prostitution and venereal disease: "Our negotiating position appears to be weak, for we have no lever to force the R.O.K. to improve their efforts."[18] Not only was the USFK leadership in the early 1960s unable to use its large and potent military presence as leverage to pressure the Koreans, it even exhibited awareness and concern for the political implications, i.e., sensitivity toward issues of Korean sovereignty, of official meddling by the U.S. in local camptown issues, primarily prostitution. A Major Saalberg, an Eighth Army official in 1963, stated with regard to prostitution control that "[t]he United Nations Command has followed a policy of non-interference in the internal affairs of the host nation."[19]

According to some of the women who worked as camptown prostitutes during the 1950s and 1960s, prostitutes of that time period were much "freer," "wilder," "bolder," and less controllable by U.S. or Korean authorities than the women of the 1970s and 1980s. They claimed that each woman's survival depended on her own tough handling of any problems she encountered because no part of the larger society could be counted on to protect her. Moreover, these women had not yet been "tamed" by strict regulations enforced by the U.S. military or Korean authorities. And in general, the "wild" behavior of the earlier generation of prostitutes reflected the unruliness and lawlessness of camptowns themselves, resulting from the Korean government's laissez-faire attitude toward *kijich'on* life. Some of the women went so far as to say that the police not only left them alone but feared them. Why did the overwhelming power disparity between the R.O.K.G. and the U.S. in the 1950s and 1960s not translate into overwhelming physical and sexual control and domination of Korean camptown prostitutes by U.S. soldiers?

We can begin to understand the changes in the attitudes and actions of both the USFK and the R.O.K. government if we view their interactions as part of a dynamic in which domination is relative rather than absolute. The exploitation and oppression of women are functions of the particular power dynamic between two countries. This dynamic may enable the patron to dominate the relationship, but it may also enable the client state to steer the relationship in its favor. In the 1950s and 1960s, at least two significant factors swung the power pendulum in South Korea's favor and served as a source of resistance to U.S. demands regarding camptown life: clear U.S. geostrategic interests and alliance commitments that compromised U.S. leverage.

From the Korean government's perspective, clear-cut Cold War rivalries of the 1950s and 1960s, with Asia serving as the major battlefield, meant firm U.S. commitments to non-Communist Asian allies and a large U.S. troop presence to back up those commitments. The strength of these commitments assured the R.O.K. that the U.S. had as much to gain from a free and prosperous Korea as the Koreans themselves. This meant that the R.O.K., though a junior alliance partner, had considerable freedom and leeway in its relations with the U.S.[20] With respect to camptown prostitution, the Korean government used the certainty of U.S. commitments to non-Communist Asia as reason to largely ignore USFK pleas for control of the health and behavior of the prostitutes. The Korean government considered camptown prostitution primarily a U.S. problem and a matter between GI and prostitute, not, as in the 1970s, a matter of state-to-state relations and security affairs.

Moreover, the general attitude of the Korean government and public toward these women during these two immediate postwar decades was "They're poor, like most of us who have survived the war. Let them make a living whatever way they can."[21] In other words, although most Koreans morally condemned these women for selling their flesh to foreigners, they pitied and sympathized with the women's poverty and their struggle to keep themselves and their families alive. In a way, these women's material needs were recognized more during the early postwar years than in the 1970s and 1980s, when Korea became economically and militarily much stronger.

Second, the unrelenting demand in the 1970s by the USFK for the cooperation of the Seoul government in controlling camptown prostitutes was a result of the loss of Korean leverage. This leverage had been provided by Korea's troop contribution of 50,000 to aid the U.S. war effort in Vietnam in the mid- to late 1960s. As long as Washington needed Korean troops to supplement U.S. forces in Vietnam, as well as the moral support of its ally, the power of the U.S. to dominate the alliance with Korea was significantly compromised. The U.S. had to accommodate some of Seoul's demands regarding the conditions for troop contribution to Vietnam and the terms of the U.S.-R.O.K. security relationship.[22] The Korean troop contribution to Vietnam strengthened the Korean government's ability to resist or downplay the demands and complaints of the USFK authorities regarding camptown issues. U.S. officials involved in the Camptown Clean-Up during the early 1970s admitted that as long as Korean troops were needed in Vietnam, the U.S. could not push its interests in cleaning up the camptowns.[23] It was with the reduction and withdrawal of R.O.K. troops from Vietnam in the early 1970s that the U.S. officials in Korea were able to gain the upper hand on camptown issues.

The Nixon Doctrine, which signaled the United States' disengagement from Vietnam and Asian land wars in general, and the consequent reduction of U.S. troops from Asia provided the opportune moment for the USFK to demand camptown improvements and for the Seoul government to oblige.

A specific disruption in the secure U.S.-R.O.K. alliance, then, drove the USFK leadership and the R.O.K. government, through the Purification Campaign, to tighten joint control over the bodies and conduct of camptown prostitutes. For the USFK, the Clean-Up efforts were a means to defend its organizational interests vis-à-vis the policymakers in Washington and a symbol of its commitment to remain in Korea, regardless of Washington's policy statements. For the Korean government, the clean-up was an integral part of "private diplomacy," a desperate resort to the use of local people and resources, in the absence of conventional carrots and sticks, to secure U.S. commitments to Korea.

The application of the Nixon Doctrine to South Korea amounted to the reduction of 20,000 U.S. troops (approximately 60,000 troops had been stationed in Korea throughout the 1960s) from Korea and highlighted the uncertain future of the U.S. forces stationed there. During the early 1970s, the USFK leadership had good reason to feel insecure. Members of Congress were unabashedly expressing their skepticism about a continued U.S. military presence in Korea. Congressman Ronald Dellums, a newly elected African-American, severely criticized the Korean government and people's treatment of black servicemen in Korea and questioned the need to aid militarily countries where Americans, i.e., black soldiers, were not welcome.[24] Given this context, the Clean-Up Campaign was a way for U.S. military authorities in Korea to demonstrate the strength and congeniality of its relationship with Koreans as well as a means to maintain U.S. congressional support of its continued presence in Korea and continued military assistance for the R.O.K. government. It was, in short, an intense and comprehensive public relations effort. According to one of the main U.S. initiators of the Clean-Up,

[it] was an opportunity for the U.S. military in Korea to put a good face on their presence in Korea . . . For the USFK, the stake in this was that it wanted to show people in Washington that we have good relations, that nothing is wrong in Korea. The military in Korea did not want to leave Korea.[25]

The Clean-Up Campaign not only assuaged critics in the U.S. but also addressed skeptics in the Korean government who were wary of the sincerity of the U.S. commitment to Korean security. Again, in the words of the main U.S. initiator,

The Koreans were feeling at the time [of the troop reductions] that it's all over for them if the U.S. leaves. So, we made it clear to the Koreans through the clean-up activities that we wanted to stay.[26]

Indeed, the R.O.K. government reacted to the departure of the U.S. 7th Division (one of the two army divisions that had been in Korea since 1955) and three Air Force squadrons with shock and panic. The *Korea Herald* reported on July 1, 1971 that the "20,000-man U.S. troop withdrawal was first regarded as a bolt from the blue sky." The *Far Eastern Economic Review* characterized the Seoul government's opposition to the withdrawal as "violent."[27] Major sectors of the Korean society—government, military, legislature, media, and the general public—opposed the U.S. cut as sudden, hasty, and provocative (of North Korean reaction). Even opposition members of the National Assembly joined the mass protest. Koreans "expressed the fear that the new attitude in America really means that the United States will abandon Korea."[28] By demonstrating its desire to improve camptown life, then, the U.S. military aimed to prove to Koreans how much it cared about Korean-American friendship, cooperation, and cohabitation.

From the Korean government's perspective, the women were instrumental to improving the daily life of U.S. soldiers stationed in Korea and in meeting the demands of the USFK for increased camptown control. Then President Park Chung Hee made the U.S. soldiers' quality of life a priority in U.S.-Korea relations. Although he was fully aware of the complex set of international and domestic factors that led the U.S.

to reduce its military commitments to Asia, Park became convinced that, given the "special relationship" Korea had long enjoyed with the U.S., negative "people-to-people relations" were at fault for the United States' change of heart. Park and his aides diagnosed Korea's problem with the U.S. as bad public relations and a negative image of Korea and Koreans held by U.S. soldiers, the Congress, and the American public.[29] To remedy this situation, the Korean government waged an aggressive campaign of "people-to-people relations" to supplement what it considered its weak and ineffective public channels of influencing U.S. policy circles.

Camptowns, in particular, were viewed by Korean officials and the Korean public to be responsible for such "negative images" of Korea. All the Korean officials (whether working for the USFK or the R.O.K. government) I interviewed repeated that the Korean government and society were always concerned that GIs were getting a distorted and erroneous impression of Korea through their interactions with the Korean nationals in camptowns, i.e., prostitutes, pimps, drug dealers, and other social pariahs. The Political Secretary overseeing the "Purification Campaign" under President Park's orders mentioned that the Blue House feared that because all that U.S. soldiers witnessed during their stay was *kkangt'ong-hwa,* or "culture of tin cans,"[30] around their bases, these same individuals would return to the U.S. with an image of Korea as populated solely with poor, thieving people, grovelling for U.S. dollars and lacking in national culture and pride. This image, in turn, would unfavorably inform Washington's political decisions regarding Korea.[31]

The work of the Korean government in the Clean-Up effort was intended to "correct" the image of Korea in the eyes of U.S. servicemen. The Ministry of Health and Social Affairs official who oversaw the various prostitution and VD control programs in 1971–72 stated clearly that the purpose of the control effort was "to give a cleaner impression of camptowns and of Korea." He emphasized that the "Purification Campaign" was not intended for the entire nation but solely for U.S. camp areas, especially those with large concentrations of troops.[32] Another medical official of MoHSA stated that only camptown prostitutes, not Korean prostitutes in general, were regularly examined and quarantined for VD infection (in the beginning of the campaign).[33]

Without doubt, not only the government, but the Korean people regarded camptown VD as *such'i byŏng,* or "disease of shame."[34]

From the perspective of the Korean government, the camptown prostitute was in a position to play "personal ambassador" to the numerous GIs she sexually contacted, and the task of the "Purification Movement" was to transform her from a bad ambassador to a good one. The Blue House secretary who oversaw the R.O.K.'s "purification" programs stressed that camptown prostitutes needed to be taught how to work correctly. In his interview, he recounted his visits to camptown areas, where he asked the women, "Why did Japan develop from nothing to greatness?" He answered for them by admonishing them to imitate the spirit of Japanese prostitutes who sold their bodies to the post-1945 U.S. occupation forces:

> The Japanese prostitute, when she finished with the GI, did not get up to go get the next GI (for more money) but knelt before him and pleaded with him to help rebuild Japan. The spirit of the Japanese prostitute spread to the rest of the society to develop Japan.[35]

Such a view clearly established camptown prostitutes' sex work as a vital form of patriotism, and lower-level Korean officials echoed such words in their regular "educational lectures" to the women. For example, women were urged during such classes in the Ŭijŏngbu area to "take charge of national prestige" (*Kugwirŭl damdang hara*).[36] One former camptown prostitute who worked in Tongduch'ŏn and Songt'an (respectively, the major camptowns for the 2nd ID and the Osan Air Base) in the first half of the 1970s recalled:

> During every "Etiquette and Good Conduct Lecture" [sponsored monthly by local Korean officials], the local mayor or local public information officer or public peace officer would . . . give the introductory remarks. They would say, "All of you, who cater to the U.S. soldiers, are patriots. All of you are nationalists working to increase the foreign exchange earnings of our country." They said that we are servants of the nation and that we should live and work with pride. And then they told us not to show humiliating things [behavior] to the U.S. soldiers, to maintain our dignity as Korean women.[37]

The control of camptown women's bodies and sexual health was integral to improving deteriorated USFK-R.O.K. relations in the early 1970s. Just as the Clean-Up Campaign in general helped mitigate tensions between the USFK and the R.O.K. government, the Subcommittee found that those camptowns which addressed the VD problem to the satisfaction of the local U.S. command leaders possessed a "spirit of mutual cooperation . . . between the Base Command and local Korean officials" and had "excellent" civil-military relations.[38]

The insecurity of Korea that ensued from the Nixon Doctrine and the withdrawal of 20,000 U.S. soldiers linked private individuals and personal conduct to public priorities, namely, the defense and security of the Republic of Korea. Like Pak Tong Sŏn and other "unofficial ambassadors" of "Koreagate" fame in the 1970s, camptown prostitutes were deployed by the R.O.K. government to transform the image of Korea in the eyes and minds of Americans: the target audience of the former was the power elite in the United States while that of the latter was the GIs in Korea. Both channels of "private diplomacy" were intended to secure the continued presence of U.S. troops in and the flow of U.S. military aid to Korea.

Gendered Roles and Policies in U.S.-Korea Relations

Power disparities and domination alone, then, do not absolutely prescribe the actions of the patron state and the client toward each other or toward the client's women. But that is not to say that power disparities and domination are completely relative. The obvious disparity in capacity to affect the relationship provides the patron with opportunities and responsibilities for dictating the structural boundaries of the relationship and constrains the client's influence on those boundaries while loading it with the burden of observing the limits.[39]

With respect to U.S.-R.O.K. relations, the United States held the role of the protector, with the opportunity and responsibility for setting geopolitical policies, and South Korea was placed in the role of the protected, with no choice in geostrategic matters but to accommodate itself to U.S. initiatives, given the lack of viable alternative alliance partners and the ever-present Northern threat. To force a change of U.S. policy or to threaten retaliation for such unilateral decision-making as the 1970s troop reduction, the R.O.K. would have had to possess significant economic, military, and/or political resources (including influence over U.S. and world opinion or a "united front" with other Asian governments opposing the Nixon Doctrine). But the only relevant "resource" Seoul possessed during this period was its troop contribution to Vietnam, and even this form of leverage was contingent on U.S. actions and lost its efficacy when U.S. foreign policy toward Vietnam changed.

Although the Seoul government and the USFK leadership, faced with a U.S. Congress that was critical and impatient, had mutual interests in cooperating to keep as large a U.S. troop presence in Korea as possible, such cooperation was not free of coercion on the part of the USFK. The U.S.'s dominance in the bilateral alliance, as manifested in its ability to dictate new terms of the security relationship, empowered the U.S. military in Korea to make demands on the Korean government and local camptown businesses. The vulnerability of the Seoul government to policy changes in Washington and its dependence, not only militarily but psychologically, on the U.S. troop presence strengthened the hand of the USFK leadership bent on imposing law and order in camptowns. They used the reality of the troop reduction and the threat of a total withdrawal in the near future to pressure the Koreans into controlling prostitutes' conduct toward U.S. soldiers and curbing the spread of venereal disease. Joint governmental "cooperation" on base-community issues, then, was a function not only of the compatibility of the USFK's organizational interests and the R.O.K.'s security interests, as mentioned earlier, but also of the USFK's successful employment of threats and coercive actions.

Power disparities among nations do appear to possess gendered characteristics in the sense that the stronger power has access to a large and diverse availability of public, "overt," resources (economic weight, military power, diplomatic influence), relative to those available to client states. The weaker power is positioned in the feminine role of resorting to domestic, "covert" and "personal" resources, including its female citizens, as instruments of power in its relationship with the patron state. Bruce Russett and Harvey Starr include in their definition of "covert" resources a state's ability to mobilize its domestic society to meet security goals, the capacity of a people to endure physical suffering and economic deprivation, and the willingness of a people to sacrifice private interests and privileges for the collective good.[40] As mentioned earlier, in the early to mid-1970s, the R.O.K.'s conventional, public tools of security policy were limited in kind, number, and efficacy. However, its unconventional, "covert" resources were not. To supplement its public diplomacy, the R.O.K. enlisted private individuals, including camptown prostitutes, in a massive public relations campaign to sell its security cause to the U.S. Congress, American public, and USFK personnel. Though the R.O.K. was constrained by U.S. domination, it made specific choices, including the use of camptown women, as means to an end. USFK's demands for law and order in camptowns could have generated a debate between the Koreans and Americans about eliminating such prostitution, but the Korean government determined the prostitutes to be the source of and solution to camptown problems rather than considering other ways to meet USFK demands.

When we consider the gendered nature of power disparities and domination in international politics, we often cite the masculine and feminine gender stereotypes attributed, respectively, to colonizers and colonized on the basis of racial hierarchy, especially the West in relation to the East.[41] What we often do not probe are the ways in which actual power disparities generate government policies that have gendered consequences. My point here is that between legally sovereign states, the weaker is not merely a passive recipient of the actions of the stronger. Consequently, exploitation of the women of a weaker state is not automatic or constant. Strong and weak states alike make calculated choices regarding women's roles and values in society at a given time. To attribute the exploitation and abuse of women to the weakness and passivity, or feminization, of a client state is to exempt that state from taking responsibility for its actions toward and regarding women. It strips the weaker state of agency and over-emphasizes the role of the stronger state.

The Korean government's use of private individuals, particularly women, and sexual relationships as instruments of foreign policy was made possible by a culture that expected and legitimated women's self-sacrifice for family and country. Confucianist values of self-sacrifice for

the good of the family and country fit handily into the Park government's scheme of women's roles in national economic development and
security enhancement. Korean history, folklore, and literature are replete
with variations on this basic scheme: girls and women who sacrifice their
labor, lives, bodies and personal aspirations for the sake of their family
and country are heroines, martyrs, and patriots.[42] In the 1960s and
1970s, women formed the backbone of the low-skilled, low-wage, light-
manufacturing export industry that launched South Korea's economic
"miracle."[43] On the security front, thousands of poor girls and women
from the countryside put their bodies to work selling sex to U.S. soldiers, increasing Korea's foreign exchange earnings from the dollars
spent by the men and contributing to security by "providing comfort"
to them. In the early to mid-1970s, such women were "lauded" by the
R.O.K. as "patriots."[44]

Additionally, South Korea's authoritarian practices, justified as
national security requirements by the Park regime, contributed to the
use and abuse of private citizens for the "national good." Park and his
cohorts' draconian grip over the ideas and activities of private Korean
citizens through the propagation of anti-Red ideology and the coercive
activities of the Korean Central Intelligence Agency (particularly in the
late 1960s through the 1970s) reflected the government's view that private thoughts and actions were closely linked to public safety and
national security. The history of suffering and deprivation from the
Korean War and the people's desire for prosperity and stability also lent
Park Chung Hee the license to demand hard work and personal sacrifice, including the sacrifice of political liberties and participation, for the
economic development of the country.

In the 1960s and 1970s, the R.O.K. relied on human resources,
rather than natural resources, technology, and indigenous capital, for
economic development. But this development did not happen "natural-
ly," owing to Korea's "weak" status with respect to the U.S. government,
and business leaders made specific choices to throw the Republic into
cheap export orientation, and it can be argued that relying on human
resources in the service of promoting security goals was a logical adjunct
to such economic practice, especially in a time of Korea's "public"
resource-shortage in its security relations with its protector. The sexual

labor of camptown prostitutes and their close proximity to U.S. service-men made these women into convenient, though unconventional, resources for pursuing the R.O.K.'s security goals.

Camptown Prostitutes Protest

For the Korean and American inhabitants of camptowns, the summer of 1971 was filled with racial, political, economic, social, and sexual ten-sions. Long-held prejudices, competition, frustration, and misunder-standings came to a head. Indeed, both USFK and R.O.K. government officials agreed that

> [t]he drawdown of U.S. forces introduced new elements of tension into traditionally friendly relationships. Accompanying base closures and restationing of U.S. Forces resulted in widespread dislocations among Koreans living in villages adjacent to U.S. bases . . . and result-ed in increased competition among bar owners, "business girls," and merchants.[45]

Authorities attempted to defuse the explosive situation, but this in effect politicized the various groups of camptown residents, inciting them to defend and assert their interests both privately and publicly. Black and white soldiers expressed their racial and racist sentiments and demands for changes in military policy through public demonstrations. Similarly, Korean nationals, including prostitutes, staged public protests to voice their grievances against the USFK. In most cases, the women reacted when their bodies and pocketbooks were severely threatened by the actions of base personnel. For example, "about 200 prostitutes carrying sticks demonstrated outside [Camp Ames] demanding immediate arrest" of a GI alleged to have murdered a camptown prostitute on July 16, 1971.[46]

Such protests against alleged GI murders of Korean women and USFK reluctance to turn the accused men over to the R.O.K. legal sys-tem were not uncommon even before the clean-up campaign.[47] What was new in the summer of 1971 was the support the prostitutes received from other residents as they protested what they all believed were USFK injus-tices toward them.[48] The most ardent and prolonged of such protests took place in reaction to the off-limits decree[49] imposed by commanders in Anjŏng-ni during the racial violence of July 9–10, 1971. What began as a protest at the gates of Camp Humphrey by 100–150 prostitutes on July 13, against the decision of the camp commander to close the compound's main gate and declare Anjŏng-ni off-limits to its men, grew to a crowd of approximately 600 prostitutes and 3,000 other villagers by August 9. During this series of protests, prostitutes demanded that the base author-ities withdraw the "cowardly retalition [*sic*]" by opening the gates; blocked Korean waitresses who worked on the base from entering the compound; hurled stones at military personnel; overturned the car belonging to the P'yŏngt'aek County Police Superintendent; and demanded to meet the base commander.[50]

The base authorities and local KNP (Korean National Police) ini-tially responded to the protests with blockades and gas grenades. The ensuing mélée between the protesters and the police (both U.S. military police and KNP) resulted in the arrest and clubbing of several prosti-tutes and other villagers by the Korean police.[51] But the protests also led to the official recognition of the prostitutes as a significant group to be reckoned with in camptown politics: Ms. Yi Chŏng-ja, "the representa-tive of [the] village's 'girlie Club,'[52] was invited together with National Assemblyman Ch'oe, Yong-hi and one other village leader, to a luncheon sponsored by Col. Best to discuss the gradual lifting of the off-limits ban on Anjŏng-ni."[53] The ban on Anjŏng-ni was finally lifted on August 8, 1971 (although seven of the twelve local bars remained off-limits owing to their failure to comply with standards agreed upon by local Korean and command leaders), after forty-eight days of social unrest and eco-nomic losses for the Korean residents. Without doubt, the prostitutes initiated and largely sustained the push to lift the ban on the village, as promised by the Humphreys command in late July. The prostitutes not only received the support of other villagers in exerting pressure on the base leadership but also the support of Koreans in the greater society. For example, in a July 29, 1971 article, *Chungang Ilbo*, one of the lead-ing national dailies, accused the Humphreys command of breaking its promise to lift the ban.[54]

Besides the protests in Anjŏng-ni, camptown prostitutes also staged demonstrations on behalf of their "human rights." In May 1971, the

Hanguk Ilbo, another major daily, reported on protests by prostitutes (in P'yŏngt'aek) against GIs' efforts to cut their rates for sex:

> Some 1,000 Korean prostitutes staged a demonstration in a camp town near Seoul Monday evening, denouncing American soldiers for attempting to beat down charges for their services by half.
> They held rallies and demonstrations in front of a U.S. Army camp in the town for three hours before breaking up voluntarily to wait for "proper measures" by U.S. Army authorities.
> In the demonstration, the prostitutes asked the U.S. Army to make an apology for the attempt.[55]

These prostitutes objected to the U.S. airmen's boycott campaign, "Do-Not-Buy-Korean Commodities," begun in mid-April of 1971; the participants were 90 percent black.[56] The boycott itself was a protest against racial discrimination by Korean residents and against the rise of local prices due to the increased demand from more servicemen redeployed to the P'yŏngt'aek region (as part of the troop reduction). Korean camptown prostitutes were outraged at the boycott and held rallies near various U.S. camps. Songt'an prostitutes "adopted a four-point resolution, calling for the withdrawal of the Korean commodity boycott drive and reverance for the human rights of the Korean people."[57]

According to Kim Yŏn-ja, a veteran of the Songt'an "Women's Association," club prostitutes were insulted by U.S. servicemen who compiled a list of prices they were willing to pay for various goods and services in town. She said the soldiers treated sex as just another object of purchase:

> [T]hey fixed the local prices—for example, $5 for a pair of shoes and $5 for a "short-time." Therefore, we demonstrated. We charged, "How is it possible that someone can set the same price for a pair of shoes and a woman's body, then print the prices and circulate them?"[58]

Kim Yŏn Ja and other prostitutes found the military men's actions not only economically damaging but morally demeaning. The boycott ended a couple months after its initiation, partly because of insufficient participation by airmen,[59] but also because of the public protests by prostitutes and other villagers. Ms. Kim recalled that someone from the U.S. command did apologize to the women, and "therefore things were appeased."[60]

The protests described above demonstrate that many camptown prostitutes, though powerless in many ways, did not remain passive in the camptown turmoils of the early 1970s. Indeed, they formed a local "bloc" with which to protest the U.S. hegemony over the economic and political life of their camptowns. Referring to the protests against the boycott, Ms. Kim stated, "[T]he shop owners and club owners joined forces with us and supported our protest because with fixed prices, the prices of their own goods fell."[61] In other words, U.S. actions, whether off-limits decrees or boycotts and *prix fixe* actions, had direct economic impact on all camptown residents who depended on the bases for their survival. In this sense, although prostitutes were the most despised of the camptown residents, their plight starkly represented the vulnerability of many local Korean residents to U.S. power. The prostitutes thus succeeded in leading other villagers to challenge that power.

The political protests of prostitutes also represent the refusal of many women, who were condemned by Korean society and abused by Koreans and Americans alike, to be treated like commodities. In short, the prostitutes' sense of dignity—however fragile or distorted—asserted itself when pushed too far by others in the camptown communities. For these women, the economic value of their labor and their human worth were intertwined. And, they merged their sense of personal powerlessness, in relation to the bases, to the violation of the human rights, or domination, of the Korean people in general by the United States.

Public protest was one of the last available weapons of influence to which the prostitutes could resort, and such mass protests on the part of camptown residents were one of the main reasons why the U.S. initiated the clean-up campaign. The military sought to prevent such public outcries and disturbances by instituting law and order in the camptown communities. Major General Joseph Perditz, the head of Korea Support Command (KORSCOM), complained of the unruliness of the local Korean population around several of his command areas in the spring and summer of 1971, listing the demonstrations that had broken out near Camps Howard (May 23), Humphreys (July 13 and 27, August 3–5 and 9), Ames (July 19), and Carroll (August 2). He and other high-ranking military officials insisted that the Eighth U.S. Army Commanding General raise the issue with the R.O.K.G. to ensure that such disturbances would no longer occur.[62] With the initiation of the Clean-Up Campaign, such public challenges to U.S. military power in camptowns became rare throughout the remainder of the 1970s. Law and order and improved communication between U.S. and R.O.K. officials were intended to avoid violent and disorderly actions by both Koreans and Americans in the camptowns, but the effect on prostitutes was further silencing of their voices and anger.

The Camptown Clean-Up Campaign, initiated in the summer of 1971 as a direct response to the civil unrest and racial violence in Anjŏng-ni, marked the end of an era of "wildness" and "freedom" for many camptown prostitutes and the beginning of official reconstruction—by both the U.S. and R.O.K.—of prostitutes' identities and roles. Beginning in July 1971, the Korean prostitutes were no longer seen as individuals forced by public crises and dispossession, namely the Korean War and poverty, into prostitution. Instead, through the Clean-Up Campaign, the personal service that prostitutes could provide to GIs made them "private ambassadors" and "patriots." The rules of the game changed as well. The prostitutes were no longer allowed to eke out a living for themselves and their family members as willfully and wilefully as they could but rather were required to submit their bodies, work activities, and homes (rooms) to the systematic scrutiny and control of U.S. military and local Korean authorities.

How did the women deal with the changes in their lives brought on by the Clean-Up Campaign? If public protest was shut off to them, how did the women give voice to their interests? Did they accept the Korean government's transformation of their sex work into a form of patriotism? The general attitude of the women toward the Clean-Up activities appears to have been one of annoyance. Most women found the mandatory VD talks imposed by some local camptown authorities to be yet another regulatory nuisance aimed at protecting the health and welfare of the GIs but not the Korean women. All of the Korean women I interviewed blamed the Korean government for failing to distribute condoms and show women how to use them. They contrasted this with USFK practice: condoms were readily available, free of charge, at the compound gates for the soldiers to take into the camptowns. The women believed that proper education and the availability of condoms were not a priority for the R.O.K. government because the physical control over the women's bodies, through the examination and detention system, served as the core of VD control.

Across the board, camptown prostitutes detested the mandatory VD examination system and its heightened enforcement. First, they found the exams deeply humiliating. The women interviewed repeatedly used the word "shame" and "dread" to describe their feelings about VD exams. A USFK community relations officer (who is a Korean national himself), then active in VD control in Ŭijŏngbu, pointed out that some of the "smarter women" told him that forced VD exams amounted to a violation of their human rights.[63] He noted that these women especially took offense at being harassed by U.S. military police (MPs)—to show valid VD cards—and at being examined by U.S. medics; they charged infringment of their rights as Korean citizens: "We're Korean. Why are American doctors and police checking us?"[64] On the other hand, one woman asserted that some prostitutes would have preferred being checked by Americans because, given that most Koreans despised these women, it was more embarrassing to expose their genitals to Korean nationals than to American foreigners.[65] Some women questioned the validity of a VD prevention system that focused only on women's genitals: "Why are the authorities cracking down on us? American GIs are half the problem!"[66]

Alongside VD registration and effective diagnosis and treatment, the Clean-Up Campaign emphasized establishing and/or reinforcing strict "contact identification" systems. The purpose was to locate the female source of VD and order her to obtain treatment so that she would not spread infection further. Nearly all the bases had some form of contact system and regularly briefed servicemen regarding the contact procedures they should follow in case of VD contraction. Most of the women found the various contact identification measures humiliating, burdensome, inaccurate, and unfair. With the "tag system," women were required to wear numbered tags on their chest so that a GI could report the number (and hence, the woman's name) to his superiors in case of

VD infection.[67] Most of the women I interviewed did wear such tags beginning in the early 1970s and remarked bitterly that they felt humiliated in doing so. One woman asserted that many of her co-workers complained among themselves, "We're not animals—why are they tagging us and rounding us up!"[68]

Some commands encouraged the infected GI to go to the club or home of the alleged VD transmitter and point her out to the relevant military officials. Accused women found such public displays condemning and degrading and would put up loud and sometimes violent resistance, causing GIs to avoid such face-to-face confrontations. In response, most commands eventually adopted less confrontational practices, such as having the infected soldier simply point out the room where the alleged transmitter lived and then have medical officials and/or police force her to get treated. The major reason for such indirect accusations stemmed from soldiers' fear of retaliation from the prostitutes.[69]

When asked about the Korean government's designation of their work and role in U.S.-Korea relations as "patriotic," all of the women stated that no camptown woman they ever knew felt that her sex work was a nationalistic or patriotic act and that economic need was what drove most women to remain in prostitution. A "Mrs. Pak" put it simply: "It was shameful work: How could it be patriotic sacrifice?"[70] Several of the women interviewed pursued the idea of patriotism and stated that patriotism requires education and the positive provision and enforcement of skills to conduct "necessary and important work" for the country. They did not view their sex work as necessary or important for the security of Korea.

Most women admitted that they were unsure of the meaning of "national security" (*kugga anbo*), for which they were supposed to use their bodies, but they were certain that actions by the Korean government generally were oblivious to their physical and economic needs. Ms. Kim Yŏn-ja, former prostitute turned activist, sharply articulated that the rationales of the Korean government and U.S. military, namely, public professions of national security requirements, had no connection to the actual needs of camptown women. All of the women interviewed stated that their greatest need for R.O.K. protection (after the Korean War) was not from North Korean threats but the exploitation and abuse by clubowners/pimps, local Korean police and VD clinic officials, and the power of the U.S. bases.

All of the women expressed anger and contempt for their own government during the 1960s and 1970s for not standing up to the U.S. to fight for the rights of Koreans. In the words of one "Mrs. Ch'oe," "Korea was a land where only idiots lived: the government could not even defend its own people's interests, vis-à-vis the U.S."[71] Many of these women also believe that camptown women were generally not interested in issues of national security or other governmental policies because they felt powerless to influence or react to them. Ms. Kim stated that "because camptown prostitutes had no political power to effect policy changes, the interest wasn't there." She immediately added, "But this refers to Koreans in general—there really isn't much that we Koreans have been able to influence vis-à-vis the U.S. Is there?"[72]

The prostitutes whose voices and experiences inform this essay all witnessed the poverty and collapse of Korean society from the days of the civil war as well as the economic and international ascendance of South Korea in the last twenty years. They identified their personal lives closely with the losses and struggles of their country. They often associated the sexual abuse and exploitation of their bodies with the political and military domination of their country by the U.S. But they also harbored what seemed to me to be an honest sense of disappointment and a clear understanding that their government and people, not only the U.S. military, were to blame for their degraded lives. In this sense, these uneducated and under-educated women displayed a more realistic assessment of Korea's problems than many of the highly educated political leaders and activists who have criticized U.S.-Korea relations and the presence of U.S. bases in South Korea. For the women, the discovery of self-worth and improved livelihoods would not come with the potential removal of U.S. military bases. The sources of their abuse and exploitation would not necessarily change with the departure of American troops: severe class stratification; Confucianist moral norms of womanhood that deemed them social and moral pariahs; and a political system and culture that do not listen to the voices and input of women and the dispossessed. Even those groups actively fighting to expose and seek compensation for human rights violations against former women sex slaves to the Japanese Imperial Army have consciously tried to keep the plight and cause of the U.S. camptown prostitutes out of their movement. Former "comfort women" protest the identification of their past victimization and current campaign for justice with those of U.S. GI prostitutes.[73] The "comfort women" do not want to be associated with such "morally decadent," "trashy" women who "voluntarily" entered prostitution.

To make analogies between the dominated and conquered state of a nation and the bodies of individual women makes sense in the case of Japanese imperialism in Korea and "comfort women" of the 1940s. The Japanese did have effective, "colonialized" control over Korea. The Japanese military did "recruit" and deploy tens of thousands of Korean women, which was humiliationg and shameful to Koreans. But in the case of U.S. camptown prostitution, such an analogy is not accurate. There is a substantial difference between the resources available to poor, uneducated, lower-class women and those available to a juridically sovereign (postwar) state with near monopoly control over the economic, political, and social levers of society, as Korea was in the 1970s. It is possible to argue that individual girls and women were forced into prostitution by pimps or dire economic circumstances, but it is not as convincing to argue that the Korean government was forced by the U.S. to prostitute their women. Despite its historical arrogance in dictating Korean camptown life, the U.S. military institution did not kidnap or force individual women into prostitution. Nor did it require the prostitution of Korean women as a requirement for defending Korean soil. Given its geostrategic interest in Korea, from the 1950s to the 1980s, the U.S. would not have exited Korea, even if there had been no women to buy sex from.

What historically grew out of the exigencies of war, Korean women as camp followers, became instituted as an economic and social system by governmental authorities, both U.S. and Korean. Such institutionalization was a function of choice—on the part of the Park regime to prostitute a segment of the Korean female population for the purpose of economic and military gains, and on the part of the U.S. military to assume that prostitution was a necessary evil and Korean women mere commodities, whose bodies and human dignity were disposable. The factor of "choice" in the policy decisions and adaptations of the R.O.K. and U.S. governments must be scrutinized and criticized if we are to advocate genuinely for the needs and interests of poor and dispossessed women. The U.S. bases will not stay in Korea forever, but neither will the sexual domination and abuse of Korean women by foreign men vanish with the departure of U.S. troops unless the Korean government and people make new and different choices about the worth of women in their society.

NOTES

1. For example, Yayori Matsui refers to the larger phenomenon of sex tourism as a North-South problem in *Women's Asia* (Atlantic Highlands, NJ: Zed Books, 1989), 71. Also, Elaine Kim, "Sex Tourism in Asia: A Reflection of Political and Economic Inequality," in Eui-Young Yu and E.H. Phillips, eds. *Korean Women in Transition* (Los Angeles: Center for Korean-American Studies, California State University, 1987). See also Maria Mies, *Patriarchy and Accumulation on a World Scale: Women in the International Division of Labour* (Atlantic Highlands, NJ: Zed Books, Ltd., 1986), 137–142. For specific explanations of the relationship between inter-state power and military prostitution in Asia, see articles by Bruce Cumings, Aida Santos, and Walden Bello in Sandra Sturdevant and Brenda Stoltzfus, eds., *Let the Good Times Roll: Prostitution and the U.S. Military in Asia* (New York: The New Press, 1992).

2. Nicholas Boronoff, *Pink Samurai* (London: Grafton Books, 1991), 217. This point and others regarding some differences between the development of U.S. military prostitution in Japan and Korea were assessed by a former Wellesley College student, Aria Lu. I am grateful to her for sharing her resources and perspectives in a paper, entitled "One's for Pleasure, the Other's for Fun: A Comparison of the Differences in the Development of the Military Prostitution Policies of Japan and Korea," written for a seminar I taught in spring 1995 at Wellesley College ("Political Economy of the Body: Sex Industries in Asia").

3. Numerous factors, such as geographic location of the base (e.g., urban or rural, war zone or peace-keeping), familiarity of the host nation's language and culture, racial makeup of and stereotypes held by both U.S. soldiers and locals, military classification of the post (e.g., hardship tour, combat zone), military sponsorship versus non-command-sponsored tour, ages of soldiers, and individual command policies influence where, how, and why military prostitution occurs.

4. Cynthia Enloe, *Does Khaki Become You? The Militarization of Women's Lives* (Boston: Pandora Press, 1988), 25.

5. Col. Robert W. Sherwood, Chief of Preventive Medicine Division, Directorate of Health and Environment, Office of the Surgeon General, U.S. Army, "Deposition Form—Trip Report to Eighth U.S. Army, Korea, 7/7/72," 7.

6. Office of International Relations, Eighth U.S. Army (EUSA), Seoul, "Psychological Operations Campaign Control Sheet," 1–2.

7. The Status of Forces Agreement (SOFA) Joint Committee, composed of a delegation from the U.S. military and U.S. Embassy in Korea and the Korean Ministry of Foreign Affairs, was established in 1967 as the central and primary body responsible for managing USFK-R.O.K. relations, in accordance with the U.S.-R.O.K. Status of Forces Agreement, on a regular basis. The Committee met monthly until 1980 and three or four times a year from 1980 to the present. The "Minutes" of the Joint Committee state that they "are considered as official documents pertaining to both Governments." The complete volumes of the Minutes can be found in the U.S. Library of Congress. The Ad Hoc Subcommittee on Civil-Military Relations was established by the Joint Committee in 1971 to address camptown problems. The Subcommittee Minutes are

kept by the Institute for Foreign Affairs and National Security in Seoul and are not available to the public.

8. Joint Committee Minutes (JCM), #69, Inclosure 2 to Inclosure 11, December 16, 1971.

9. Ŭijŏngbu, Tongduch'ŏn, and Songt'an are the three main U.S. camp areas mentioned in this paper. Ŭijŏngbu and Tongduch'ŏn, north of Seoul, respectively house the I Corps (R.O.K./U.S.) Group at Camp Red Cloud and the Second Divsion at Camp Casey. Songtan serves as the camptown for U.S. personnel at Osan Air Base.

10. "Psychological Operations Campaign Control Sheet," 3.

11. Five hundred flyers containing such instruction were distributed to club women in July, 1971 by EUSA Psychological Operations officials. A copy of the flyer is recorded as Inclosure B of the Psychological Operations Memorandum by Col. Sasfy. The translation from Korean to English is mine.

12. Office of the Chief of Staff, Headquarters, USFK, "Problems in Civil-Military Relations in the R.O.K. and the First Year of the Operation of the U.S.-R.O.K. Joint Committee's Ad Hoc Subcommittee on Civil–Military Realtions," 1972, 1. (This report was attached to a letter written by Lt. Gen. Robert Smith, Chief of Staff, USFK and U.S. Representative to the Joint Committee, and sent to Philip Habib, U.S. Ambassador to the R.O.K., 1971–74.)

13. Interview, Uijŏngbu, June, 1992. This Community Relations officer for the USFK noted that for reasons of national dignity, a name like "National VD Purification Movement" would have been inappropriate.

14. Base Community Clean-Up Committee, "Woegukkun giji jŏnghwa jonghab daech'aek" (Comprehensive Policy for the Purification of Foreign Troop Bases), July, 1972, enclosed in Subcommittee Minutes, #12, July 31, 1972; Subcommittee Minutes, #8, March 20, 1972; Ministry of Foreign Affairs, "Kijich'on jŏnghwarŭl wihan woemubu sihaeng gyehoek #1" (MOFA Plans for the Purification of Camptowns), enclosed in Subcommittee Minutes, #6, January 24, 1972; Ministry of Health and Social Affairs, VD Control Programs, enclosed in Subcommittee Minutes, #10 (submitted to MOFA upon MOFA's solicitation of information from relevant ministries, to be reported to the 70th meeting of the SOFA Joint Committee).

15. Conversations with Yu Pok Nim, co-founder of Turebang (My Sister's Place), a counselling center in Ŭijŏngbu and Tongduch'ŏn for GI (Korean) wives and camptown prostitutes, 1991–92; Migun kiji bandae jŏnguk kongdong daech'aek, Yangki go hom (Yankee Go Home), (Seoul: Migun kiji bandae jŏnguk kongdong daech'aek, 1990); Pusan minjok minju undong yŏnhap (Federation of Pusan People's Democracy Movement), Nŏhiga mullŏnaya uriga sanda (You Must Withdraw So That We Can Live), (Seoul: Toso Publishing Co., 1991), Part II, Chapter 2; Malji (Mal Magazine).

16. Letter by Lt. Gen. T.W. Dunn, Commander of I Corps (Group) to EUSA Commanding General Hamilton Howze, July 19, 1964.

17. EUSA (Eighth U.S. Army), "Civil Affairs Handbook," #530–4, January 11, 1968, 68.

18. Memorandum from EUSA IO to EUSA Deputy Chief of Staff, Re: "Construction of Medical Clinics," May 3, 1963.

19. Memorandum by Maj. Saalberg, EUSA G-1 Action Officer, Re: "Report on Venereal Disease," January 14, 1963.

20. Astri Suhrke, "Gratuity or Tyranny: The Korean Alliance," in *World Politics,* 25:4 (July 1973).

21. Interview, Uijongbu, 6/4/92.

22. Sungjoo Han, "South Korea's Participation in the Vietnam Conflict: An Analysis of the U.S.-Korean Alliance," in *Orbis,* 21 (winter 1978).

23. Telephone interview with U.S. Representative to the Joint Committee, 1973–75, on October 31, 1991. This official noted that when he asked the then U.S. Ambassador to Korea, Philip Habib, why camptown problems had not been resolved before his tenure on the JC, Habib responded that because "Korea was fighting our war for us in Vietnam—with their best division, the U.S. could not push too hard." (These words were paraphrased by the interviewee.)

24. *Korea Herald,* July 17, 1971.

25. Interview, Connecticut, October 24, 1991.

26. Ibid.

27. *Far Eastern Economic Review,* August 6, 1970.

28. *Korea Herald,* January 31, 1971.

29. U.S. House of Representatives, *Investigation of Korean-American Relations,* Hearings before the Subcommittee on International Organizations of the Committee on International Relations, Part I, June, 1977, 34.

30. *Kkangt'ong* literally means tin can in Korean. The term has been used since the Korean War. The popular use of the cans began with the influx of canned goods brought by the U.S. military. *Kkangt'ongmunhwa* refers to flimsy, tacky, and cheap culture.

31. Interview, Seoul, June 11, 1992.

32. Interview, Seoul, May 14, 1992.

33. Telephone interview, Seoul, June 15, 1992.

34. Interview, Uijŏngbu, June 4, 1992.

35. Interview, Seoul, June 11, 1992.

36. Interview, Uijŏngbu, June 12, 1992.

37. Interview with Kim Yŏn Ja, Songtan, May 3, 1992.

38. Ad Hoc Subcommittee on Civil-Military Relations, "Nineteenth Report," January 23, 1975; JCM, #101, January 30, 1975, Inclosure 19.

39. Glenn Snyder refers to such dominance on the patron's part as the "preponderance

of influence" in "Alliance Theory: A Neorealist First Cut," in *Journal of International Affairs*, no.44 (1990).

40. Bruce Russett and Harvey Starr mention such "internal" capabilities of weak states in transforming the resources within a state's borders as instruments of foreign policy: "Intangibles such as leadership, belief in a cause, and especially cohesion resulting from a threat to survival are important assets for smaller states in unequal, or asymmetric, conflicts." *World Politics: The Menu for Choice*, 4th ed. (New York: W.H. Freeman and Co., 1992), 147.

41. David Henry Hwang, *M. Butterfly* (New York: Plume, 1988), 83; Andrew Rotter, "Gender Relations, Foreign Relations: The United States and South Asia, 1947–1964" in *The Journal of American History* (9/94), 518–542. For a discussion of gender identities of colonizing and colonized nations in general, see Ann Tickner, *Gender in International Relations: Feminist Perspectives on Achieving Global Security* (New York: Columbia University Press, 1992), 47–51.

42. Numerous stories contain this basic theme of self-sacrifice for the family's and country's good, but the story of Nongae best captures the totality of woman's sacrifice—body, chastity, and life—for the love of her country. The story of Nongae has been taught in Korean schools and celebrated as an example of Korean women's personal contributions to Korea's historical fight against Japanese encroachment. According to the legend, Nongae, the concubine of General Ch'oe Kyŏng-hoe, governor of Chinju in the late 1500s, seduced a Japanese commander, Rokusuke Kedanimura, during the Japanese invasion of Korea and siege of Chinju in 1592, in order to kill him. While dancing with him, she led him toward the edge of a cliff and threw herself and Kedanimura into the river beneath. It is said in Korea that every June 29 of the lunar calendar, *kisaeng* and others go pay respects to Nongae at the shrine established by government authorities in Chinju.

43. Kyung-Ae Park, "Women and Development: The Case of South Korea," in *Comparative Politics*, 25:2 (January, 1993).

44. In their survey of R.O.K. legislative records regarding prostitution, Hyung Cho and Pil Wha Chang found that members of the National Assembly demonstrated a "pragmatic permissiveness" toward *kijich'on* and other foreign exchange-oriented prostitution in Korea. "Perspectives on Prostitution in the Korean Legislature: 1948–1989" in *Women's Studies Review*, v. 7 (December 1990) (in Korean).

45. The quoted portion appears in capital letters in the Minutes of the Ad Hoc Subcommittee on Civil-Military Relations, Meeting #11, June 30, 1972.

46. *Pacific Stars and Stripes*, July 28, 1971.

47. For example, more than 300 prostitutes "staged a protest funeral march in front of 8057 American Unit [in Pup'yŏng], demanding a Sgt. Teni [phonetic] appear before them. They charged the American responsible for the death of one of their friends called Miss Yi Ŭn-ja," 23 years of age. "The hearse carrying the girls in white mourning dress, [*sic*] stopped in front of the unit's front door en route to a burial site and shouted: 'Come out Teni. Let him appear before us.' They also attempted to enter the unit compound and were stopped by about 50 American military police and 30 Korean police." *Korea Times*, May 15, 1969.

48. For example, according to a letter by Maj. Gen. Joseph Perditz, Commander of KORSCOM, "Several females penetrated the area between the inner and outer gates when a CID [Criminal Investigation Division] vehicle entered the compound. These KNs [Korean Nationals] were exchanged for two U.S. soldiers held hostage by the crowd." By mid-afternoon, four more soldiers were held hostage, and the crowd, led by prostitutes, demanded to speak to the installation commander, who agreed to do so. Letter from Perditz to EUSA Commanding General, Re: "Lack of Control of Civilian Populace," August 10, 1971.

49. The then Commander of Camp Humphreys placed the town indefinitely off-limits to U.S. personnel at 1 a.m. on July 10. Off-limits placed on individual bars or camp areas meant that no U.S. personnel was permitted to enter, hence patronize, the area(s). As a consequence, Korean camptown residents whose incomes depended on U.S. military patronage suffered economically.

50. *Pacific Stars and Stripes,* August 12, 1971; *Chungang Ilbo,* July 29, 1971 (EUSA translation); *Taehan Ilbo,* July 13, 1971 and August 10, 1971; letter from Perditz to EUSA Commanding General, Re: "Lack of Control of Civilian Populace," August 10, 1971; Letter from Col. F. Best, Commander of Camp Humphreys, to Maj. Gen. J. Perditz, February 7, 1972 (in letter from Perditz to EUSA Commanding General, Re: "Continuing Harassment by Korean Officials in Attempts to Place Back-Alley Clubs On-Limits," February 7, 1972).

51. Letter from Perditz, Re: "Lack of Control of Civilian Populace."

52. Yi Chŏng-ja was the then president of the Anjŏng-ni prostitutes' "Women's Association." According to her colleagues and friends, she had served in this capacity since the 1960s and had been an advocate of prostitutes' interests until recent years. Kim Yŏn Ja, a former leader of the "Women's Associations" in Kunsan and Songt'an, told me that Ms. Yi would have been able to describe in detail the camptown politics of Anjong-ni during the 1970s, but when Ms. Kim and I tried to locate Ms. Yi, we found out that she had passed away. Most of the large camptowns had "women's associations" which were supposed to serve as intermediaries between the numerous prostitutes and local officials. Although they were supposed to represent the women's interests, most such organizations did not have autonomy but rather served to convey the local Korean and U.S. authorities' interests to the women. These associations required their members to pay dues and served as emergency support for those in need of financial help, for example, in the case of illness. The organizations also helped pay for funerals of prostitutes whose relatives were unwilling or unable to pay. The relative strength and independence of such associations to represent and assert the interests of prostitutes depended to a great extent on the strength, authority, and capabilities of the association leaders. Both Ms. Yi and Ms. Kim were recognized by other prostitutes and local USFK and R.O.K. officials as strong, aggressive women who helped bring about some positive change for the women in their camptowns.

53. *Korea Herald,* July 30, 1971.

54. *Chungang Ilbo,* July 29, 1971 (EUSA translation).

55. *Hanguk Ilbo,* May 4, 1971 (EUSA translation).

56. *Overseas Weekly,* August 14, 1971.

57. *Chosŏn Ilbo,* May 4, 1971 (EUSA translation).

58. Interview with Kim Yŏn-ja, Songt'an, May 3, 1992.

59. *Overseas Weekly,* August 14, 1971.

60. Interview with Kim Yŏn Ja, Songtan, May 3, 1992.

61. Ibid.

62. Letter from Perditz, Re: "Lack of Control of Civilian Populace," August 10, 1971.

63. Interview with community relations officer, *Ŭijŏngbu,* June 4, 1992.

64. Ibid.

65. Interviews with Community Relations officer, Uijŏngbu, June 4, 1992 and Kim Yŏn Ja, May 3, 1992.

66. Interview with Kim Yŏn-ja, Kunsan, May 14, 1992.

67. Most medical offices and Provost Marshall Offices kept a book or file of records containing information regarding each registered woman in the base area. The information included the name, photograph, VD card registration number, local address, and the club name in which each woman worked. The tag number would accordingly be matched with the woman's file.

68. Interview with Kim Yŏn-ja, Songt'an, May 3, 1992.

69. Regarding soldiers' reluctance to name prostitutes face-to-face, one *Pacific Stars and Stripes* article (November 2, 1971) noted, "Some of the soldiers fear retaliation the next time they go into the village [for having accused a woman]. However, each is assured [by the medical office] that he will only have to point out the girl's residence and will not make eye-to-eye contact with her if he doesn't want to. We [U.S. medics] drop the KNP [Korean National Police] at the hooch and then take the GI back to his unit or dispensary."

70. Telephone interview with "Mrs. Pak" via "Mrs. Smith" (pseudonyms), April 2, 1993. "Mrs. Smith" served as an intermediary.

71. Telephone interview with "Mrs. Ch'oe" via "Mrs. Smith" (pseudonyms), April 2, 1993.

72. Interview with Kim Yŏn-ja, Songt'an, May 3, 1992.

73. Conversations with a *Chosŏn Ilbo* correspondent who has actively followed the "comfort women" issue, spring, 1995.

8

HYUN SOOK KIM

Yanggongju as an Allegory of the Nation:

The Representation of Working–Class Women in Popular and Radical Texts

There is no space from where the subaltern (sexed) subject can speak.
—Gayatri C. Spivak, "Can the Subaltern Speak?"

Far from being natural, . . . bodies are "maps of power and identity": or, rather, maps of the relation between power and identity.
—Gillian Rose, *Feminism and Geography*

In February 1995, a former sex worker (Kim Yŏn-ja) and two activists from Korea (a female, feminist writer and a male videomaker/photographer) led a three-week tour through eight major cities in the United States. The purpose of the tour was to raise Americans' awareness about the problem of militarized prostitution with foreigners in Korea and its impact on the lives of Korean women and their children. I was among many activists on the East Coast who helped to coordinate the speaking tour and in particular to organize a public forum for Korean Americans in Boston, which was their next-to-last stopping point.

The night before the activists were scheduled to address the Korean Americans, they were engaged in another forum at one of the major academic institutions where the audience was comprised of mainly feminist students and faculty. Feeling excited about the rare opportunity to meet with activists from Korea and discuss the militarized prostitution issue, I attended that evening forum. It had been three years since I had first met Kim Yŏn-ja in Songt'an, Korea, where another Korean-American activist and I had gone to investigate and write about two young boys who had been murdered by their American GI father. At that time, Kim Yŏn-ja had welcomed us to her home and shelter for bi-racial families called True Love Shelter (*Chamsarang Simtŏ*);[1] she fed us, introduced us to the women who work in bars and clubs surrounding the U.S. military base in Songt'an, and openly discussed life stories of sex workers of Kijich'on (military camptowns), including her own.[2]

The evening forum in Boston began with the Korean feminist writer's lengthy analysis of U.S. militarization of Korea since 1945, followed by the videomaker's slide show displaying the images of poverty-stricken Korea and Koreans from the 1960s and 1970s and the photos of U.S. military installations. The forum concluded with Kim Yŏn-ja's presentation of her experience of working and living in Kijich'on. Kim spoke in detail about the physical, psychological and economic hardship she endured in sexual labor for twenty-five years, from 1964 to 1989. She also discussed the importance of her religious faith as a source of self-empowerment which, she said, helped her to sustain hope and eventually to escape the life of a sex worker. Kim also mentioned that ever since becoming a preacher in 1989 she has used her missionary role to advocate the rights of working-class Korean women and their children living in military camptowns in Korea.

On the whole, the forum was successful in conveying important information about the history of U.S. imperialism in Korea since 1945 and the destructive impact of U.S. militarism on the lives of Korean civilians. However, as a Korean-American academic-activist sitting in the audience, I observed that the activists and the audience had very different ways of approaching the question of militarized prostitution. For example, the audience invited Kim to elaborate on her daily coping strategies in sexual labor, her views about the circumstances that forced her into sexual labor, and her views on patriarchy and militarism. Several students of liberation and feminist theology begged Kim to expand upon her description of how religious faith had guided her survival in (and eventual escape from) sexual labor. However, the young Korean American woman interpreter, who was responsible for providing simultaneous translation of questions and answers from English to Korean and vice versa, screened and censored the questions directed to Kim. Insisting that the forum time be devoted to the delivery of the group line, which aimed to "educate" Americans about the impact of U.S. imperialism and militarization on Korean lives, the activists overlooked and neglected to translate questions addressed to Kim. Attempts from the audience to ask about Kim's personal experience in Kijich'on were repeatedly ignored. The activists judged Kim's talk as "testimonial" and "evangelical" because her focus on the personal and daily struggle in sexual labor left no room for discussing the larger and, in the activists' eyes, more significant dimension of imperialism and domination of Korea by the United States.

Kim Yŏn-ja's testimony was relegated to the margins of this forum because the writer and videomaker analyzed the problem of military prostitution simply in terms of U.S. militarism and imperialism, thus locating the blame on Americans for the exploitation of Korean women working in Kijich'on. Their emphasis on the United States' culpability left little room to discuss the intricate relations of economic, cultural, and ideological hierarchies that reinforce women's subordination, including militarized prostitution among Koreans, in which Korean women provide sexual service to Korean soldiers near Korean military installations, and the role that the Korean dictatorships and patriarchy have played in encouraging Korean women into prostitution. Unlike Kim Yŏn-ja's story, which puts forward an alternative, "bottom-up" view of poor and working-class sex workers,[3] the activists' elitist, "top-down" perspective privileges their own subject positions as nationalist, middle-class experts with "critical knowledge." Their perspective can be characterized as a nationalist-feminist view. Throughout this essay, the term "nationalist-feminist" will be used to refer to what I call "the conscious-

177

ness of decolonization." This phrase effectively captures the sentiments of contemporary Korean feminist groups who share the nationalist views of social movement groups opposing neo-colonialism, militarism, and imperialism. The nationalist and feminist groups point to the problem of class and gender oppression as stemming solely from the structural domination of imperialism. Within this framework, Koreans are categorized as a unified subject occupying the victim position vis-à-vis the American oppressor.

The conflict between elite and working-class positions presents a fundamental challenge to middle-class Korean women, both feminist and non-feminist, when we speak of and about the poor and working-class women engaged in sexual labor, especially with foreigners. We must, however, ask the following theoretical and political questions: which ideological framework(s) should inform our discussions with American audiences about the problem of Korean prostitutes and foreign soldiers? Who gets to speak of, for, and about the working-class Korean women working in Kijich'on? Which boundary markers—i.e., the nation, gender, sexuality, ethnicity, and/or class—help shed light on the complex problem of militarized prostitution?

Historically, the term "Yanggongju" has referred to Korean women who engage in sexual labor for foreign soldiers. We need to problematize the social construction of this term, which does not refer to women working with or for Korean men. Used derogatorily, it means "Yankee whore," "Yankee wife," "UN lady," and/or "Western princess." This epithet, "Yanggongju," relegates Korean women working in militarized prostitution with foreign men to the lowest status within the hierarchy of prostitution. Since the end of the Korean War, this category has been extended to include Korean women who marry American servicemen (perjoratively called "GI Brides"). In postwar Korea, the epithet "Yanggongju" has become synonymous with "GI Brides," so that Korean women in interracial marriages are also viewed as "Yanggongju."

In the 1990s, a growing number of both popular and radical political texts that incorporate representations of "Yanggongju" have been produced and circulated. These include popular novels, films, and TV programs for the mass market, as well as radical political texts such as pamphlets, newsletters, journals, and books produced by leftist nationalist groups fighting for national sovereignty—specifically, the national unification and independence of, and democracy in, Korea. Like the Korean activists who spoke at the Boston forum, the popular and radical texts focus only on militarized prostitution with foreigners and do not acknowledge or problematize militarized prostitution in Korea, which includes Korean women providing sexual service to Korean soldiers. The texts also use the term "Yanggongju" unquestioningly and uncritically, in its pejorative connotation.

I will interrogate this categorization of Korean working-class sex workers by examining how specific texts construct and sustain the notion of "Yanggongju." Curiously, critical studies of sexual labor with foreigners in Kijich'on remained few and far between until the 1990s,[4] and negative images of working-class Korean women as "Yanggongju" have left a deep imprint in the minds of Koreans. My essay emphasizes two main arguments: one, that although the term "Yanggongju" is used by middle-class nationalists and feminists to symbolize the nation, this use simultaneously erases or vilifies the lives and experiences of working-class women; and two, that despite being essentialized as "Yanggongju," working-class Korean women engaged in sexual labor with foreigners have agency, subjectivity, experience, and an autonomous point of view. Their self-representations contest and challenge the dominant representations of them as mere victims, as the oppressed.

To develop these arguments, this essay's first two sections will analyze Ahn Jung-hyo's novel *Silver Stallion* (1990) and Kang Sŏk-kyŏng's short story "Days and Dreams" (1989), respectively. Translated into English[5] and introduced to the American mass market, these two texts present stereotypical, unidimensional representations of "Yanggongju" as "victims" of militarism and imperialism. The women are portrayed in terms of their object-position as poor, working-class, raped, abused "whores" for American GIs. The third section analyzes texts produced by radical movement groups, discussing specifically how these texts utilize the figure of Yun Kŭm-i, a young Kijich'on sex worker murdered in 1992 by an American soldier. How do the images of Korean military prostitutes in radical texts differ from those put forward in popular texts? (Throughout the essay, the word "radical" refers to the leftist nationalist consciousness that opposes [neo-]colonialism and U.S. militarism and seeks national independence and unification of two Koreas.) I will argue that while radical social movement groups with nationalist and/or feminist consciousness have won some mainstream support to discuss militarized prostitution, largely because of the Yun Kŭm-i murder incident, they nevertheless discuss militarized prostitution only in relation to foreigners, particularly American soldiers. Not only is the issue of Korean women providing sexual services to Korean men thus ignored, but these radical groups are reinscribing and reconstituting elitist and patriarchal views of working-class Korean women of Kijich'on as "Yanggongju"— vulgar, low, dirty, and shameful social objects. Finally, the paper's fourth section returns to a discussion of the speaking tour. I will contend that although they have not been well received by nationalists and feminists, Kim Yŏn-ja's speeches about her religious spirituality as a source of self-empowerment cannot be dismissed as politically incorrect. Neither can we appropriate her experience to assert a false unity of heterogeneous Korean women while relegating the working-class, female sex worker(s) to marginality. In fact, the elite-versus-working-class conflict described above cautions us about the privileging of class and "expert" knowledge that occurs when middle-class academic-activists and working-class women join together.

In the late twentieth century, in the age of global or transnational capitalist culture, it becomes particularly urgent for us diasporic Korean women to recognize the differences among us in terms of class, ethnicity, nationality, and power relations. Korean women do not compose a monolithic group as "Koreans," "women," or "Korean women"; we do not share a unity of "Korean womanhood"; and the traditional understanding of our locations in terms of the oppressed and the oppressor or the periphery and the metropole is inadequate. Thus, in re-thinking the politics of representation, elitist (feminist or nationalist) academics and activists must not assert a single, unitary identity constructed in terms of Korean nation, ethnicity, or womanhood and should not contribute to the silencing of the working-class women engaged in sexual labor with foreign soldiers. Instead of reproducing totalizing, unidimensional images of working-class Korean women who work in sexual labor for foreigners as victims of militarism and neo-colonialism, this essay emphasizes the importance of recognizing the self-representations of working-class women and their everyday resistance to the patriarchal and military-capitalist systems of power hierarchy. When considering the position of working-class Korean women, we need to deconstruct the essentialized category of "Yanggongju" and "speak to" the working-class Korean women who have been culturally and historically muted in the dominant narratives of the middle class, both nationalist and feminist. Imperial violence and male violence need to be theorized, but not in terms of middle-class cultural and political norms. Theoretically and politically, we need to understand Korean women, especially and working-class women as heterogeneous, material subjects making their own histories.

The Son-Centric View of the Raped Mother in
Ahn Jung-hyo's Silver Stallion

Ahn Jung-hyo's *Silver Stallion* is a story about how the Korean War transforms traditional mother-son, familial, and community relations.[6] Ahn's popular novel represents prostitutes who service foreign soldiers as "Yanggongju" and allegorizes them as symbols of the nation. With his narrative of the "suffering mother" and the "victimized nation," Ahn vilifies the lives and experiences of the raped mother and women engaged in sexual labor.

The plot centers on the protagonist's mother, the widow Ollye, who is ostracized by fellow villagers after being raped by an American soldier when UN forces move into the small village of Kumsan. The author frames Ollye as a vulnerable woman who has neither husband nor father to protect her from the intruding soldiers. In Kumsan, no shops, inns, bathhouses, or boatmen serve a widow as their first customer because she is considered less than half of a person and is assumed to bring bad luck. Doubly stigmatized as a widow and a raped woman, Ollye is ultimately ex-communicated from her community. The villagers blame her for her own tragedy, ostracizing her and her children, although they dare not challenge the UN soldiers who intruded on their village and committed the crime to begin with.

At the beginning of the story, Old Hwang, the village patriarch, is portrayed as powerless and emasculated because he has failed to protect

181

the local women from the soldiers. This image of helpless Old Hwang suggests that the local patriarchal order is threatened by the soldiers' arrival. The author does not explicitly equate the rape with the struggle between nations and patriarchies, but we can clearly see how the story inscribes the unequal power relations between Korea and the United States and points to the ways in which such a rape can lead to the disruption of social relations among the villagers and can challenge traditional notions of Korean femininity and masculinity.

Ahn also (rather duplicitously) portrays the village women as prurient "Yankee prostitutes" who threaten and destroy the village mores by openly displaying sexual acts and relations. For example, the author paints a lengthy scene of village men, women, and boys taking pleasure in, gossiping about, and ridiculing how Ollye enjoyed being raped by the "*bengkos*." With the use of salacious language and sexual scenes, the author creates stereotypes of sex workers as titillating, erotic objects. For example, in the story, the village boys beg for C-ration cans and chocolates from the "*bengkos*"; they also become aroused as they watch Ollye and other sex workers "play" with the soldiers. Ollye's son, Mansik, does not understand the impact of rape on his mother, and when Ollye becomes a "UN Lady," he is also ashamed of her body which he views as dirtied and sexed for the first time. By trying to prevent the village boys from watching her sexually engaged with the soldiers, he attempts to protect and hide his mother's shamed body (227–237). Ahn dramatizes and derides "UN Ladies," including Ollye, as sex temptresses who drink and sell beer, smile, use tricks, and enjoy sexual intercourse with foreign (including black) soldiers, and imitate and speak broken and unintelligible English. The women constantly blurt out, "okay, okay," "hubba-hubba," "namba wang," "namba teng," "drink," "kiss, kiss," etc. (146–150).

In contrast to Ahn's parody of sex workers, the so-called "UN Ladies," in my view, can be read as defiant women who rebel against traditional patriarchy and challenge the patriarch whose authority has been attenuated. When the soldiers move into Kumsan, they are followed by women from outside whom the villagers call "UN Ladies." When Old Hwang tries to prevent them from opening a brothel in Kumsan, they proudly defy him, mocking and ridiculing him because they consider him impotent and incapable of dealing with the changes set off by the war and the arrival of UN soldiers. To challenge his authority further, they assert themselves in terms of the pejorative labels attached to them by the villagers. On several occasions they exclaim boldly: "We're Whores!" (106).[7] Although these labels are pejorative terms that both the villagers and the text assign to female sex workers servicing foreign men, we see that the women themselves appropriate these terms to challenge the patriarchal and nationalist stigmatization of the women's bodies and their labor.

Like the other so-called "UN Ladies," the protagonist's mother, Ollye, faces an uneasy conflict between the economic and survival needs of her family and the patriarchal taboo that marks her as a widowed, raped woman. When Ollye turns to sex work for American soldiers after being raped by one of them, she finds herself additionally castigated by the villagers. She is not like the other village women, according to the author and in the villagers' eyes, because her body has been "damaged" and "dirtied." However, we can interpret her decision to work in militarized prostitution with foreign soldiers as being strategic and rebellious, albeit contradictory. Her fear of the patriarchal social taboo turns into rage when she is directly confronted by villagers' ostracism and ridicule; she feistily refuses to be mocked or stigmatized as a "fallen" woman. Her rage makes her determined to fulfill her maternal duty, and she turns to sexual labor in exchange for money and canned goods offered by American soldiers.[8] Here, Ollye is caught between this double desire— on the one hand, to be freed from the Confucian patriarchal values that mark her as an outcast, and on the other hand, to fulfill her maternal duties as prescribed by patriarchy. Thus her engagement in sexual labor can be understood as a rebellion constituted within the constraints of a wartime economy and Confucian patriarchal notions of womanhood, as well as a forced choice.

With its fetishized descriptions of Ollye, the text collapses together the figures of the chaste, respectable mother and the sexualized "fallen" women even further. When Ollye becomes a "UN Lady," she discards the plain peasant clothes that hide her body, donning colorful Western dresses that expose her legs and arms in public for the first time. Her bare face is made over with powder, eyeliner, and lipstick. High heels, permed hair, a few broken words of English, and the drinking of alcohol further masquerade Ollye as a "modern UN Lady" who inhabits a landscape quite different from the rustic village world that has abandoned her (175). Wearing make-up and Western clothing may be read as Ollye's efforts to free herself from stigmatization and victimhood under her particular relation to patriarchy. At the same time, however, the Western dress and make-up serve to legitimize the brand as a "Yanggongju." The text imagines her as "showy," "gaudy," "noisy," "garish," and "colorful," pejorative views that render her more a commodified object of play than a self-determined subject.

At the end of the story, the raped woman achieves redemption by returning to a traditional maternal role. Ollye's conflicting female identities—the raped woman, the "UN Lady," and the mother—are reconciled only when she leaves sex work and resumes conventional motherhood, thereby regaining respectability in her son's eyes. In collusion with Confucian patriarchal mores, Ahn here reconstitutes a closed binary construction of Korean women in terms of the "good mother" and "bad Yanggongju"—mutually exclusive and essentialized roles for Korean women.

The last image we see of Ollye is that of a redeemed peasant woman wearing farm clothes—"loose *chŏgŏri* blouse" and "baggy *monpe* pants" (116; 265). *Chŏgŏri*, a traditional Korean blouse with sagging sleeves, and *monpe*, pants adopted from Japan, together suggest the layering of precolonial, colonial, and post-colonial Korea. Ollye herself symbolizes the changing Korean nation and a hybrid Korean culture that is both "modern" and "traditional." We can read in her image the uncertain possibility of hybridity in the postwar Korean nation.

This popular Korean novel fixes at the center of its allegory the fallen (raped) Korean woman whose vulnerability mirrors the nation's own "effeminacy" in contrast to Western masculinity (embodied by the wealthy, militarily powerful agents/soldiers who bring modernity and capitalist culture to the small, "backward" village of Kumsan). Literally and figuratively, therefore, Ollye represents a contested terrain for reconfiguring the meanings of what and who is a Korean woman. The foreign soldiers, the local patriarch, the villagers, the outcast woman herself, other "UN ladies," and the son identify and mark the raped woman in contradictory terms. In the end, however, Ahn's text sustains and supports the Confucian patriarchal notions of femininity—such as the qualities of duty, self-sacrifice, devotion, and respectability— assigned to the "good woman."[9]

Violence and Poverty in Kang Sŏk-kyŏng's "Days and Dreams"

In contrast with *Silver Stallion*, which chronicles the protagonist's view of his raped mother, the protagonist in "Days and Dreams" is the "outcast" woman herself, a Korean woman whose childhood memories are grounded in the period of American occupation of Korea, from 1945 to 1948, and during the Korean War. Lured by signs of wealth offered by American GIs, she runs away from her poverty-stricken family.[10] She is resigned to the life she takes up doing so-called "Yanggongju" work, but expresses rage, angst, and a desire to be emotionally rooted in the family and the nation.

From a complex, nuanced, middle-class feminist perspective, Kang weaves a story of social dislocation, economic exploitation, and sexual violence in which poor Korean women are victims of both local/national and foreign/Western patriarchies. Unlike Ahn Jung-hyo, Kang does not vilify women engaged in militarized prostitution with foreigners. However, like Ahn, she essentializes the women of Kijich'on as symbols of the nation, thereby erasing their agency and subjectivity.

Whereas the rapist in *Silver Stallion* is a Western soldier, Kang presents the perpetrator of sexual assault and murder as the Korean male pimp who kills Mi-ra, one of the many women who work in camptown bars. Anticipating the actual, not fictional, barbaric murder of Yun Kŭm-i, which will be discussed in the following section, he mutilates Mi-ra's body by sticking a pair of coal tongs between her legs. As summed up by one "bar woman," "[a] Korean man took her for all she was worth, and she ended up dead" (20). With the portrayal of the Korean male pimp, who is also a drug user and a gang member, Kang raises the spectre of misogyny and exploitation of women under Korean patriarchy. Yet she is also fair enough to explain this misogynistic behavior in terms of the man's poverty, economic dependence on sex workers, and emasculation. In the pimp's police confession about the murder of Mi-ra, we learn that the psycho-social motivation behind his anger and hatred stems from his wounded masculine pride. The pimp states that Mi-ra "would live it up with the GIs" and then "give him leftover sex." Receiving money and secondhand clothes that Mi-ra obtained from American GIs damages the pimp's self-esteem and makes him feel impotent. The sex workers are sympathetic toward the Korean pimp because although he controls and exploits women's sexual labor, he has lost his "manliness" and is materially dependent on American GIs. Indeed, the "bar women" understand the humiliation and damaged pride of Korean men who are forced into economic and military dependence on America. They also express defiant contempt for Korean men: "Why should we sacrifice our money and hearts to these Korean pricks?" "What good are they?" Of the pimp accused of murder, the women ask, "Is he the only one who's eaten leftovers? This whole country's been living off other countries' leftovers" (20). Such statements are illustrative of the range of ambivalent emotions and contradictory allegiances held by the women. On the one hand, they resent Korean men, who abuse, exploit, and dominate them; on the other hand, they yearn for communication with men who share the same culture and language.

Ultimately, however, the women in this text are fully conscious of Korea's subordination to America. Kang suggests that Korea's poverty and economic dependence on the West force women engaged in sex work for foreigners to gravitate towards America. Kang presumes here that Korean masculinity and patriarchy are less powerful, less caring, and more oppressive than American masculinity and patriarchy. America, meanwhile, is seductive. One of the women working and living in Kijich'on says, "GIs are cold as ice when they turn their backs on you, but they'll propose if they like you. Basically they care for women. Can you think of a Korean man who would propose to one of us?" (21). Kang suggests that going to America may be the only hope for these women, depicting Sun-ja as a sex worker who dreams of America as an escape from Korea and Korean patriarchy: "I have to get to America. You think I came to this godforsaken area for my health? At my age? I'm not going to live in this country anymore. I want to leave any way I can" (13).

While postwar poverty and the omnipresence of American soldiers in Korea has nurtured longings among many Koreans to emigrate to America, Kang's version of America as the ultimate escape route from Korean poverty is unsettling because none of the women seems to be conscious that her oppression stems from class inequality and Korean patriarchy. By focusing on the dream of escape, Kang evades the real problems of socioeconomic, cultural, and social dislocations faced by poor women who engage in sexual labor for foreign soldiers. At the end of the story, none of the women marries an American soldier or moves to the United States. In fact, no one gets married at all. The possibility of a lesbian marriage is flirted with in the text, but lesbianism is treated only as an abstract idea, a fantasy. For example, the narrator rejects the young black lesbian soldier named Barbara; Sun-ja also dies before she can escape to America with Barbara, who had proposed to Sun-ja. Why does Kang make lesbian marriage impossible? Is it because Barbara is a woman, because she is black, or because she is an American GI?

In Kang's story, there is no escape for the women from poverty, sexual violence, and sexual labor. Kang represents sex workers in the context of victimhood, as sites of death, destruction, and despair. Instead of rejecting marriage and patriarchal family ideals, her characters long to fill traditional feminine roles and identities. Kang romanticizes heterosexual female identity and desire for the love of and marriage to men. The choice she gives to her women characters is between death and acceptance by Korean men, through which they can gain a sense of belonging to the Korean nation. Needless to say, both are extreme and problematic options.

In the conclusion, we also find Kang's allegorization of the "bar women" and the camptowns as "islands"—the sex workers inhabit landscapes which, as geographically and physically suspended areas, belong to no nation. These nation-less women thus act as spatial metaphors. The women experience extreme sexual violence and poverty, but the author is silent about the possibility of resistance and struggle to gain dignity through sexual labor. Instead, Kang's middle-class, heterosexual feminist treatment of the women of Kijich'on deploys the woman as victimized sex workers who are place markers and materials to symbolize the subordination of Korea to America.[11]

Reading Gender and the Nation in Radical Texts

What are the images of Kijich'on sex workers as presented in the literature (books, pamphlets, poetry, newsletters, magazines, and newspapers) produced by radical nationalist groups? What do these images reveal about the subject positions of working-class sex workers as constructed in the trope of the nation? How do these representations of the working-class sex workers in radical texts compare with representations in popular texts? To answer these questions, this section examines recent radical nationalist publications such as the *Hangyŏrae Sinmun* (One People Newspaper) and *Mal* (Talk) monthly journal, which represent two key voices of the radicalized nationalist opposition to the U.S. military establishments and military crimes in Korea. The aim here is not to analyze the history of Korean nationalist movements but to examine how radical texts create representations of women as "Yanggongju."

Yankee Go Home! (1990), *Make Us Sad No More!* (1990), and *To the Sons of Colonialism* (1989), published with the support and endorsement of *Hangyorae Sinmun* and *Mal* journal, document the crimes that U.S. military troops have committed in Korea since 1945. These crimes include murder, rape, physical and sexual assault, arson, mugging, all of which are considered to be racially and sexually motivated. In *Make Us Sad No More!*, journalist O Yŏn-ho describes the changing attitudes of Koreans toward American troops between September 1945, the end of Japanese colonialism and the beginning of American occupation of Korea, and the 1990s. He states that in 1945, those Koreans injured or assaulted by U.S. soldiers quietly endured the military crimes. During the 1960s and 1970s, victimized Koreans began to challenge soldiers verbally and shout back: "Why do you hit instead of talking?" Since 1987, with the rise of strong anti-American sentiments, Koreans have begun to cry out, "Yankee Go Home!"[12] O Yŏn-ho asks:

> Until when must we repeat these words to the U.S. Armed Forces in Korea? . . . But the U.S. Armed Forces in Korea have not listened to our cries. Today in 1990, from It'aewŏn to Tongduch'on, P'aju, Osan, Kunsan, the history of pillage and plunder continues . . . this land [of Korea] is a land of sin. A land of disgrace.[13]

Similarly, in *To the Sons of Colonialism* (1989), another collection documenting military crimes, O Yŏn-ho asks, "The America that is inside the Korean peninsula—who are they to us?" From the "critical" stance of "the mass" (*minjungŭi ipchang*), the preface of the book states that its aim is to confront "the historical reality in which we face the national issues of self-determination, democracy, and reunification." Within this anti-U.S. and anti-imperialist framework, Korean male and female victims of military crimes are memorialized and personified as symbols of Korean collective national suffering. With the nation held up as a primary concern, this trope occludes the gendered nature of such crimes as rapes and sexual assaults. The limitation of this trope is revealed in the following murder case.

On October 28, 1992, a Korean woman named Yun Kŭm-i, who had worked in sexual labor in Kijich'on, was killed by an American soldier named Kenneth Markle. Yun was mutilated by a bottle stuck into her vagina, an umbrella stuck into her rectum, matches pushed into her mouth, and detergent powder spread all over her body. Her body was found in a pool of blood in the small room that she rented in Kijich'on. This incident certainly was not the first case of assault or crime committed against sex workers by American soldiers in Korea. However, given the escalation of anti-American sentiments among Koreans since the Kwangju massacre of 1980[14] and the gruesome nature of Yun's murder, the incident awakened Korean consciousness about the brutality of U.S. military crimes.[15]

For feminists in Korea, the Yun Kŭm-i incident created a new arena for discussing gender and sexual politics.[16] Yun's mutilated body was material evidence of imperialist violence against the bodies of Korean women. These bodies were allegorized as the "victimized" and "suffering" Korean nation.[17] By linking sexual violence against working-class sex workers in military camptowns to the victimization of the Korean nation, female bodies were subsumed symbolically into the national body politic. The body of Yun Kŭm-i became a metaphorical boundary for the nation.

When alive, however, Yun Kŭm-i was shoved to the margins of Korean society and viewed derogatorily as a "Yanggongju."[18] The brutal way she was killed led Koreans to remember and reconstruct the image of her as a "good woman" passively victimized by "beastlike" (*maengsu*) American soldiers.[19] This re-shaping of Yun's image is unusual: typically, Koreans and Korean Americans consider "Yanggongju" as "crazy women" (*mich'inyŏn*), "loose women" (*baramkkiga itnŭn yŏja*), and "women plagued by the longing-for-America-sickness" (*migukbyŏng gŏllin yŏja*). Children born of Korean "bar women" and American GIs are similarly viewed as "bastards of the Western Princess" (*yanggongju saekki*), "seeds sown by GIs" (*gunindŭri ppurigogan ssi*), and "darkies" or "niggers" (*kkamdungi*).[20] Thus the stigma for Korean women labeled as "Yanggongju" involves both being a sex worker and associating with American male soldiers.

Similarly, the documents published by the Committee on the Murder of Yun Kŭm-i by American Military in Korea (*Chuhan Migunŭi Yun Kŭm ssi Salhae Sagŏn Gongdong Daech'aek Wiwŏnhoe*) (hereafter, the Committee) also reveal radical and feminist nationalist delineation of who or what is "Yanggongju." The diverse spectrum of feminist groups include Christian women's groups, women's rights groups, labor and human rights groups.[21] In a Committee document titled *Our Kŭm-i* (1993) Yun Kŭm-i is invoked as a symbol of the underprivileged Korean woman: she is "the daughter of poor family," "our (the Korean) daughter," "a female factory worker," "poor prostitute," and "our nation's daughter who dreamed for America" (5). A poem dedicated to Yun titled *Tongduch'ŏn Kŭmi*, for example, memorializes and sentimentalizes her in the following ways: "your life hellish, your breath a pain itself"; "wretched was Kŭm-i's life, pitiful is ours"; "a *Tongduch'ŏn*-woman is not a citizen of this nation"; "under the Stars and Stripes, the colonized bodies of our women are thrown about"; "how did you get here [a military camptown], Kŭm-i?"[22] As reflected in these lines, Yun Kŭm-i embodies the collective suffering of Koreans and the Korean female. In this slippage between ethnic/nation and gender identities as composed by the committee, Koreans are homogenized into one unitary subject.

In this particular document dedicated to a Kijich'on sex worker, nationalist and feminist views coincide. The nationalist-feminist view emphasizes that Korean national sovereignty has been compromised by neo-colonial political and economic relations, whereby the U.S. political and economic domination is maintained by the division of Korea and the presence of the U.S. military bases on the southern half of the peninsula. Women's movement groups share the nationalist platform of the larger, leftist national democratic movement—participating in anti-U.S. military base rallies, human rights campaigns, and campaigns to institute social reforms such as better wages, the right to organize unions, the elimination of police brutality and corruption, etc. The overarching nationalist agenda, supported by women's groups, calls for the preservation of a common Korean ethnic-national identity that unifies men and women, regardless of class and gender differences, as common victims of U.S. imperialist oppression.

Feminist activist Pak Sun-kŭm, the Committee representative and the Chair of the Korean Church Women United, describes Yun Kŭm-i's death as a symbol of the collective suffering of the nation:

> The crime by the American soldier provoked the heart of this nation; this crime made us experience the stark reality of being completely robbed of our national sovereignty and dignity.[23]

She adds that the dead body of Yun is like a weak animal that has been pierced severely by a cruel beast[24] and with this simile Pak also memorializes Yun as a victim and a symbol of national sovereignty.

Similarly, Chŏn U-sŏp, a renowned minister of Tabitha House (*Dabitaŭi Jip*), expresses an equally sentimentalized view of the nation: "The death of Yun Kŭm-i is not the death of an individual. It is the death of national sovereignty; the death of national [human] capital!"[25] In Chŏn's analysis, Yun symbolizes the lack of sovereignty and independence for Korea as a nation. The murder of Yun, in Chŏn's view, indicates the urgent need for the divided Koreas to be unified, the Korean peninsula to be de-militarized, and the American troops to be withdrawn as soon as possible.

Again, in these nationalist views, both feminist and non-feminist, the crime is U.S. imperialism. There is no mention of how Korean patriarchy, class inequality, and the state's economic policies have contributed to the re-colonization and marginalization of sex workers.[26] Instead, masculinized nationalism is recuperated by activists, including nationalist-feminists. And in this recuperation, no space is opened to view sex

191

workers in their class, gender, and sexual positions; the contestation, resistance, and challenge by sex workers to both the international and local capitalist-military patriarchy are also occluded. In short, discussions of working-class sex workers in radical texts do not counter or contest their representations in popular texts. The radical narrative about working-class women in militarized prostitution with foreigners is the same as the popular narrative in that the speaking subject at the center is the privileged activist and the local patriarchal power remains unquestioned. In both radical and popular texts, working-class sex workers are recognized only after gruesome death and violence, and when they do become visible, they are categorized as victims oppressed by U.S. imperialism/militarism. In short, any historical specificity of women's locations in particular social and cultural power relations as subordinate, marginal, or powerful, is effectively erased.

Viewing the Politics of Yanggongju from Within

Returning to the speaking tour with which this essay began, we have seen that activist Kim Yŏn-ja poses some important challenges to feminist and nationalist activists. Kim asserts that militarized prostitution and women engaged in sexual labor in Kijich'on will probably not be eliminated right away after the U.S. army withdraws. Simply, her view is that the military prostitution problem should rightly be solved through the elimination of American military establishments in Korea. However, that is not enough. She also tells us that the role that the Korean government and police play in punishing women and regulating prostitution is no less problematic. She challenges the Korean government's support of militarized prostitution for U.S. soldiers and speaks personally about her own experience of sexual violence, exploitation, and oppression stemming also from Korean military-capitalist-patriarchal culture. She is part of a protest wave building in a nation where critiques of military prostitution in general and Korean patriarchy in particular are not widely embraced or supported.[27]

Furthermore, in her testimonies, Kim also articulates another dimension of oppression connected to sexual labor—namely, discrimination based on unequal class positions. She states with disappointment that during the twenty-five years of her life in Kijich'on, from 1964 to 1989, not a single movement activist or feminist visited her or other women:

> Without hearing the voice of the women working and living the life [of a sex worker], how can women's problems be solved? I don't know what a women's movement is, but the problem is that the person playing the leading role is always the woman-activist and the ancillary or support-ing actors are us, the women in the sex industry. Are we simply frogs or materials for clinical demonstrations? The activists use us, the women of Kijich'on, as research materials, but how much effort did they honestly make to bring improvement of the lives of Kijich'on women?[28]

What might be learned if women like Kim could position themselves at the center of political narratives, rather than being assigned to the periphery of politics? If we view working-class women in military pros-titution from Kim's perspective, it is not difficult to recognize that her speaking personally about her life in Kijich'on is indeed political.[29] We hear her challenging not only U.S. imperialism but more directly the repressive Korean government and the police, the Confucian patriarchy, and the classism and elitism of nationalist and feminist activists. As Kim Yŏn-ja has clearly delineated, both nationalist and feminist activists need to elucidate the ways working-class women of Kijich'on struggle to define the personal meanings of Korean womanhood and their self-rep-resentation as subjects of the Korean nation.

For example, in the booklet *Great Army, Great Father (Widaehan gun-dae, widaehan abŏji)* (1995), we find nationalist-feminist activists speak-ing with patronizing kindness about military prostitution: "The most victimized persons by the U.S. troops are 'Kijichon women' and 'women who are interracially married to American soldiers.' We must protect the rights of Korean women" (83). Challenging this construction of prosti-tutes as passive victims, a short article in the same booklet on Kim Yŏn-ja shows evidence of Kim's anger, protest, and resistance against the ways women of Kijich'on are treated in Korean society. In *Great Army, Great Father*, Kim states that she cannot control her rage when the women of Kijich'on are judged from the perspective of anti-Americanism and labeled as "pitiful" or "wretched." In her view, when we inscribe the American military as "evil" and "Yanggongju" as objects of pity, we only cover up the roots of the problem. She insists that we also examine the psychological and emotional crises that sex workers face stemming from their experiences of sexual abuse, rape, and assault perpetrated by Korean men. These men, she points out, include Korean soldiers, Korean pimps, and Korean police and government officials. Furthermore, debt, drug addiction, alcoholism, and psychological, emotional, and sexual abuse trap the women in sexual labor and eliminate any hope of alternatives. Kijich'on is a "quicksand," Kim states, because once a woman falls in, she usually cannot get out.[30]

While political protests have been organized by sex workers, they have received scant public attention. However, a few significant examples of collective action are worth mentioning. In May 1971, Kim and other sex workers organized a protest in Songt'an. The American soldiers had distributed leaflets that read, "Shoes $5, Short-time $5, Long-time $10." Equating women's bodies with merchandise, the soldiers were demanding that the price of sexual service be reduced. Kim played a key role in mobilizing over one thousand sex workers to demonstrate in front of the army base. "We are not shoes! We are human beings!" The women demanded that the soldiers who distributed the flyers be forced to resign. The women's demands were not only ignored, but they were forced to disperse by the Korean and military police.

In June 1977, in "America Town" in Kunsan, a sex worker named Yi Pok-hi was strangled to death and her body scorched. A month later, another sex worker named Yi Yŏng-sun was killed. An American soldier, Steven Warren Towerman, admitted to killing both women, but at the time of the incident, neither the Korean police nor the U.S. military police investigated the murders.[31] Instead, the Korean police covered up the incident, declaring that there was "insufficient evidence." Then, apparently, no activists stepped forward to hold up these sex workers as national symbols, but Kim Yŏn-ja mobilized sex workers to demonstrate against the indifference and apathy of Korean and U.S. military police.

As Kim Yŏn-ja and her fellow organizers have demonstrated, the sex workers of Kijich'on are not simply victims; they are social actors who interpret and shape their own lives. With their brave acts of protest, they have called for critical engagement and moral agency, challenging the material and social circumstances that bind them. They have also fought against the further degradation of their commodified bodies and demanded that their rights be protected. However, women's collective resistance has always been suppressed by both Korean and the U.S. military authorities, and sex workers have not received material or emotional support from Korean authorities or from the public at large. In Kim Yŏn-ja's personal struggle, for example, she turns to the Christian faith, which she says has been her single source of hope and strength. She says she has also found spiritual healing by mobilizing other sex workers together in Christian fellowship. Kim founded the True Love Shelter (*Ch'amsarang Simtŏ*) and continues to work as a missionary to promote hope in other sex workers and their children. It is in this personal-political context of everyday struggle against class, gender, nation-state, and imperialist subordination that we may find Kim Yŏn-ja's actions and words as being strategic and historically specific.

Conclusion

This essay has examined representations of working-class sex workers for U.S. military in popular and radical texts, both of which fix the identities of the women as "bad"/"good" and treat the female body as a metaphorical map of the Korean nation. Their contradictory representations indicate that women engaged in militarized prostitution for foreign soldiers have become a battleground for nationalist-feminist politics in the 1990s.

Specifically, both popular and radical texts portray women engaged in sex work for foreign men as victims: the women are widowed, abused, raped, prostituted, and murdered. And within this construction of the female subject as passive victim, there is no space to view the woman engaged in sexual labor as a speaking and resisting subject; instead, her speech is muted, censored, and silenced. If what she says contradicts and challenges dominant representations of her subjectivity, she is further marginalized as an outcast—as were Ollye, Mi-ra, Yun Kŭm-i, and Kim Yŏn-ja. Popular and radical discourses create and sustain the subject position of women in militarized prostitution with foreigners as "Yanggongju" and as an allegory for the Korean nation. Using the victim trope, these texts also treat the sexual-class subject position of military sex workers as secondary or subordinate to national identity. No space is allowed for discussing military sex workers in terms of their gender, sexual, and class positions simultaneously. Instead, the construction of this allegory for the Korean nation is premised on "masculinized memory, masculinized humiliation and masculinized hope."[32]

In sum, we must recognize that military sex workers have not been completely colonized by patriarchy, militarism, and imperialism or neo-colonialism; the women do assert agency and subjectivity as Korean women. In what ways do the outcast military sex workers resist, reject, and try to invert the power hierarchy that relegates them to the lowest social standing? Do we retain the metaphor of nation as the representative discourse for collective unity and female identity, or can we develop an alternative discourse on/for military sex workers that will not re-colonize or subordinate their bodies and identities? This essay raises these unresolved questions and emphasizes the need to further investigate the ways in which the subject positions of working-class women in sexual labor are constructed in defense of the nation. The first step towards "pivoting the center"[33] may be to chart the multiple, fragmented subjectivities of working-class Korean women, such as military sex workers who have historically been excluded from scholarship and represented as passive objects in popular and radical representations. Answering these unresolved questions would thus require a critical feminist analysis of the power relations inscribed in the reading, writing and public presentations of women as the *victim*, the *oppressed*, and the *exploited*. Instead of essentializing the experiences of the women of Kijich'on as categorically "Yanggongju," we must begin acknowledging the agency, subjectivity, and resistance of working-class women.

NOTES

1. *Chamsarang Simtŏ* (True Love Shelter), located in Songt'an, Korea, was founded by Kim Yŏn-ja in October 1992. The shelter provides various after-school programs for bi-racial children of "bar women" who are discriminated against in Korean society; English and Korean language classes for "bar women" and American GIs respectively; counseling on family, marriage, divorce, battering, and racism issues; and Bible and spiritual renewal classes. Kim uses her role as a missionary to provide a safe and nurturing sanctuary for "bar women." Personal information noted about Kim Yŏn-ja is based on my communication with her during my visits to the shelter in July 1992 and in Boston in February 1995.

2. I use the term *sex workers* throughout this essay critically, to refer to women, especially working-class women, engaged in sexual labor while not attempting to legitimize or reify sexual labor. Even with its problems, I prefer the term over *prostitute* or *yanggongju*.

3. Foucault and Deleuze have stated that, if given the chance and via alliance politics, "the oppressed" of the First World "can speak and know their conditions." Gayatri Spivak asks whether the subaltern, "on the other side of the international division of labor from socialized capital," can speak. See Gayatri C. Spivak, "Can the Subaltern Speak?" in *Marxism and the Interpretation of Culture*, ed. Cary Nelson and Lawrence Grossberg, Urbana and Chicago: University of Illinois Press, 1988: 283.

4. In the 1990s in the United States, various feminist perspectives on Kijich'on women have emerged, including two Ph.D. dissertations, two documentary films, and one book. See Diana Lee and Grace Lee, *Camp Arirang* (28 min., video, 1995); Katharine Moon, "International Relations and Women: A Case Study of U.S.-Korea Camptown Prostitution, 1971–1976," Unpublished Ph.D. Dissertation, Princeton University, 1994; Hei-soo Shin, "Women's Sexual Services and Economic Development: The Political Economy of the Entertainment Industry and South Korean Development," Unpublished Ph.D. Dissertation, Rutgers University, 1991; Saundra Sturdevant and Brenda Stolzfus, ed., *Let the Good Times Roll: Prostitution and the U.S. Military in Asia*, New York: The New Press, 1992; and J.T. Takagi and Hye-jung Park, *The Women Outside* (58 min. documentary film, 1996, distributed by Third World Newsreel). The two documentaries, *Camp Arirang* and *The Women Outside*, are important resources providing an intimate view of military sex workers living in Kijich'on. The former focuses especially on racialization of sex—Korean women and American GIs offer their perceptions of each other's race and sexuality. The latter questions the presence of American troops in Korea and the role that sex workers play in global geopolitics, and attempts to convey the strength and resiliency of female sexual laborers.

5. *Silver Stallion* was translated from Korean to English by the author, Ahn Jung-hyo, himself. Kang Sŏk-kyŏng's "Days and Dreams" was translated and published in English by Bruce and Ju-chan Fulton in *Words of Farewell*. See Kang Sok-kyong, Kim Chi-wŏn, and O Chŏng-hŭi, *Words of Farewell: Stories by Korean Workers*, Seattle: The Seal Press, 1989.

6. Ahn Jung-hyo, a reporter and columnist, has recently gained notoriety in South Korea and in the United States because of his two war novels, *Silver Stallion* on the Korean War, and *White Badge* on the Vietnam War. *Silver Stallion* was first published in Korean

in 1984 but curiously did not become popular among Korean readers at that time. Subsequently, in 1990, after the author's own translation of the novel into English for the American market, it received recognition in Korea. *Silver Stallion* was also made into a feature film in Korea in the late 1980s under the title of *The Silver Stallion Is Not Coming (Ŭnmanŭn oji anŭnda)*, produced by Chang Kil-su.

7. This statement needs a qualification. Although Koreans often single out those Korean women who engage in sexual labor with foreigners as being different from women who engage in sexual labor with Koreans, this boundary is not always clear. When business in camptowns surrounding U.S. military bases in Korea is slow, the same women who provide sexual service to foreign soldiers service Korean men, including Korean soldiers. The author of *Silver Stallion*, Ahn Jung-hyo, implies in this sentence that the so-called "UN Ladies" work "only for the Yankees," but even during the Korean War, there may or may not have been separate groups of women catering to foreign and Korean men.

8. In this context, the predicament of Ollye or the raped woman is analogous to the subordinate position of Korea to the U.S., as in Korea's dependence on American economic and military aid after the Korean War.

9. Recent scholarship analyzes similar gendered constructions of motherhood/womanhood linked to nationalism. For example, the Nazi German state ideology defined women as the preservers of the family and the childbearers. See George Mosse, *Nationalism and Sexuality*, Madison: University of Wisconsin Press, 1985. In colonial India, nationalist leaders also constructed Indian women as bearers and preservers of cultural values of sacrifice, devotion, and spirituality/religiosity. See Partha Chatterjee, *The Nation and Its Fragments, Colonial and Postcolonial Histories*, Princeton: Princeton University Press, 1993, and Parma Chatterjee, "Colonialism, Nationalism, and Colonized Women: The Contest in India," *American Ethnologist* 16 (1989): 622–633. For related discussions on gender, sexuality, nationalism, and feminism, see : Andrew Parker, Mary Russo, Doris Sommer, and Patricia Yaeger (eds.), *Nationalisms and Sexualities*, New York: Routledge, 1992; Rajeswari Sunder Rajan, *Real and Imagined Women: Gender, Culture and Postcolonialism*, New York: Routledge, 1993; and Kumkum Sangari and Sudesh Vaid (eds.), *Recasting Women, Essays in Indian Colonial History*, New Brunswick: Rutgers University Press, 1990; Katheleen Uno, "The Death of 'Good Wife, Wise Mother'?" in *Postwar Japan As History*, ed. Andrew Gordon, Berkeley: University of California Press, 1993: 293–322.

10. Like Mansik, the protagonist in *Silver Stallion*, the nameless narrator in this story, a child of the postcolonial Korean war period, remembers eating American hard candy, yellow cornbread, and C-ration leftovers to fill her hungry stomach. Like Mansik, her physical contact with American GIs also occurs at a young age, when she is in the eleventh grade; an old school classmate who works at an American military base entices her into sexual labor.

11. On discussion about the female body as a place marker, see : Gillian Rose, *Feminism and Geography*, Minneapolis: University of Minnesota Press, 1993; Anne McClintock, "Family Feuds: Gender, Nationalism and the Family," *Feminist Review* 44 (Summer 1993): 61–80; Catherine Nash, "Remapping and Renaming: New Cartographies of

Identity, Gender and Landscape in Ireland," *Feminist Review* 44 (Summer 1993): 39–57.

12. O Yŏn-ho, *Make Us Sad No More! (Tŏisang urirŭl sŭlp'ŭge hajimalla!)*, Seoul, Korea: Paeksan Sŏdang, 1990: preface.

13. Ibid.

14. In May 1980 the citizens of Kwangju demonstrated against Chun Doo Hwan's military rule and for democratic elections. Korean military troops, whose power is ultimately controlled by the U.S. military command, massacred over 2,000 protesters and recaptured the city. The killing and repression, which was authorized by the U.S.–R.O.K. (Republic of Korea) Combined Forces Command, led many Koreans to question American military presence in Korea. For more discussion, see *The Kwangju Uprising*, ed. Donald Clark, Boulder: Westview Press, 1988.

15. Initially, the U.S. military refused to extradite Kenneth Markle to Korean judicial authorities for a trial, and this arrogant injustice outraged Koreans. Approximately fifty organizations, including political parties, feminists and women activists, clergy, students, youths, workers, farmers, academics, and human rights activists formed the Committee on the Murder of Yun Kum-i by American Military in Korea (*Chuhan migunŭi Yun Kŭm-i ssi salhae Sagŏn Gongdong Daech'aek Wiwŏnhoe*). Through the protests, the collection of petition letters, and press conferences as well as visits to prosecutors at the Korean Ministry of Justice, the U.S. Ambassador, and the Commander of the U.S. military in Korea by the Committee and its supporters (both inside and outside Korea), Kenneth Markle was finally tried and received a fifteen-year sentence. Since April 21, 1994, Markle has been imprisoned in the U.S. Army prison in Pyŏngtek, Korea. For more discussion of this case, see *Our Kŭm-i (Uridŭrŭi Kŭm-i)*, the Committee on the Murder of Yun Kŭm-i by American Military in Korea (*Chuhan migunŭi Yun Kŭm-i ssi salhae Sagŏn Gongdong Daechaek Wiwŏnhoe*), Seoul, Korea: 1993.

16. Politically and conceptually, the problem of militarized prostitution, or Korean women selling sexual labor to American GIs, has not been connected to the problem of generalized prostitution for non-military Korean men.

17. Gayatri Spivak discusses this point about the homogenization of subject positions in the narratives of nationalism. She notes, "the elite culture of nationalism participated and participates with the colonizer in various ways" (246). In the process, various subject positions are "reactively" homogenized in terms of nationalism and ethnicity. See *In Other Words, Essays in Cultural Politics*, New York: Methuen, 1987.

18. For analysis of this "bad woman"/"good woman" dichotomy in the U.S. context, see *Bad Girls/Good Girls*, ed. Nan B. Maglin and Donna Perry, New Brunswick: Rutgers University, 1996.

19. See *Our Kŭm-i* (1993), published by the Committee on the Murder of Yun Kŭm-i by American Military in Korea (*Chuhan migunŭi Yun Kŭm-i ssi salhae Sagŏn Gongdong Daech'aek Wiwŏnhoe*).

20. An Il-sun discusses how the Yun Kŭm-i's murder case was an important moment of

political awakening which transformed her view of "Yanggongju." As she ventured into *Kijich'on* to write about the life of Yun Kum-i, An met Kim Yŏn-ja; their meeting served as a catalyst for An Il-sun to problematize military prostitution as a nationalist-feminist issue. Visiting Kunsan, Tongduch'on, and Songsan for the first time, An says she became conscious of her own prejudices about "GI towns" and "Yanggongju." Based on An's communication in Boston, February 1995.

21. The Committee has been endorsed by groups such as Korea Church Women United (*Hanguk Kyohoe Yŏsŏng Yŏnhaphoe*), Korea Women's Associations United (*Hanguk Yŏsŏng Danch'e Yŏnhap*), Korea Women Theologians Association (*Hanguk Yŏsinhakcha Hyŏpŭihoe*), Catholic Women's Welfare Commission (*Katorik Yŏsŏng Bokjihoe*), Korea Women's Hotline (*Hanguk Yŏsŏngŭi Jŏnhwa*), Korean Sexual Violence Counseling Center (*Hanguk Sŏngp'ongnyŏk Sangdamso*), My Sister's Place (*Turebang*), Special Commission for the Law Regarding Sexual Violence *Sŏngp'ongnyŏk T'ukpyŏlp'ŏp che-chongchujin T'ukbyŏlwiwŏnhoe*), National Committee of University Students (*Chŏnguk Taehaksaeng Daep'yŏjahyŏpŭihoe*), National Committee of Labor Movement (*Chŏnguk Nodong Undong Danchehyŏpŭihoe*), National Coalition of Democracy and National Unification (*Minjujuŭi Minjok T'ongil Jŏnguk Yŏnhap*), and the women's committees of political parties, to name a few.

22. This three-page-long poem, "Tongduch'on Kŭm-i," was written in Korean by An Il-sun, November 13, 1992. The lines translated and quoted here have been taken from an unpublished copy of the same poem, given to me by An Il-sun. I would like to thank Hyun Joo Yim for translating these lines. An abridged version, in Korean, is published in *Our Kŭm-i*, by the Committee on the Murder of Yun Kŭm-i by American Military in Korea (*Chuhan migunŭi Yun Kŭm-i ssi salhae Sagŏn Gongdong Daech'aek Wiwŏnhoe*), 1993.

23. See *Our Kŭm-i*, 1993: preface.

24. Ibid.

25. A statement made by Chŏn U-sŏp, the minister at Tabitha House (*Dabitaŭi jip*). See *Our Kŭm-i*, 1993: 6–7.

26. For an analysis of how the South Korean and American governments have used sex workers as instruments of foreign policy and economic development, see Katharine Moon's essay, "Prostitute Bodies and Gendered States in U.S.–Korea Relations," in this volume.

27. Ever since the U.S. military has occupied South Korea in September 1945, approximately 35,000–40,000 troops have been stationed there in a given year. There are one hundred military bases in South Korea (see An Il-sun, "Great Army, Great Father" in *Great Army, Great Father*, 1995: 16). While the number of camptowns servicing the "needs" of American soldiers and the commodification of sexual labor of Korean women have expanded rapidly since the 1960s, no social movement or feminist movement has focused specifically on this issue until recently. Unlike the "Comfort Women" problem, which has become a national political issue since 1991, the problem of "Yanggongju" or militarized prostitution, as discussed in this essay, has not been embraced as a political issue on national and international levels.

28. See An Il-sun's interview of Kim Yŏn-ja, "The Yanggongju I Met, The World of American Military Crimes" (*Naega kkyoun Yanggongju, Migunpŏmjoeŭi Segye*), in *Mal* (*Talk*), a monthly journal from Seoul, Korea (December 1993): 148–155.

29. Katharine Moon has pointed out to me that the women working and living in Kijich'on see themselves as "the real women" or "the macho women" of Korean society because they feel they have the license to behave in ways other Korean women cannot. For example, it is considered a norm for "bar women" to drink and smoke, behavior considered taboo for middle class women. This is an important point to consider in the further development of our feminist analysis about the different meanings embodied in Korean womanhood.

30. Based on talks given at the Massachusetts Institute of Technology and the Korean Methodist Church of Boston, and my communication with Kim Yŏn-ja during their three-day tour, from February 11–13, 1995.

31. SOFA (Status of Forces Agreement), which is a mutual defense treaty between South Korea and the United States, first signed in 1967 and revised in 1991, provides the U.S. armed forces in Korea with the legal jurisdiction and authority. This unequal treaty relegates the Republic of Korea (or South Korea) as a subordinate to the U.S. and gives no authority to intervene in the U.S. military territories inside Korea. See *Great Army, Great Father* (1995).

32. Cynthia Enloe, *Bananas, Beaches and Bases*, Berkeley and Los Angeles: University of California Press, 1990: 44.

33. Karen Sacks, "Toward a Unified Theory of Class, Race, and Gender," *American Ethnologist* 16 (1989): 543.

9

YOU-ME PARK

Working Women and the Ontology of the Collective Subject:
(Post)Coloniality and the Representation of Female Subjectivities in Hyŏn Ki-yŏng's *Paramt'anŭm Sŏm* (*Island in the Wind*)

I was sitting in front of Seoul Railway Station, proud but also somewhat intimidated to be part of the sea of students. I kept looking towards the other side of the station where my brother was. Appearing easy and confident, he had become part of the demonstration. A rumor about an impending crackdown by military troops had reached us hours earlier. Concerned about his safety as well as mine, I wondered whether we would be back home that evening, back to our "normal" domestic coziness. I also wondered if, once we were back in our everyday space,[1] he would reassume his usual benignly protective, yet still authoritative position and advise me, his younger sister, against taking part in mass demonstrations. When we were younger, he used to make sure I stayed home when he played outside so that he wouldn't have to worry about my "well-being." Thus my solicitude for his well-being on that day felt incongruous and even presumptuous. Later that day, when we returned home together holding hands, I didn't quite realize how what happened that day would change how I related to him as well as how I conceptualized women and men in struggle in general. The day was May 15th, 1980, just a few days before the government's massacre of Kwangju citizens.

So as not to relinquish as a moment of transient glory the revolutionary fervor that occurred during the Kwangju Uprising of May 1980, we need to continually re-evaluate and re-conceptualize what happened in May 1980 in terms of our personal histories as well as in terms of global and local political and economic circumstances.[2]

In this essay, I propose to read three texts, all published in 1989, at a moment of unprecedented global historical change that required serious reevaluation of the South Korean political movement. The writers of these texts had been at the vanguard of that movement. I am attempting a critical intervention by examining the gendered and gendering representations of political struggle and the omission of women's political agency in these texts.

The first text I address is Hyŏn Ki-yŏng's narrative *Paramt'anŭn sŏm* (*Island in Wind*), a historically based novel dealing with women divers' organized struggles against Japanese colonialism. The narrative raises questions about gender and organized mass struggles in order that, as Hyŏn himself suggested, "we can rightly understand the revolutionary movements today." Then I look at a review of *Paramt'anŭn sŏm* by Ch'oe Wŏn-sik, one of the most prominent and progressive critics of Korea who, I argue, in "innocent" or well-meaning complicity with the text, trivializes and circumscribes women's agency. The last text I discuss is an 1989 issue of *Yŏsŏng* (*Women*), a journal devoted to socialist feminism that raises apt questions about the status of women workers in terms of social, economic, and cultural formations in Korea in the late 1980s.

I read these texts side by side to perform a conjunctural analysis of the moment. Bringing together these discourses illustrates how these different genres of writing that share the discursive space of oppositional cultural movements define, relate, and negotiate concepts such as revolution, organized struggle, gender, nation, colonialism, neocolonialism, and class. In addition, I detail how we read and negotiated cultural, literary, social, economic, political, and everyday discourses in the late 1980s so that we can construct a paradigm of struggle for the present day.

I place specific emphases on the issue of gender because I believe that struggles against patriarchy, which is imbedded in neoimperialist, exploitative social formations, will offer us an opportunity to unhinge the entire complicated structure. By reading Hyŏn's *Paramt'anŭn sŏm* in the context of the discursive formation of the period, I problematize certain masculinist traditions in Korean national discourses which attempt to subsume the issue of gender in discussions of class or neocolonialism. According to my reading, the main question becomes: how do we talk about the agency of working women fighting (neo)imperialism and patriarchy in political, organized, and even violent ways?

Hyŏn Ki-yŏng's *Paramt'anŭn sŏm* depicts an organized struggle of women divers in Cheju Island against the Japanese colonial regime. With over 17,000 participants, the 1932 uprising was the biggest mass uprising of the period. Hyŏn reads this uprising as "a result of the grafting of radical ideology imported from the mainland onto the specific tradition of resistance in Cheju Island" (394). The revolutionary protagonists neatly fall into two categories: women divers and male radicals. Through representations of three young women divers (Yŏ-ok, Yŏng-nyŏ, and Chŏng-sim) and three male radicals (Si-ho, Si-jung, and Ho-il), the author constructs an image of a community suffering from the exploitative Japanese militarism and colonialism as well as from native capitalists in complicity with the colonial regime.

Despite their conflicting political beliefs (Si-ho is an anarchist, Ho-il a communist and Si-jung a nationalist), the three male protagonists join together to organize and lead resistance movements. As the narrative develops, the three women divers (Yŏ-ok, Yŏng-nyŏ, and Chŏng-sim)—supposedly under the influence and tutelage of the men—go through phases of doubt, despair, and awakening as they participate in the struggle. The text suggests that these women divers are able to carry out the mass uprising against the Japanese colonial regime by drawing from their traditional sense of community in Cheju Island, their experi-

205

ence as female migrant workers, and the leadership provided by radical men. It is assumed that the women characters needed to learn and mature to become political agents but the men were already there as finished products.

Here I deliberately accentuate the seemingly programmatic plot of the narrative, with a view to addressing the ideologies of gender roles and gendered subjectivities that emerge as Hyŏn attempts to conceptualize and represent struggle—especially *organized* struggle. Actually Hyŏn manages to create an atmosphere of generosity, laughter, and love as well as a realistic sense of how working people coalesce, despite the grim impact of Japanese colonialism. I believe it is important to recognize how Hyŏn contributes to postcolonial Korean resistance literature by providing a paradigm for a people's struggle against (neo)colonial power that does not reduce the masses to one-dimensional characters or signs. However, it is the responsibility of those working for liberation and decolonization to critique in a caring yet thorough way his visions and assumptions about political agency and the organization of mass struggle.

In *Paramt'anŭn sŏm*, Hyŏn not only posits women divers as subjects of resistance, mobilized and active; at certain points in the narrative, he represents them as autonomous beings with their own work, desires, and spaces. In her pivotal work on women and politics in the postcolonial world, Rajeswari Sunder Rajan demonstrates that "the typical female subject of feminism has been the subaltern woman, or specifically the woman-as-victim, whose subjectivity post-structuralism has helped to conceptualize as discontinuous, changing, and contingent—or, as we may say, less than one."[4] Hyŏn's representation, on the other hand, creates women who are multi-faceted and yet autonomous political agents with collective identities. Thus he offers the model of the female subjectivity Sunder Rajan calls for—"the ontology of collective subject,"[5] which is necessary for the conceptualization of a viable anti-imperialist feminist movement.

How do women come to read and conceptualize themselves as political agents unless both their understanding of "everyday" work, space, and life, as well as their perceptions of macropolitical history, are radically transformed? This question is especially relevant for those women located, collectively and as individuals, at the nexus of patriarchy, imperialism, and capitalism. Thus, the women divers in Hyŏn's narrative (and women workers in rapidly "developing" postcolonial Korea) are able to transform their individual lives and the social formations in which they are exploited only by negotiating their subjectivity and their collective identity.[6] What Kwangju taught, not only to Kwangju citizens but also to Koreans in general, is that the masses *can* govern themselves peaceably. (For example, during the ten days of self-government during the Uprising, there were no incidents of violent crimes). What is missing, or at best problematic in Hyŏn's narrative is the notion of people's (or more specifically women's) power and leadership being rooted in actual experiences of struggle and resistance.[7]

Throughout the narrative, three women divers, Yŏ-ok, Yŏng-nyŏ, and Chŏng-sim, are literally and metaphorically taught by the male radicals. From them, the women learn how to read and, by extension, how to read their position in society.[8] As suggested earlier, these women divers share similar family backgrounds and work experience as divers, which Hyŏn equates with the "natural cycle of life." Hyŏn also presents the three women's consciousness of social injustice and Japanese imperialism as indistinguishable. In contrast, the three male protagonists struggle with one another over their readings of the situation as well as possible corresponding strategies. Thus Hyŏn reinscribes notions of gendered subjectivities and work (women learn and know "instinctively," while men teach and know ideologically), inevitably casting the women divers in the role of "Natural Women." For example, it is significant that the three male characters' arguments about how to lead mass movements take place against the background of the sea, where "tens of women divers were working in groups" (135). Not coincidentally, this scene ends with a call for the three men to "work together in the friendship of Song-san and Jug-am—two male activists famous for their friendship" (159).

The text describes the women divers as "natural," uneducated, and primarily sexual beings, taught and desired by male protagonists with a homosocial vision of male bonding as a prerequisite of viable political leadership. This representation not only raises questions about the relationship between gender and political agency/leadership, it also undermines the text's otherwise sensitive critique of patriarchy. Especially during the first half, the narrative represents women divers as part of the landscape and as symbols of nature and idealized tradition. Unlike "modern girls," whose sexual desire and "immodesty" the text condemns (119–120), the divers make sure that "the source of fire, the source of life in the family does not die out" (19). "The source of life" in this particular instance is explicitly and unproblematically defined by patriarchal definitions of gender roles within the family. Yŏ-ok must remember that "there is only one man in her family left, her twelve-year old brother, Man-gi" (19). Thus, even towards the end, it is he who "gives the order" to students to participate in a mass uprising.

Hyon's reluctance to represent Yŏ-ok and other women divers as political leaders may be due in part to the fact that he opted not to represent the central female figures as mothers. In Korean culture, mothers are highly respected. Almost supernatural fortitude is demanded of them. If Hyŏn's female protagonists had been mothers, they could have easily been presented as strong, autonomous agents. Instead of biologizing womanhood and circumscribing politically mobilized female subjectivities within patriarchal definitions of women,[9] Hyŏn chose to experiment with the figures of strong, non-maternal women in struggle, in recognition of the Korean women's labor movements in the 1980s. These movements were carried on primarily by young, unmarried, women workers.

Young female divers in *Paramt'anŭn sŏm* are at least partly defined by their alignment with a tradition that is, in turn, based on patriarchy. They are represented as antithetical to "bad," new women who abandon tradition and thus nation.

> Nowadays it is a deplorable custom that educated young men everywhere abandon their "ignorant" wives given to them by their parents as if they were worn-out shoes and get new women. Whoever are these educated new women? Aren't they the ones who have long fingernails like parasites, flatter men with sweet words as if they would cut off their tongues for their men, and sing Schubert's lullaby to their babies instead of our own lullaby? (51)

This dichotomy between good, traditional women who are victims, and bad, new women who are perpetrators of coquetry and falsehood, is unproblematically inscribed earlier on. We need to note the way the responsibility of destroying traditional family structure is quickly moved from young men who abandon their wives to educated young women with *false bodies* (as we can see from the grotesque imagery of their "long fingernails like parasites" and their tongues, which seem to be false and unreal). The text also suggests that these "new women" are responsible not only for undermining the family, but also for undermining national cultural identities as well, since they are bad mothers who fail to inculcate their children with national tradition and culture.[10]

Thus, Hyŏn unproblematically reinscribes a fundamentally conservative and masculinist conceptualization of femininity, tradition, and family: national integrity and the future seem endangered by false women with false female bodies. I would argue that this conflation of genuine femininity/motherhood with "good" national identity, as well as conferral of actual/ideological power on bad women is complicitous with masculinist nationalist discourse, which in turn deflects attention from the disempowerment and oppression of women. In the end, this conflation also is responsible for the text's failure to represent young women divers as fully developed political agents, capable of educating, organizing, and leading themselves.

This is not to argue that Hyŏn is oblivious to the problems patriarchy poses to the mobilization of the masses, especially but not exclusively to women. He does not idealize or romanticize native communities or the traditional culture of Cheju Island. He draws attention to patriarchal violence and how it undermines anti-colonial movements. When To-a, one of the most progressive and active divers, comes home after having been detained for participating in a demonstration, her brother, a lowly official of the colonial government, beats her severely.

> That day, after she was released late in the afternoon, To-a spent time with her friends who came to console her. As soon as the friends left, her brother suddenly pounced on her and ruthlessly whipped her while she was tied to a pillar. They say he beat the hell out of her while screaming that she would ruin the whole family as well as herself if left alone, and that she was crazy to become a traitor. (348)

The scene is followed by a representation of village women rescuing To-a from her brother and contesting the use of the term "traitor": according to those women, a colonial regime does not have the legitimacy to name people who participate in oppositional movements "traitors." The scene is narrated from the point of view of an impersonal communal subject ("they say"), so that the reader senses that there are "other" communal values countering patriarchal violence. These implied alternative views evoke the sympathy of the author and readers. Hyŏn also points out that the problem is not just of To-a's "bad" brother but of patriarchy's complicity with colonial, capitalist force and male violence against women.

> The biggest enemies were within the family. Prior representatives of women divers were chained by their husbands, fathers, and brothers, who have stooped to become tools of the police. How could they tolerate ruthless blows, and how could they endure threats of abandonment! (361)

We need to ask, however, if Hyŏn's representation of certain kinds of patriarchal violence deflects attention from other types of injustice to and oppression of women. For example, the only form of patriarchy Hyŏn represents as objectionable is the one that is complicit with Japanese or pro-Japanese forces. We can sense that the problem goes deeper when Yŏ-ok argues, "They say letters are power. Men are all alike. They monopolize learning and keep us illiterate so that they can have us as servants . . . How can we not be slighted outside when we are slighted thus at home?" (213). This insight about the relationship between literacy and power, as well as between women's status in society and at home, however, is not more fully explored and explicated in the narrative. Instead, it unproblematically privileges Man-gi over Yŏ-ok, and Si-jung over his sister Chŏng-hwa who is introduced to readers mainly through the smell of her hair and her burgeoning sexuality, as political agents and structural centers of the family. *Paramt'anŭn sŏm* reinscribes the traditional and patriarchal positioning of gendered subjects. Both within and outside of the family structure, the text only condemns the fortuitous violence of patriarchy gone awry instead of raising questions about fundamental premises of patriarchy, such as definitions of ideal femininity and masculinity, what constitutes a "healthy" family structure, or why dichotomies between the public/masculine sphere and the private/feminine sphere exist and are continually reinforced.

The ending of the narrative, however, "revises" many assumptions about gendered revolutionary subjects and traditional femininity that were inscribed on the text earlier.[10] For example, when Si-ho's dream about "Cheju people running together on the newly made road, filling it with their cries" (296) comes true, it is the women—To-a, Kŭm-ch'un, Yŏ-ok, Yŏng-nyŏ, and Chŏng-sim, who "ran down the road, pounding on gongs," (367) and led people in the mass uprising. Even the men were "all disguised as women in skirts, jackets, and head kerchiefs" (378).

These women do not remain within traditional definitions of femininity, either. Just before they depart for the uprising, they "reaffirmed their determination to each other by joining hands, tore out their coat strings as a token of solidarity and sewed on buttons. At the last demonstration, their coat strings caused problems as they kept becoming untied" (365). The coat strings of Korean women's traditional clothes have always been deployed as a symbol of passive, fragile, yet seductive female sexuality. For example, the blouse ties function as a sign of a husband's access to the virginal body of his bride on the first night of marriage, or as a convenient piece of clothing a young woman can put in her mouth and chew on when she is shy; consequently, the image infantilizes and sexualizes her at the same time. Thus, by tearing out the symbol of their traditional femininity and sexuality for the practical purpose of preparing for a physical confrontation with colonial forces, these women sever the string that links them to patriarchal oppression as well.

Nonetheless, the text still adheres to the assertion that Ho-il, Si-jung, and Si-ho are the ones who staged the fight and ultimately authored the uprising. Si-jung continually "assures" Yŏ-ok before the breakout of the uprising, that "we men are ultimately responsible for everything" (325); Ho-il, when he parts with Si-jung who chooses to go to jail, exclaims "it was quite a fight. Women divers who were submerged in the state of nature have turned into women in history!" (387--8) Thus these male radicals, by assuming "ultimate responsibility," not only preempt any possibility of these women being recognized as authors of their own struggle but also claim to have authored these women, because it was they who transformed them from beings of nature into historical subjects.

Ch'oe Wŏn-sik's review of *Paramt'anŭn sŏm* reiterates male claims of exclusive authorship of history. Such authorship is made possible by turning women divers who are, as Ch'oe himself points out, "the genuine protagonists of the text" into part of timeless nature.[11] Ch'oe, an intellectual who opposed cultural militarism and neo-imperialism all his life, is a prominent critic and literary historian who authored and edited such influential and groundbreaking works as *Minjokmunhagŭi nolli* (Theories of National Literature), *Chŏnhwangiŭi dongasia munhak* (East Asian Literatures in the Era of Change), *Hanguk kŭndae sosŏlsaron* (The History of Korean Modern Novels), and *Hanguk kŭndae munhagsaŭi jaengjŏm* (Conflicted Issues in the History of Korean Modern Literature). Ch'oe's review deserves our close attention as we struggle to construct a site of dialogues related to women's and men's genuine liberation and decolonization.

Ch'oe argues that "beyond the linguistic fragments of intellectuals emerge women divers, who are the genuine protagonists of the text, like blue-back fish, fresh and refreshing" (380). He exalts and thus separates women divers from "intellectuals," as well as from their interpretations of political, historical reality, and ultimately from language itself. Ch'oe employs a demeaning imagery of fresh fish to refer to these women whose work, suffering, and uprising the text vividly represents. It is no coincidence that most of Ch'oe's discussion of colonial history and the political context of the text addresses the ideologies of male characters. In contrast, his discussion of the women divers addresses them as solely beings in harmony with the nature, with a lengthy quote from the text which compares the life cycle of women divers to the cycle of tides. The only other episode about Sunju's elopement with Musang involves their sexual intercourse. Ch'oe defines Sun-ju's elopement as an act of "rising up to be an owner of her own destiny, shaking off fetters" (381).

Ch'oe privileges Sun-ju's defiance of patriarchy (her abusive husband, to be more precise) by deeming it worthy of greater note than the mass uprising led by women as a collective. By privileging a necessarily local and contained, if defiant, act over the political acts of women revolutionaries, Ch'oe trivializes women's political agency while indulging in a gesture of liberal humanism (that is, by noting that fortuitous acts of violence of an uncontrolled patriarchy are understood to be deplorable by the author and Ch'oe alike.) He declares that "the novel is not as interesting as the plot develops, that is, as the struggle of women divers become substantialized" (381) for, as far as he is concerned, the novel was never about the women divers' political action and struggle. As a result, Ch'oe's interpretation of Hyŏn's narrative flattens out the conflicts between women and patriarchy, the representation of women's political agency, and the need to conceptualize mass organization and struggle in a non-masculinized way.

When we read this review alongside the third issue of *Yŏsŏng* (*Women*), a socialist feminist journal, published in the same year that *Paramt'anŭn sŏm* came out (1989), it becomes clear that Ch'oe's review is not just a matter of an incompetent reading or the limitations of the time which is not "mature" enough for deeper understanding of women's issues. *Yŏsŏng*, published by Yŏsŏngsa yŏnguhoe (the Association for the Studies of Women's History) since 1985, is part of a larger oppositional feminist movement that blossomed in the mid to late 1980s. As a journal that aspires to be attuned to real-life struggles and praxis, it covers wide areas in women's studies, literature, education, media studies, Marxist theories, and reportage.

The 1989 special issue is devoted to Korean women's labor realities and movements, and addresses issues of women workers' health, low wages, labor organizing, as well as cultural representations of women, particularly of women in struggle. The issue attempts to forge coalitions among different groups of women. A range of articles deals with strategies for organizing housewives and report on homeless women's struggles against evictions from their temporary shelters as well as discussing more traditional labor movements.

Interestingly, the issue also includes two articles that address women's political struggle in the 1930s: the first is an article by Yi Ae-suk on Chŏng Chŏng-myŏng, a woman activist who led the women's anti-colonialist movement of the 1920s and 1930s, and the second is by Yi Sang-kyŏng on literary works by Marxist writers that represent women in struggle during the same period. By highlighting anti-colonial movements led by women, the journal emphasizes the tradition of women's struggle and suggests that these movements have had more political significance than scholars have previously bestowed on them.[12] Reports on the life history of Chŏng Chŏng-myŏng, together with an excerpt from *Kŭnu*, a publication from the woman's group that Chŏng helped lead, fundamentally undermine masculinist notions about femininity and political agency, as well as patriarchal versions of nationalist discourse (which presume the dichotomy between good/traditional/"natural" women and bad/educated/false women), a discourse that Hyŏn's *Paramt'anŭn sŏm* and Ch'oe's review unproblematically reiterate and perpetuate. Thus the article on Chŏng in *Yŏsŏng* is an example of Korean feminist scholars' attempts to "read" for women's resistance and struggle, as well as leadership and organization, during the colonial period. To that end, these scholars reclaim and articulate history from women's perspectives and demonstrate how women choose to read for evidence of the process whereby women's struggles led them to organize and adopt leadership roles. Such a reevaluation and reclamation of history problematizes complacent assumptions about gender roles and the sexual division of labor evidenced in Ch'oe's review as well as in Hyŏn's narrative, both of which represent a larger masculinist trend in Korean revolutionary/reform movements.

In Yi Sang-gyŏng's "Hangil hyŏngmyŏng munhagŭi jŏnt'ong" ("The Tradition of Anti-Japanese Revolutionary Literature"), two literary works produced in the 1930s are discussed: *Kkot p'anŭn ch'ŏnyŏ* (*A Woman Selling Flowers*) and *Minjungŭi bada* (*People's Sea*). After introducing these works and offering critical interpretations of them, the article suggests that the future of the women's movements depends on the following:

> We understand Mother in *People's Sea* as a model of a female subject who breaks out of the framework of "woman's life," meaning being forced to remain in exclusively private. It also embodies the double contradictions of economic and gender exploitation, and begins to lead a life as an autonomous subject in social, historical space. It goes without saying that we need to create another "vision of women who assert themselves as autonomous subjects" in our era with its own set of contradictions. (240)

Yi Sang-gyŏng's call for autonomous female subjects who understand themselves—through a recognition of their social and historical positions as well as their private selves within domestic space—provides us with a conceptual framework with which to evaluate Korean oppositional movements in the 1980s and 1990s, including Hyŏn's *Paramt'anŭn sŏm* and critical discussions of his text. I concur with *Yŏsŏng's* editorial collective that genuine decolonization and democratization of Korea can only be possible when those who work towards these aims are willing to constantly reevaluate their goals and strategies so that patriarchal oppression as well as other forms of political/economic exploitations are named, criticized, and successfully dealt with.

At this point, I want to discuss the significance that critical readings of oppositional literature from places like Korea can assume in postcolonial studies, so that we can stake out a more open and liberatory space for the discipline. I want specifically to focus on the concept of "migrancy," which has been widely discussed among postcolonial theorists, as one of the most characteristic and suggestive postcolonial phenomena and experiences. As detailed discussions of those theorists go beyond the scope of this paper, I merely wish to point out some problems in the ways these critics employ the term to "define" postcoloniality, and to suggest that Hyon's treatment of the issue of migrancy in *Paramt'anŭn sŏm* disrupts the harmonious tone of the discussion going on among these critics.[13]

In spite of the various voices and viewpoints involved in the discussion, there has emerged a tacit agreement concerning what defines postcolonial migrancy. That is to say, while these theorists argue about the ways the concept of "migrancy" can be signified and interpreted, they assume that "we" all know what "it" is. Accordingly, migration is used to refer to the experience of "hybrid hyphenations" derived from "the interstitial, erratic movements that signify culture's transnational temporalities."[14] Thus, the task for postcolonial subjects/critics (another problematic conflation) is defined as follows: "To revise the problem of global space from the postcolonial perspective is to move the location of cultural difference away from the space of demographic plurality to the borderline negotiations of cultural translation."[15]

Postcolonial migrancy as an experience of cultural translation has its own significance and thus calls for intellectual investigation. Yet when the term, defined in this specific way, becomes a model for "representing" postcoloniality as both metaphor and metonymy, there emerges a danger of privileging certain textualized cultural experiences over other types of distinctly colonial/postcolonial phenomena/experiences, such as the forced—or seemingly voluntary, yet virtually forced due to the lack of other options—circulation of workers (especially female workers with a view to exploiting their sexuality as well as their labor power) on a global scale. How do we discuss the cases of comfort women, the export/import of prostitutes from Myanmar, the Philippines, South Korea, and Thailand, the sales of young girls as "child brides" from India to the Middle East, as well as more recognizable patterns of migrant laborers crossing national boundaries as various "versions" of postcolonial migrancy?[16] As the case of comfort women on the list calls into question—is "migrancy" really a characteristically postcolonial condition to begin with? Haven't colonized people been circulated on a global scale to suit the "needs" of colonizing force?[17] If "volition" is the criterion which separates colonial migrancy (such as the removal of Africans from their homes) and postcolonial migrancy (for example, the cosmopolitan subjectivity Appiah discusses), why do we privilege certain types of migration such as that of postcolonial intellectuals over the experiences of women coerced into prostitution, or those of domestic workers?

Hyŏn's *Paramt'anŭn sŏm* not only deplores the inhumane treatment of Korean migrant laborers in various Japanese colonial territories but also suggests that what made possible the mass uprising on Cheju Island was the migrant labor experience that Cheju workers had had in Japan and China. Hyŏn makes sure to stress the scope of the problem:

> Those young women who used to weave with their friends, singing while they worked, have migrated to Japan to become factory workers with pale faces in weaving and rubber factories that resemble dark caves. Out of fifty thousand workers who went to sell their labor in Japan, twenty-five thousand were female factory workers. (105)

Yet he also suggests that the migrant labor experience contributed to radicalizing these workers: "The miserable labor conditions suffered by forty thousand workers in Japan produced three hundred fighters, who were beginning to mobilize the workers" (219) and also radicalized the resistance movements in Cheju Island, as "most of these young people had had the experience of organizing and participating in labor movements" (293). Women divers in the narrative also become conscious of their position within the colonial "order" due to their experiences as migratory workers:

> Yŏ-ok herself could feel that she had grown tremendously during the last half year while she was away from her mother for the first time. The experience of working as divers in Ulsan was that ruthless . . . Yŏ-ok had left her girlhood behind and opened her eyes to cold and cruel reality as a woman diver and also as a worker. (315)

Hyŏn goes on to argue that the mass uprising at the end of the narrative would not have been possible without this kind of awakening on the workers' part, which allowed them to clearly read their positions in the global order and Japanese colonialism.

In conclusion, I would like to suggest that Hyŏn's text may provide leverage to unhinge some postcolonial studies' assumptions that privilege certain textualized and in many cases masculine renderings of postcolonial conditions and experiences as the paradigm of postcoloniality. These assumptions are privileged at the expense of other types of experiences and representations of (post)colonial migrancy, such as those of female (sex) workers and women participating in anti-imperialist struggles. By representing Korean women workers whose consciousness about Japanese imperialism and economic exploitation matures due to their experience as migrant workers, Hyon opens up a discursive space in which discussions of gender, class, imperialism, and migrancy can be brought together. Reading *Paramt'anŭn sŏm* in the context of postcolonial debates on the concepts of migrancy and (gendered) subjectivities offers opportunities for feminists to discuss women as political agents and organizers rather than as mere victims, for Korean studies scholars to benefit from discussions of the process and strategies of decolonization and social change in other parts of the world, and for postcolonial scholars to implode the strictly "cultural" rendering of a "postcolonial" world order. I believe that, in order for postcolonial studies to become part of a genuinely progressive and liberating global movement for decolonization, it must embrace the stories and voices of subaltern women, working, loving, and fighting in "small places." Only then may the postcolonial studies become genuinely *post*colonial.

Fifty years after Korean "independence" from Japan and fifteen years after that pivotal day in May, I wonder about the identities and locations of "postcolonial" Korean women. Who are we? Where are we? When do we as women learn to dive into a sea of our own making?

NOTES

I would like to thank Chungmoo Choi, Daniel Moshenberg, and Rajeswari Sunder Rajan for their close readings of the text, insightful suggestions, and friendship.

1. Here I am using the terms "everyday" or "normal domestic coziness" not as transparent words, but as culturally and politically constructed concepts, especially from the viewpoints of women and/or the third world. I argue that these terms normalize and erase certain social practices in terms of spatial divisions and assignments of labor based on gender and class, such as who defines the "normality" of various domesticities, who adjudicates who is eligible for "everyday life," and whose labor is subsumed under the category of normal everyday life. For a discussion of the term "everyday," see Henri Lefebvre, *Everyday Life in the Modern World*, trans. S. Labinovitch (New Brunswick: Transaction Book, 1984). For a text which uses the term from a specifically gendered perspective, see Swasti Mitter and Sheila Rowbotham eds., *Dignity and Daily Bread: New Forms of Economic Organising among Poor Women in the Third World and the First* (London and New York: Routledge, 1994).

2. For a discussion of incidents that led to the Kwangju Uprising, see "80nyŏn gwangjuŭi ŭimi" (Significance of Kwangju in the 1980s)—a transcript of a formal debate on the Kwangju Uprising, in *Ch'angjakkwa bip'yong* 17.2 (Summer 1989) 323–333. In the debate, Kim Se-kyun argues that the withdrawal at Seoul Railroad Station on May 15 was one element that caused the Kwangju massacre because the oppositional force's decision to avoid physical confrontation in Seoul created a "temporary vacuum of oppositional power" (326) which, in turn, provided the military group in power the perfect opportunity to carry out their coup-d'etat. For a general understanding of the Kwangju Uprising, see Donald Clark (ed.), *The Kwangju Uprising: Shadows over the Regime in South Korea* (Boulder: Westview, 1988). Also see my "And They Would Start Again: Women and Struggle in Korean Nationalist Literature," *Positions: East Asia Cultures Critique*, 3.ii (Fall 1995): 392–414.

3. Hyŏn, *Paramt'anŭn sŏm* (*Island in Wind*) (Seoul: Ch'angjakkgwa bip'yong sa, 1989), 394. Since the novel has not been translated into English, the translation of the text is mine. Further references appear in the text.

4. Rajeswari Sunder Rajan, *Real and Imagined Women: Gender, Culture, and Postcolonialism* (London: Routledge, 1993), 119.

5. Sunder Rajan, 120.

6. In that sense, Sunder Rajan's diagnosis about "most Marxist and feminist thinkers" in whose theoretical work "collective praxis is still primarily conceived of as an aspect of struggle and resistance, not of power and leadership" (121) raises some questions. Even though I agree with Sunder Rajan that Marxism and feminism should not privilege the "subject-as-victim" as the only desirable political agents of social transformation, I argue that "struggle and resistance" are not separable from, let alone antithetical to, "power and leadership." On the contrary, different (non-tyrannical and non-repressive, for instance) ways of conceptualizing "power and leadership" based on actual "struggle and resistance" are necessary for developing political movements for further transformation that do not romanticize and idealize struggle per se.

7. For a discussion of the ways in which South African women, for example, organized and led themselves as well as resisted and struggled against patriarchy and the violence of apartheid, see Daniel Moshenberg, "Starting Quietly, Often Disguised," *Forward Motion* 14.ii (Spring 1995): 30–32, 47.

8. Here what Hyŏn argues to be radical intellectuals' social vocation resembles Paulo Freire's "pedagogy of the oppressed": Freire advocates teaching illiterate peasants of South America to tear apart and reassemble social reality as well as phonemic combinations. See *Pedagogy of the Oppressed* (New York: Continuum, 1990).

9. Motherhood in general has become a site of contestation where right wing advocates of "family values" and Marxist feminist critics stage their battles and stake their respective claims on motherhood. For a discussion of the ways in which political/cultural discourses conflate political power with the familial/psychoanalytical trope of "mother of the nation," see Sunder Rajan, 103–128.

10. *Paramt'anŭn sŏm* was written in a serialized form for a daily newspaper. When it was published as a book, Hyŏn substantially revised the ending of the novel, emphasizing moments of liberation and glory as well as the women divers' roles in the uprising.

11. Ch'oe Wŏn-sik, "Yŏnhapchŏnsŏnŭi munhakjŏk hyŏngsanghwa" (Literary Represent-ation of Political Coalition), *Ch'angjakkwa bip'yong* 18.1 (Spring 1990): 374–382.

12. For example, the editorial collective argues that the women's group, Kŭnu, had more cohesive power than the largest nationalist group of the period, Singanhoe. Moreover, Singanhoe failed to produce its own publications, while Kŭnu managed to publish its own journal, *Kŭnu. Yŏsŏng* (Women) 3 (Seoul: Ch'angjakkwa bip'yong sa, 1989): 298–329.

13. The writer whom these theorists discuss most extensively in order to address the issue of "migration" or "migrancy" is Salman Rushdie. *Shame* and *The Satanic Verses* have been interpreted in various ways by critics who profess different, and sometimes conflicting, theoretical positions. See Homi K. Bhabha, "How Newness Enters the World: Postmodern Space, Postcolonial Times and the Trials of Cultural Translation," *The Location of Culture* (London: Routledge, 1994), 212–235; Aijaz Ahmad, "Salman Rushdie's Shame: Postmodern Migrancy and the Representation of Women," *In Theory: Classes, Nations, and Literatures* (London: Verso, 1992), 123–158; and Anthony Appiah, *In My Father's House: Africa in the Philosophy of Culture* (New York: Oxford University Press, 1992).

14. Bhabha, 219.

15. Bhabha, 220.

16. See Maria Mies, *Patriarchy and Accumulation on a World Scale: Women in the International Division of Labor* (London: Zed, 1986); James Blaut, *The National Question: Decolonising the Theory of Nationalism* (London: Zed, 1987); Chungmoo Choi, "Korean Women in a Culture of Inequality," Donald Clark, ed., *Korea Briefing 1992* (Boulder: Westview, 1992); Sunder Rajan, "Ameena: Gender, Crisis, and National Identity," *Oxford Literary Review* 16.1, 147–176, and in *Real and Imagined Women;* Cynthia Enloe, *Bananas, Beaches, and Bases: Making Feminist Sense of International*

Politics (Berkeley: University of California Press, 1989), and *The Morning After: Sexual Politics at the End of the Cold War* (Berkeley: University of California Press, 1993); E. San Juan, *Crisis in the Philippines: The Making of a Revolution* (South Hadley: Bergin & Garvey, 1986).

17. For example, Nancy Abelmann and John Lie, in *Blue Dreams: Korean Americans and the Los Angeles Riots* (Cambridge: Harvard University Press, 1995), point out that the global Korean diaspora is a colonial as well as a postcolonial phenomena:

> The global Korean diaspora includes communities throughout East Asia, Soviet Central Asia, Australasia, the Middle East, Europe, and the Americas, which by 1982 accounted for 10 percent of the global Korean population. . . . This displacement is not new: at the end of Japan's colonial reign in Korea (1945), 11 percent of the Korean population lived abroad. Indeed, all Koreans are mired in dislocation as the North-South division engulfs them in a diaspora of sorts, displaced from families, homeland, and landmarks. As the division persists as a geopolitical reality, so does the symbolic legacy of colonial period dispersals remain alive in the political ideological workings of contemporary South Korea. (50)

Thus, Abelmann and Lie link colonial migrancy and postcolonial migrancy with the division of the Korean peninsula (and the subsequent migrancy) and with the problems of Korean immigrants in the United States.

10
≡

Mother Load
Photo Essay

Mother **Load** is a four-part sequential sculpture. The images refer to traditional *pojagis,* square pieces of cloth used by Korean women for wrapping and carrying various objects. Each of these *pojagi*-like forms constitutes a patchwork, a collage of personal and historical photographs as well as modified pieces of traditional and contemporary clothing. These collages function as receptacles for Korean and Korean American history.

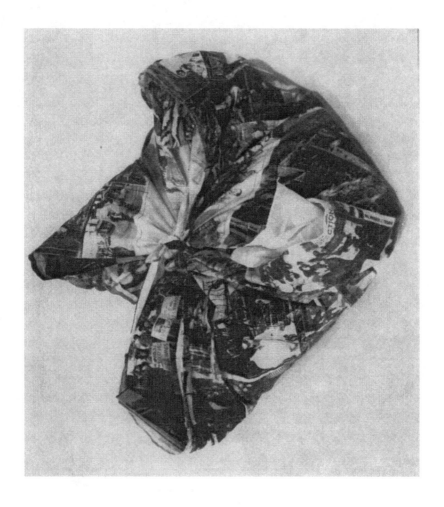

11

HYUN OK PARK

Ideals of Liberation:
Korean Women in Manchuria

Although Korean migration to Manchuria dates back to the seventeenth century, it became substantial in the 1880s, following a series of natural disasters and crop failures in Korea. As many peasants and small landowners lost their tenancy or land during the Japanese colonial rule, the Korean population in Manchuria swelled from roughly 202,070 in 1910 to 1.5 million in 1945. In the 1930s, Korean women participated in the riots and the ensuing revolutionary and nationalist movements. The riots of 1931 and 1932 were typical grain riots, similar to the food riots and tax rebellions in Europe and Japan in the eighteenth and nineteenth centuries.[1] Korean peasant women cooperated with both Korean and Chinese Communists throughout the 1930s to achieve the conjoined goals of changing economic conditions and liberating both Korea and China from the Japanese rule.[2]

These revolutionary and nationalist movements in Manchuria fell far short of a feminist vision of social change: the Chinese Communist Party's (henceforth CCP) attempts to expand women's independence from the family and to change the family structure were short-lived. As Johnson and Stacey observed in other parts of China, such policies were replaced in 1934 by pro-family policies that discouraged divorce and stressed family harmony.[3] As a result, the movements in Manchuria seemed to serve men rather than women, despite equal participation and commitment on the part of women. Economic and national exigencies of revolutionary change seemed to proliferate women's oppression.

A different conceptualization of women and their identities may, however, suggest an alternative meaning for the participation of women in the revolutionary and nationalist movements. As deconstructionist gender studies argues, women are not a homogeneous group, lacking any unity due to different social positions; nor is women's identity unidimensional, given their diverse social positions and ensuing influx of experience.[4] In light of these theoretical insights, it is not feasible to assume unified and general interests of women in revolutionary and nationalist movements. A single form of liberation may not be shared by all women in different national and class positions and in different historical contexts. Awareness of differences among women raises some questions regarding what groups of women might have felt deluded by, or agreed with, the Communist policies to preserve the family structure and existing gender relations. Questions of whether women's identities changed during the process of movements also need to be addressed.

Pursuing these issues, I will analyze variations in women's social positions, interests, and political activities in Manchuria. In the early stage of the movements, variations are most evident when Korean Communist women are compared with Korean married peasant women. The political activities of the two groups of women merged as they acquiesced to family policies of the Chinese Communist Party. Tracing the process of their activities will inform about us when and how the politics of these two groups of Korean women differentiated and coalesced.

Communist Women's Vision
Becoming Communist

The women in Manchuria who joined the Chinese Communist Party tended to be unmarried Korean peasants. This national, class, and gender background is indicated by three documents on Korean women's participation in the Chinese Revolution: Volumes I and III of *Changbaek ŭi t'usadŭl* (*Heroes of Changbaek Mountain*) and *Hangil yŏ t'usadŭl* (*Heroines in the Anti-Japanese Struggle*).[5] According to these sources, Korean Communist women, like their male counterparts, came from poor peasant families that barely survived cultivating rented land or smallholdings. Sixteen of twenty-five female guerrillas shared poor peasant family backgrounds. Most women joined the Party between the ages of 18 and 23. At the time they encountered Communism, they tended to be unmarried or about to be forced into an arranged marriage. Their age and marital status contrasted with those of other Korean peasant women a great deal, as I will discuss later.

Arranged marriage or forced early marriage triggered these women's support of Communist activities, as many anecdotes suggest. Hong Hye-sun[6] was the daughter of a doctor and among the most highly educated Korean women. In 1925, at age of eighteen, she chose to become engaged to a committed revolutionary named So Sŏng-gyu over her parents' objections. Her engagement put her village into shock. Hŏ Sŏng-suk,[7] another well-known revolutionary woman, left her family upon hearing the news that her wedding had been arranged by her parents. She attempted suicide by jumping into a river. She was saved by a guerrilla and started living with the guerrilla army, using a new name, "daughter of guerrilla army." Yi Chŏng-in,[8] a *minmyŏnŭri*, child bride, escaped from her husband's family after an unbearable two years. While staying at her uncle's home, she joined the 1931 uprisings and participated in guerrilla activities. She remembered her experience of being sold at age fourteen as a *minmyŏnŭri*, and contrasted that with her life in the guerrilla army, where she was treated like a human being with dignity and freedom.

The Korean Communist women's experiences corresponded to those of the Chinese Communist women. The Manchuria Committee of the Chinese Communist Party (henceforth the Manchuria Committee) implemented what the CCP had enacted across the rest of China. In Communist language, arranged marriage, early marriage, daughter-in-law adoption, concubinage, and footbinding constituted diseases of the old society, and these diseases were a defilement of women's rights and blasphemies against humanity. The CCP declared absolute freedom in marriage and divorce as the central means of instating women's equality. The Manchuria Committee applied the same gender policies to both Chinese and Korean peasants in Manchuria. Conceiving of Chinese and Korean women as belonging to the same category of women, the CCP made no reference to ethnic or nationality differences. The Manchuria Committee's inability or unwillingness to evaluate ethnic or national differences in gender relations stemmed from the CCP's desire to enforce uniform policies all across China to maintain unity across the country as well as among Korean and Chinese Communists within Manchuria. To prevent nationalist divisions and conflicts within the Manchuria Committee, the CCP and the Manchuria Committee suppressed expressions of national identity among Korean Communists, who comprised the majority of the Chinese Communist Party in Manchuria.

Although the CCP lacked an understanding of Korean culture, its gender policies challenged the oppression of Korean peasant women too, because family systems were similar in Chinese and Korean communities. Except for the practice of footbinding, which was unique to the Chinese, other practices that the Manchuria Committee identified as oppressive feudal traditions were shared. In both national communities, marriage was arranged by the kin or the fathers of the two families, without consent from either the bride or the groom. Divorce was hardly ever allowed to women for any reason, although a woman's inability to give birth to a son or her inadequate care of her husband's family were enough reason for a man to divorce his wife.

Minmyŏnŭri, the practice of child-bride marriage among Korean peasants, and daughter-in-law adoption practices among Chinese peasants were similar in origin and form. In both cultures, the marriages of young girls from poor families were in fact transactions exchanging their labor for material benefits to the families involved. These practices originated in patrilineal family systems in rural villages where unmarried daughters became a burden because they were less likely to bring income to the family than were unmarried sons. Meanwhile, the groom's parents could ensure that their son would have a bride as well as low marriage costs. For example, *minmyŏnŭri* was prevalent among the Koreans during the poor economic conditions in the 1930s. When Korean families with some economic and financial means lacked labor power either for agricultural production or for housework, they paid cash for the daughters of poor families who were anxious to reduce their family size because of the lack of income. A girl was sent to the expected husband's family at the age of seven or eight and married after several years of working in that family. The Chinese practice of daughter-in-law adoption was similar. Kazukuo[9] explains it as the most oppressive feudal practice widespread across China, including northeast China. At a low cost, a bride could be provided for a son by adopting a future daughter-in-law while she was a child. In Shanxi province, prices were set according to the girl's age: the older she was, the higher the market price. Adoption of a daughter-in-law served two purposes at once: the girl's parents were not only spared the expense of her board, but also received a small sum from her sale. The daughters-in-law so purchased were frequently older than the boys for whom they were intended. This was done so that the family could get at least some useful labor from the girl early on.

Whether the Manchuria Committee intended it or not, its declarations for free love and marriage and against trafficking in women seemed to challenge both the Chinese and Korean patriarchal systems. Protection of women's rights defied two long-standing pillars of the Confucian morality: "Man is respected and woman lowly (*namjon yŏbi*)"; plus "three subordinations of women (*samjongjido*)"; and "three fundamental principles and five moral disciplines in human relationship (*samgang oryun*)." The CCP's critique of patriarchal authority over women's marriage was designed to dismantle the authority codes of the old society. Since marriage was decided according to the authority of the father and kinship, challenges to feudal arranged marriages and the advocacy of free love and free divorce seemed to pose a significant threat to the existing peasant society.

Overturning Gender Policies

The radical gender policies of the Communists were short-lived. Although the rhetoric of "women's liberation" and "the guarantee of equality regardless of sex" continued to appear in the platforms of the People's Governments, what was evident in the specific guidelines of the Manchuria Committee and the women cadres was the abandonment of "free marriage and divorce" and an emphasis instead on family harmony. The reversal was as abrupt in Manchuria as it was in other regions of China.

As the initial gender policy of the Manchuria Committee followed the central policies of the CCP, the retreat of the Manchuria Committee once again corresponded to the course and logic followed by the CCP beginning in 1934. The radical measures of freedom of marriage and divorce invoked antagonism, mistrust, and resentment among male peasants and the elderly in Manchuria. The peasants seemed to believe that the Communists had denounced family relations, instigating young people to defy the family. They also were suspicious that the Communists were luring young women to abandon their virtue and join a group of indecent people who advocated sexual freedom. In response, the CCP determined that marriage reform threatened the class unity that was essential to its vision of rural revolution, since the family was a crucial unit of economic production and socialization and women played the key role in reproducing family relations. To build strong ties with the peasants, the Chinese Communists withdrew those policies that threatened to deprive male peasants of their two most valuable possessions—land and women. The drive to enforce freedom and equality in marriage and divorce was replaced by the pro-family principle, which was further reinforced by the united front with the reformist Guomindang Party during the Chinese-Japanese War (1937–1945).

Japan's symbolic war also contributed to this setback in Communist gender policies. The Japanese incited the peasants by spreading rumors that Communists were bandits who burned houses, plundered food and property, and kidnapped women. To prevent misunderstandings, the CCP took extra precautions not to allow young people to join without their family's approval.[10] As the behavior of women cadres became a

Japanese pretext for fanning the flames of suspicion among the peasants, the Manchuria Committee called on women cadres to pay respect to patriarchal values so as not to confirm the image of Communist men and women as morally corrupted seekers of unrestrained sexual pleasure.

The Manchuria Committee made every attempt to retain the trust and support of the peasants in the villages. It embraced "tradition," defining chastity and subordination as women's primary virtues. Female "beauty" now meant women's traditional, nurturing roles, which offered absolute respect for elders and unquestioned commitment and sacrifice for the well-being of the husband's family. The principle of "true love and true marriage" replaced slogans of "free love, free marriage, and free divorce." "True love" was defined as serving the collective interest of achieving revolution and/or the liberation of the nation, while free love was criticized as a selfish pursuit of individual freedom. "True love" was possible only in relations within the boundary of revolutionary struggle—whether the love was between husband and wife or between comrades—and only when people's minds were committed to the highest love, love for the nation, which entailed even a willingness to sacrifice one's life for it. Ch'un-hyang and Sim Ch'ŏng, two of the best-known heroines of Korean folklore, were elevated as models and virtuous beautiful women. The story of Ch'un-hyang was the best representation of the virtue of chastity, while the story of Sim Ch'ŏng extolled the virtue of filial piety.[11] Even the short haircuts of women, which had symbolized defiance of tradition and the beginning of modernity in China since the May Fourth Movement in 1919, were now under attack.

According to a number of records, Korean women cadres tried hard to become accustomed to, instead of restraint, the peasant woman's life.[12] Korean Communist women helped peasant women in doing such work as washing clothes at the river, pounding grain, and collecting vegetables and edible grass in the mountains. Ann Sun-hwa,[13] a well-known Korean woman cadre, visited every peasant household to explain revolutionary work while she helped them with weaving and other housework. Fearing criticism that she neglected housework herself and thus undervalued the woman's role as wife and mother, she carried out her own housework more diligently.

Pak Nok-kŭm[14] visited wells and rivers where village women often gathered to fetch water and wash clothes. To please the elders in the village, she made efforts to learn village customs, such as the way women carried pots on their heads when they fetched water from the well, and the way that they walked. Only after these precautions and services brought her trust from the village people did she begin to organize "*toenori,*" a village custom where people sat together and made food. While women peeled potatoes and cooked, they listened to what she told them about the revolution. She was praised for her wisdom in convincing elders who had previously objected to their daughters-in-law's involvement in study groups and in Women's Committees (*Punyŏhoe*). Pak organized meetings at houses where the parents were reluctant to accept Communist teaching. While making thread and weaving together with them, she explained to the young women that they had to respect their parents-in-law, serve their husbands, and take good care of children. These strategies often turned out to be successful in earning the trust and permission of the elderly, as intended.

Peasant Women's New Imagined Society
Migration and Women's Work

Married Korean peasant women differed from Communist women in terms of their understanding of the movement, their age, and their family experience. The married Korean peasant women were drawn by class and national issues rather than gender issues. Their concern for the survival of their families led them to their commitment to the movements.

The Korean migration to Manchuria reinforced changes in work patterns, which involved women in agricultural work. This migration created an environment unfavorable to the revival of collective work practices, such as "*ture,*" which had been in decline since the late nineteenth century in Korea. As *Contemporary Manchuria,* a Japanese journal, reported in 1940, the tradition of "*ture*" was regenerated to the extent that it was organized to carry out occasional collective work that individual families could not accomplish alone, such as drawing water from a river, changing the course of a stream, or digging holes for irrigation systems. The Korean community also revived practices of mutual help in such events as funerals and weddings.

While farming could be done with hired labor, those who could afford it were few. Most Korean peasant households instead spread the burden among household members. When the individual family became the unit for tilling land, gender relations framed the farming experience. Before the migration to Manchuria, Korean farming was done mostly by men, who exchanged labor and planned with neighbors the detailed timing and cooperation necessary for cultivation, while most women managed the housework and took care of the elderly and the children. After migration, reliance on family labor brought more women into growing crops such as beans and rice, an involvement that must have been extended as their husbands and other male adults left for wage jobs in railway construction and mining.

Yet not all Korean peasant women were brought into farming. The boundary between women's work and men's work was crossed to the extent that married women were incorporated into the field labor force. The relative absence of unmarried women's or girls' work in agricultural production was shaped by both gender- and class-specific dynamics. Demand for female chastity and sex segregation after age seven constrained unmarried women from engaging in contact with men other than family members and led peasants to consider an unmarried daughter the last person to work in the fields. Furthermore, limiting the potential contributions of unmarried women to agricultural production was also a class-specific phenomenon. Families with small holdings required only a limited number of people to work in agricultural production and were consequently less likely to employ unmarried women in the fields.

Multifaceted Meanings of Motherhood

How peasant women interpreted the experience of intense work depended on how they viewed marriage, the family, and giving birth. Under the patrilineal system, the natal family was only a temporary place for women. Marriage was the ultimate fate for women of all classes. The family that a woman made after marriage was not considered her own, but her husband's family. Frequent visits back to her parents' home after the wedding were regarded as a signal of her lack of commitment and loyalty to her husband's family, a development that would embarrass both families. The husband's family was a strange place for a newly wed woman and one from which she could not escape. Marriage was not the place to find affection. Women's plight in the peasant family was heightened by the physical burden of work and discipline. Folk songs and labor songs, which Korean peasant women sang while at work, best illustrate this. "*Milmae norae,*" a song about wheat, crystallized a woman's life in her new husband's family and the hardships that she had to endure:

> Sister, sister, my sister. How is married life in the home of your husband's parents? Although peppers are said to be very hot, they cannot be compared to the hard life of married women. In three years of hard work in my husband's family, my silky hairs were turned into a chestnut bur. My white hands, which used to be soft as a silky hair brush, wore out and turned into the foot of a duck. My sisters-in-law are like little mice. What is this all about?[15]

Giving birth to a child and becoming a mother transformed the meaning of work and life in the husband's family. Whether a Korean woman married the son of a peasant or a landlord, giving birth to a son secured her position in her husband's family. She was then no longer a stranger to the family, but a mother of sons who would pass on the family name, if not its wealth, to the next generation. Her newly acquired identity as a mother and therefore a key member of the family brought new meaning to her exhausting work both in the fields and in the landlord's house. If before having children Korean peasant women endured overwork and exhaustion out of helplessness, as mothers they now did so for the sake of assuring the survival of their children and other family members.

Motherhood also shaped a Korean peasant woman's class experience when they leased land from the landlord. For these women, motherhood was not confined to delivering children; nor did it necessarily mean always giving immediate attention to the needs of babies and children.

Motherhood for the peasant woman, especially a woman from a poor tenant family in Manchuria, often meant denying the body's basic need to recover from delivery. Pak Kyŏng-suk recalls that her landlord harassed her mother to work in the fields immediately after she had given birth, and her mother was ill afterwards.[16] Landlords wanted to maximize the use of peasants' labor power in order to increase the harvest, since the rental rate was set as a percentage of the harvest.

Motherhood also meant enduring the pain of separation when a family had to be broken up because of poverty. When high rents and increasing tax burdens threatened the subsistence of the peasant family and their hard work was not enough to support them, a common strategy of individual families was to reduce their family size by sending children to live with other families as servants. Men in the family left for work as agricultural laborers or as miners and construction workers in urban areas or in Japan or Russia. Young boys and girls also worked as servants for their landlord's family. Sometimes they were paid in cash or in kind for their work; sometimes they worked to pay off family debts to buy food. Boys helped with agricultural production, tended livestock, and did jobs such as collecting wood and cleaning house. Young girls were sent to the landlord's family or some other relatively wealthy family to do childcare, carry water, cook, wash dishes, pound grain, and clean house.[17]

Motherhood and Women's Politics

The experience of mothering itself influenced the collective political action of Korean peasants. As Bohstedt demonstrated in his study of English riots, motherhood is not always the origin of women's political empowerment.[18] Instead, several political, economic, and gender factors coalesced to bring married Korean peasant women in Manchuria to revolt. With worldwide economic depression, inflation, high interest rates, and rising rent and taxation, the peasant family economy deteriorated. As much as married peasant women shared agricultural work with men and became key household members taking responsibility for the survival of the family, they considered this family economic crisis as their own and joined the riots and the revolution. Similarly, as much as they continued to be subject to Japanese harassment, surveillance, and arrests even after they moved to Manchuria, their struggle was directed against the Japanese.

The married peasant women's involvement was promoted by the moral standing which positioned them as mothers and wives. They were to be brought into the social struggle by family members, especially sons and husbands. When the men insisted, the women reluctantly came to support their activities on the grounds that it was better to try to protect the lives of their sons and husbands by helping rather than criticizing and interfering with their activities. The women kept watch to see whether strangers were coming near their houses when their sons held secret meetings there. They sent their young children to the village entrance to watch for the approach of policemen. They hid secret documents inside the kitchen fireplace or in the walls. They offered secret agents a place to hide, such as in the root cellar under the house, or in a mountain tunnel. They cooked for and nursed the guests of their sons and husbands, and even washed and sometimes made the clothes for the visitors. These women were also asked to help with work outside of the family. They distributed propaganda flyers in markets and streets and posted them on village walls, or ran errands to the Communist agents or to Communist organizations in other villages.

The experience of Kim Myŏng-hwa[19] exemplified this process. Before she joined the Chinese Communist Party in 1932, her first experience was to cook for the "revolutionary people" who visited her husband and brother-in-law. Being persuaded by her husband, she began to help her son, Ma Tong-hwi, a well-known Communist. Disguising herself as a chili merchant, she delivered her son's messages to other guerrillas and underground activists across the Amnok River, going back and forth from Hamgyŏng province of Korea to northeast China. She sometimes brought books published by the guerrilla army, such as *Hwajŏnmin* and *Sam'ilwŏlgan,* to the village. Whenever secret agents came to her house late at night, Tong-hwi's wife cooked with care so as not to make smoke in the chimney, which would make neighbors suspicious. Hyŏn Kŭm-son, the wife of well-known Korean Communist, Pak Tal, recalled that "the more my husband participated in the revolutionary activities, the more documents I had to hide, from small black memo books, to packages, to a big box full of secret notes and documents. I had to hide them in holes covered with snow, bunches of grain, and bushes."[20]

Arrest of family members by the Japanese and Chinese armies spurred the Korean peasant mothers toward more active participation. These women adopted the revolutionary commitment of their husbands and sons as their own. "I observed and watched how cruel the Japanese are," Kim In-suk said.[21] She explained that her will for revenge motivated her activities:

> My son, Tong-gi, and his friends were arrested as suspects in the harvest uprisings. Right after being released by the police due to lack of evidence, Tong-gi and his seven friends went to the mountains to join the guerrilla armies. I heard later that they engaged in attacks of the pro-Japanese, pro-landlord Self-Defense Group (*Chawidan*) in 1932. My second son and 12 other village people, including my daughter-in-law, were convicted. My second son was tortured and killed during the investigation. Since then, I always carried a hand-made bomb and a knife hidden in my clothes. I was determined to avenge the death of my son. That was 29 years ago [in 1932] and I was 45 years old. I received military training, carrying my baby on my back. I worked in the Storm Corps and the Red Defense Corps. In October 1933, I became the leader of the Women's Committee in Namgol, Pon'gaedong.

Kim Myŏng-hwa was determined to fight the Japanese, saying that "although my husband could be killed before the day of liberation comes, I have to fight. If he dies before the revolution succeeds, I have to see it through on his behalf. Even if I cannot see the liberation, I have to fight so that my children can see it."[22] Chang Kil-bu recorded how a letter her son sent from prison rescued her from despair after the deaths of her daughter and daughter-in-law:

> After sending my daughter-in-law and daughter to the guerrilla army, I returned to Korea with my mother-in-law. Several years later, I heard that Kuk-hwa, my daughter, died in the battle at P'aldogu. Kim Yong-gŭm, my daughter-in-law, lost her life in a fire set by the Japanese while she was making army clothes as a member of the sewing batch at Chiyanggaegol. I was subjected to continuous torture by the Japanese

police whenever there was labor strike or tenant dispute among the peasants. Because of my pain and suffering over the death of my daughter and from my torture, I attempted to commit suicide.

However, I changed my attitude after receiving the letter my son sent me just before his death in prison: "Kind and strong mother, please follow the flag of Kim Il Sung's army, even by surviving as a beggar. Supporting and following the army is the only way to liberate Korea and establish a new society for workers and peasants. I, your son, dedicate my life to this. Our enemy can end my life but cannot take my commitment from me. Mother, please live and enjoy a new society that I cannot see." My son's last letter provided me with great strength. I became fearless whenever I thought of my son's courageous death.[23]

The sons' and husbands' activities rekindled married women's political consciousness and sustained them through hardship. Misfortunes spurred mothers and wives with anger, desire for revenge, courage, and the will to survive and struggle. In contrast, there are few records that daughters inspired them to do similar works. The asymmetrical relations of mother-son and mother-daughter can be attributed to the character of the "uterine family," which Wolf characterizes as mothers who exercise their power through a grown-up son, a head of the household.[24]

Solidarity among Women

The married Korean peasant women's supportive activities stirred their consciousness and carried them to the point of trying to find their own ways of contributing to the struggle. The helping activities women engaged in for their sons and husbands, or their assumption of their sons' and husbands' roles, created the context in which married Korean peasant women widened the boundaries of their social relationships with other women. Accumulated experience and contact with other women in the struggle led them to broaden their perspective beyond individual household boundaries, as they understood that the personal goal of reintegrating their families was common to all of them. The construction of a new society in which families could be united would be achieved only by carrying out the struggle and winning the war against the Japanese and the landlords. The married peasant women who participated in the struggle at this stage were no longer simply accomplices under the domination of their husbands and sons. Although their identity as mothers was the basis of their solidarity around the Women's Committee, their own families were not the sole source of their identities and strength. Their sense of responsibility had moved beyond their own family relationships.

The deepened sentiment of solidarity was expressed in the formation and activities of the Women's Committee. The Women's Committee carried out various assignments, such as producing crops; supplying guerrilla armies with food, clothing, and other necessities; and conducting reconnoitering missions. Since many male householders had joined the guerrilla armies at their bases or were involved in other secret activities, the women were responsible for planting, harvesting, and threshing crops. The Committee also opened a night school for peasant women. Along with the principles of the revolutionary and national liberation of Korea, reading and writing were also taught. Another important achievement of the Women's Committee was organizing and training the Children's Corps, which was crucial for standing sentinel and delivering messages to other subdivisions of the Manchuria Committee of the Chinese Communist Party, as well as for performing dances and plays to entertain and inspire the guerrilla armies. The group was organized with about twenty children, most of whom had lost their parents or family members.

Whenever women sent food and crops to the armies, they worked all night for several nights in a row. They risked being caught by the Japanese or the landlords, since the Japanese watched for peasants who bought large amount of food in the markets, or threshed and pounded grains. A memoir noted:

> When village people had to send rice or other crops to the armies, mother and sisters hulled rice in the mortar at night when it dropped to 30 degrees Centigrade below zero. We pounded the wet barley, while they dried it. In 1936, our village sent a lot of barley and potato powder to the army. It was not easy because we all were suffering from hunger. However, we helped the army because we knew that the army would fight for the new society in which peasants and workers would live better.[25]

Ch'oe Chae-ryŏn describes the difficulties of carrying out clandestine activities:

> We were in charge of providing food, supplies, and secret communications. It was hard to carry out such jobs. We did not have any money to buy cloth to make army uniforms, because policemen, the punitive forces, and the pro-Japanese (Koreans and Chinese) searched the village and threatened and arrested people day and night. Core members of the Women's Committee visited nonmember women and asked for donations. We bought cloth little by little in different markets in order to prevent the merchants from suspecting us. We even had to lie to the merchants that we were buying cloth for marriages, ceremonies, or anniversaries, since buying a lot of fabric led them to suspect us. The Japanese often investigated those who bought a lot. We made clothes at night, not sleeping for several days, since we had to make all the uniforms by the date the army had set.[26]

Carrying out reconnoitering missions, delivering messages, and providing and buying necessities for the guerrillas were risky jobs that endangered the lives of entire families, not just the lives of the women. Their activities were watched by *Minhoe,* pro-Japanese Korean committees organized by landlords under the supervision of the Japanese police and army. *Minhoe* collected information about village people and identified revolutionaries. For example, when the Japanese police found out that Eun-bok communicated with the army, they killed her mother-in-law and her son and burned their house.

In successfully carrying out tasks and responsibilities in the Women's Committee, motherhood was a strategic resource that the peasant women resorted to. The members of the Women's Committee took advantage of the tendency of Japanese police to relax their supervision of women based on their perception that women were not politically dangerous, and especially that mothers with babies were not aggressive enough to do anything violent. The members volunteered for work such as reconnoitering, delivering messages, and buying necessities for the guerrilla armies, claiming that they would not be suspected by the Japanese police and army. The members were mothers and grandmothers who were proud of their sacrifice for the revolutionary cause. Disguised as merchants, they approached policemen who guarded railway construction sites and spent weeks getting acquainted with them to get confidential information regarding imminent attacks on guerrillas and peasants at the bases. Women also utilized their practice of foraging for mountain vegetables and edible grasses to hold secret meetings or to organize the Women's Committee, away from the surveillance of the police.

The mother-in-law of Yang Chŏng-suk volunteered to blast railroads with bombs, insisting that the police guard near the railroads would not suspect an old woman.[27] Women also gained access to police stations near the Japanese armies in the mountains and forests, under the pretense of grubbing for vegetables. Han Mae-mul was selected to buy necessities for the army because the Japanese would be less suspicious of a woman with a baby. Carrying her baby on her back, Han had to walk all night on dangerous mountain paths across the Amnok River to buy mimeograph paper, sewing thread, and needles.[28]

Conclusion

The Communist policies in Manchuria followed patterns that feminists have observed in other revolutions. The Communists' anti-family policies were quickly replaced by pro-family measures. After a brief period of enforcing measures to promote free marriage, divorce, and an end to trafficking in women, the Communists began to uphold the traditional family. In 1933, they dropped the signifier "new liberated woman," replacing it with "true revolutionary woman." Ideals of revolutionary militancy were grafted onto traditional views of virtuous Korean womanhood. The new Communist utopian vision of women's liberation was thus couched in terms of filial piety, chastity, and motherhood. These values became the moral basis for commitment and loyalty to the new state/nation. The return to tradition was a corrective to potentially still powerful resistance from the Communists' constituency—the peasant family in revolution. As a result, the family came to be understood as a source of collective unity, rather than an oppressive space where women occupied a low and dependent position. Accordingly, the issues of women's own rights over their bodies and sexuality hardly appeared in the revolutionary struggle.

Communist women and Korean peasant women rarely resisted the Party's reversion to conservative family policies. Their identity and interest in the movements, however, differed in terms of marital status, especially at the beginning of the movements. It was young, unmarried women who were attracted to early Communist proclamations of women's freedom in marriage and divorce. Korean peasant mothers' identities were bound to their families, and their own interests overlapped with those of male peasants and the Communists. The choice between resistance against class exploitation and gender struggle against male domination was not available to Korean peasant mothers. Instead, what explains the dilemma of Korean peasant mothers in Manchuria is their class/national experience and interests, as they were embedded in patriarchal relations. For agricultural production in the Korean peasant community in Manchuria, the family became the unit of production. Since family relations were shaped by patriarchal relations, the logic of work and regulation was rooted in patriarchal relations. As a result, gender identity begot class experience and class interests. One gender-specific class interest for which Korean peasant mothers struggled was the reintegration of the family. Gender struggle against male domination was something that Korean peasant mothers in these historical circumstances could not undertake, since their class interests were built upon such patriarchal relations.

Korean Communist women acquiesced to the Party's new family policies, which stressed more the family harmony than women's rights in the family. Their activities were thus merged with those of Korean peasant mothers. However, their later similarities should not elide the fact that acquiescence to the Party's conservative policies occurred not because these women shared a single form of liberation. Instead, their investments in the family stemmed from very different experiences of work and family relations.

NOTES

1. Bohstedt, John. 1988. "Gender, Household and Community Politics: Women in English Riots 1790-1810." *Past and Present* 120: 88–122; Dekker, Rudolf. 1987. "Women in Revolt: Popular Protest and its Social Basis in Holland in the Seventeenth and Eighteenth Centuries." *Theory and Society* 16: 337–362.

2. North Korean historiography has considered the peasant revolts in Manchuria, including Kando, as parts of the Koreans' national liberation movement. This experience in Manchuria has been glorified as the origin of the North Korean revolution and the national ideology of self-reliance (*Juche sasang*).

3. Johnson, Kay. 1983. *Women, the Family, and Peasant Revolution in China*. Chicago: University of Chicago Press; Stacey, Judith. 1983. *Patriarchy and Socialist Revolution in China*. Berkeley: University of California Press.

4. Butler, Judith. 1990. *Gender Trouble*. New York: Routledge; Riley, Denise. 1990. "*Am I That Name?" Feminism and the Category of 'Women' in History*. Minneapolis: University of Minnesota Press; Spelman, Elizabeth. 1988. *Inessential Woman: Problems of Exclusion in Feminist Thought*. Boston: Beacon Press.

5. Yŏnbyŏn inmin ch'ulpansa. 1982. *Changbaek ŭi t'usadŭl (Heroes of Changbaek Mountain)*. Vol. 1. Yŏnbyŏn: Yŏnbyŏn inmin ch'ulpansa; Yŏnbyŏn chosŏnjok chach'iju punyŏ yŏnhaphoe. 1984. *Hangil yŏ t'usadŭl (Heroines of the Anti-Japanese Struggle)*. Yŏnbyŏn: Yŏnbyŏn Inmin ch'ulp'ansa.

6. Yŏnbyŏn chosŏnjok chach'iju punyŏ yŏnhaphoe. 1984. *Hangil yŏ t'usadŭl (Heroines of the Anti-Japanese Struggle)*. Yŏnbyŏn: Yŏnbyŏn Inmin ch'ulp'ansa.

7. Yŏnbyŏn chosŏnjok chach'iju punyŏ yŏnhaphoe. 1984. *Hangil yŏ t'usadŭl (Heroines of the Anti-Japanese Struggle)*. Yŏnbyŏn: Yŏnbyŏn Inmin ch'ulp'ansa.

8. *Chosŏn Yŏsŏng* 1960 (3): 9–10.

9. Kazukuo, Ono. 1989. *Chinese Women in a Century of Revolution: 1850–1950*. Stanford: Stanford University Press.

10. Hwang, Ryong-guk et al. 1988. *Chosŏnjok hyŏngmyŏng t'ujaengsa (History of the Korean Revolutionary Struggle)*. Ryoryŏng: Ryoryŏng minjok ch'ulp'ansa.

11. Kim, Myŏng-hwa. 1962. "*Yŏdaewŏntŭl kwa tamhwaesŏ* (Conversations with Women Members)." *Chosŏn Yŏsŏng* 1962 (3): 4–6.

12. This lack of resistance could be attributed to the politics of writing official memoirs, which might have suppressed information about any resistance against the Communist Party. It could be an effect of the political environment in northeast China, which as a northern frontier was less part of the feminist movement accompanied by the May Fourth Movement across China.

13. *Chosŏn Yŏsŏng* 1961 (5): 10–14.

14. *Chosŏn Yŏsŏng* 1965 (2): 9–10.

15. *Chosŏn Yŏsŏng* 1962 (4): 6.

16. Pak, Kyŏng-suk. 1963. "Ch'ong'ŭl japgikkaji (Until I hold the Gun)." Chŏsŏn Yŏsŏng 1963 (7): 2–5.

17. Ch'oe, Pong-ho. 1963. "Musanja ka kalgil ŭn ohjik hangil hyŏngmyŏngŭi kilbakke ŏpda (There Is Nothing But the Struggle for Revolution)." Chŏsŏn Yŏsŏng 1963 (12): 13–16.

18. Bohstedt, John. 1988. "Gender, Household and Community Politics: Women in English Riots 1790–1810." Past and Present 120: 88–122.

19. Kim, Myŏng-hwa. 1961. Hyŏngmyŏng ŭi giresŏ (On the Road to the Revolution). P'yŏngyang: Chosŏn nodongdang ch'ulp'ansa.

20. Hyŏn, Kŭm-sun. 1960. "Pich'ŭl ddara (Following the Light)". Chŏsŏn Yŏsŏng 1960 (5): 14–17.

21. "Kim In-suk ŏmŏnie taehan yiyagi (A Story About Kim In-suk)". Chŏsŏn Yŏsŏng 1961 (3): 10–13.

22. Kim, Myŏng-hwa. 1961. Hyŏngmyŏng ŭi giresŏ (On the Road to the Revolution). P'yŏngyang: Chosŏn nodongdang ch'ulpansa.

23. Choi, Chŏng-ok. 1959. "Pulgŭn kibarŭl ddara (Following the Red Flag)." Chŏsŏn Yŏsŏng 1959 (2): 2–6.

24. Wolf, Margery. 1972. Women and the Family in Rural Taiwan. Stanford: Stanford University Press.

25. Chŏsŏn Yŏsŏng 1959 (1): 3.

26. Chŏsŏn Yŏsŏng 1960 (8): 4–5.

27. Kim, Kyŏng-suk. 1959. "Kŭdŭl ŭn yŏngwŏnhi sal'lira (They Will Live Forever)." Chŏsŏn Yŏsŏng 1959 (5): 6–9.

28. Kim, Kyŏng-suk. 1958. "Hyongmyonge ch'ungjik han choguk ŭi ddal (Daughters Who Were Loyal to the Revolution)." Chŏsŏn Yŏsŏng 1958 (12): 8–11.

12

HYUN YI KANG

Re-membering Home

"**G**o back home."

This xenophobic slur has always puzzled me in its facile command to some magical retraction across great distances and lengthy separations. Bearing the double-edged implications of (once and future) belonging and of (present) repudiation for the immigrant subject, the concept-word-space "home" thus invoked holds out additional paradoxes for those whose gender, sexual, and class positionings would have precluded any secure, comfortable habitation *in the first place.* This essay attempts to track such awkward movements through four cultural productions by Korean immigrant women: Myung Mi Kim's poetry volume, *Under Flag,* Theresa Hak Kyung Cha's book *DICTEE,* and multimedia piece *EXILÉE,* and Kim Su Theiler's film *Great Girl.* These works map a knotted topography of Korean-American imbrications that contest any neat temporal or spatial distinctions. By looking at the representational strategies by which they remember and imagine "Korea," I seek to foreground recurring tensions between an expressed desire for this "home" and an historically sobered acknowledgment of its manifold inaccessibility. The quotation marks around the two words are deployed to signify their multiple enfigurations as objects of memory, yearning, and imaginary projection, as well as a specific geographical location with a unique history of colonial dominations, internal conflicts, and transnational migrations.[1]

Articulated from and disseminated in the U.S. yet significantly oriented towards Korea, these works, both independently and in my provisionally conjoined chorus, problematize the imperative to cohesive, exclusionist national identification in both geopolitical locations. On this side, the teleology of "Americanization" undergirding the conceptualization of immigrant cultures in the U.S. figures racial-ethnic difference as largely a matter of something "left behind." Within this trajectory, the nationality of "American" stands as a more ontologically solid noun that succeeds the (merely) adjectival ethnic marker. Yet, the disenfranchisement of Korean immigrants in the U.S. affords only an incomplete and precarious naturalization. Against the state's demand for a decisive transfer of national loyalties, the works under consideration manifest a sustained, if terribly strained, investment in the Korean homeland. However, they also scrupulously point out how there is no radically *other* side to "go back" to in any reassuring fashion. Each work tellingly illustrates how the multiple attenuations of Korea as a noun-place and Koreans as an ethno-national collectivity in the twentieth century have made this gesture of transnational affiliation less a compensatory return to primordial origins than a difficult reckoning with broader historical and social fissures of the Korean homeland.

These critical interrogations of both "American" and "Korean" identifications proceed by highlighting the contentious position of women in relation to the nation. As many feminist thinkers have pointed out, nationalisms often point to the importance of women in their rhetorical appeals even as their regimes of power perpetuate conditions of social, economic, and political gender inequalities.[2] Then too, the word-concept-place "home" has also borne promising and problematic implications for feminist politics. Like its invocation as an exclusionist slur against the immigrant who, for her part, may often defensively nurse a yearning for such an impossible repatriation, "home" has offered the comforting dream of safety, freedom, and belonging even as it has more often been deployed as the rationale to confine and exploit women on various levels of the nation-state's political and symbolic economy.[3] Bespeaking a heterogeneous range of belonging and "being at home," their socioeconomic circumstances in Korea and in the U.S. dictate the forcible and enabling terms of both emigration and return *amongst* Korean immigrant women. Kim, Cha and Theiler offer powerful critiques and reformulations of gender in the Korean nation-scape, even as they lay claim to specific genealogies of diverse forms of domination and alienation, as well as strategies of resilience and survival, for women.

Beyond the binary of fragmentation and wholeness, against the linearity of separation and reconciliation, these women's enduring, if doubtful, attachments to the homeland reject nationalist nostalgia for pure origins in favor of interweaving their own displacements in the broader Korean history of colonizations, socio-political conflicts, and economic stratifications. In addition to noting their lingering significance for a Korean American female subject, these powerful invocations of Korea also force attention to the crucial imbrications of the U.S. in those defining moments, thereby reconfiguring the presumed distance and difference of these two locations. This then may be a necessary paradox of Korean immigrant identification—that we can most confidently stake a position in relation to both Korea and the U.S. in drawing out not just dissimilarities but formative connections and continuities and in re-membering the terms of such collective displacement through the peculiar trajectories of migration and reculturation wrought by that history.[4]

The articulation of such twists and detours is no easy and simple undertaking. It necessitates a critical interrogation of both knowledge and representation. In addition to the lapses and distortions of personal memory over time, Korean American women must often try to gain access to the homeland through the tinted lens of "American" cultural and pedagogical accounts of Korea. Then too, these scattered and conflicting accounts must be represented with the linguistic and cultural means available in those discursive traditions and terrains squarely located in the U.S. Acknowledging such irrevocable alienation, these works repeatedly point to the enduring gaps and forceful translations that mediate any efforts of recall and reconstitution. Rather than presenting a coherent and progressive narration of self and nation, all four of these textual and cinematic articulations are fragmented, faltering, and internally conflicted. Authoritative declarations and evocative traces are repeatedly unsettled by highly self-conscious qualifications of doubt, misrecognition, and deliberate construction on the part of the authors. Then too, what could be autobiographical details and personal expressions are set alongside and against a host of competing accounts and official documents. Signaling these Korean American women's specific estrangements from the homeland, their variously fraught compositions contest both the discreteness of national identification and the easy certainty of its articulation. In addition to the connotations of memory, such efforts awaken other possibilities of re-membering, as redefining given terms of ethno-national membership as well as inherited conventions of artistic representation.

I have written elsewhere on Theresa Hak Kyung Cha's *DICTEE*, but I want to recall the text here along with a very resonant video-film text, in an effort to place Cha's work in a more collective conversation. Like Cha, Kim and Theiler comprise that strange grouping of Korean Americans known as *il-chom o-se* or "1.5 generation," those who were born in Korea but who emigrated to the U.S. as children at an age young enough to become acculturated but old enough to retain some memories of the Korean homeland, its language, and its history. Although they were produced a decade later, both *Under Flag* and *Great Girl* strikingly echo *DICTEE* and *EXILÉE* in their prevailing orientation towards a real and imaginary Korean homeland and in their evidently stylized and keenly self-conscious construction.[5] Rather than advocating the superiority or effectiveness of experimental techniques that evince a (greater) theoretical sophistication, I choose to read their fragmented, halting, and intertextual composition as highlighting the very doubts and dilemmas that confront any attempt to grasp or re-present a homeland in the face of formidable separations. Against any progressive mapping from originary source to indebted citation, I have decided to position my discussion of *DICTEE* and *EXILÉE* between those of *Under Flag* and

Great Girl because Cha's concerted engagement with both the printed text and the projected image also displaces the demarcations of expressive media.

I

The title of Myung Mi Kim's 1991 poetry volume *Under Flag* announces the text's central explorations of citizenship and national identification. However, the force of political subjection in the pithy phrase is deflated by the unspecified nature of this national emblem— which flag?—ultimately interrogating instead of affirming its decidability. The language of the volume is similarly indistinct and multiply significant. Any attempt to discern an individual poetic voice is challenged by mechanical lists, transliterated yet untranslated passages of Korean, Latin words, excerpts from citizenship examinations, and journalistic accounts of the Korean War. Historical and geographical references slide from visceral specificity to generic terminology. While the volume repeatedly deploys the vocabulary of geography—"the sea," "the fields," "gulch, mesa, peak." "The continent and the peninsula, the peninsula and the continent"—the proper names of specific locations are rarely and very strategically invoked, emphasizing both the uprooted placelessness and the selectively obsessive memory of the refugee and the emigrant. Grammatical demarcations of time are also shifting and ambiguous with past, present, and future temporalizations disrupting and then bleeding into each other. Marking its overwhelming prominence as defining historical moment, the Korean War is inscribed not in the simple past but alternately in the present and in the conditional perfect tenses, admitting the lingering effects of what Benjamin calls "a past charged by the time of the now . . . blasted out of the continuum of history" (261).[6] Furthermore, the conditional perfect and the recurrence of "if" inscribe an imaginary negotiation of all that *could have been* under different historical formations. Pronouns and adverbial markers lack clear antecedents as well as the words "it," "them," "us," "then," and "there," which literally hang at the end of each line; their ambiguous syntactical positionings seem to express the uncertainties and the sense of ruptured suspension of personal and ethnonational displacements; and then too, they appear to declare their taken-for-granted meaning within a very particular collective consciousness. Many of the lines reverse the order of subject and verb, deflating any sense of human agency; yet, they are without even the small sense of finality and clarity afforded by the question mark, further amplifying the mood of longing and curiosity wracked by doubts permeating the volume. All these details contribute to an abiding sense of estrangement from language itself, set against the historical backdrop of successive colonizations, diasporic movements, and immigrant reculturations.

The first poem in the volume, "And Sing We," begins with a compelling need for expression: "Must it ring so true/So we must sing it" (13). Although "it" lacks a definite antecedent, the volume's title suggests an anthem.[7] Emphasizing the vulnerability of the collective "we" against the ideological and sentimental weight of this nation-song, the reversed ordering of subject and verb figures national identification as congealed in and through such forceful deployments of language. This surge of patriotic spirit may be situated within the nation-state borders of the U.S. but strains those boundaries in reaching for a remote elsewhere:

To span even yawning distance
And would we be near then

What would the sea be, if we were near it (13)

The "then" concluding the second line suggests not a geographical place but a temporal moment, either in the past or a conditional future. Even though the exiles' great yearning for the homeland would extend across such an expanse, the uncertainties surrounding this gesture, phrased as interrogation and then with this object of longing marked with an unspecified "it," underscores its elusiveness. As much as this desirous singing is held out as a compelling vehicle against total estrangement—so much so that it can unsettle the sea's position as interstitial barrier—such linguistically expressive acts have their limitations. After all, the poem describing that transnational reach is written in

English, itself an unavoidable by-product and glaring sign of emigration and reculturation.

As in several other poems in the volume, the enduring insight of "And Sing We" is that while it repeatedly gestures towards Korea and Korean history, it just as persistently reminds the reader of its own situated inscription and dissemination *in the U.S.* Immediately following the expansive lines quoted above is a lone word, "Voice," off to the right side of the poem, and then: "It catches its underside and drags it back/What sounds do we make, 'n,' 'h,' 'g'/Speak and it is sound in time" (13). The possible significance of the three letters are many, but some immediate and obvious associations are *Hanguk* (Korea) or an even more intimate *naŭi Hanguk* (my Korea) and *k ohyang* (home village). Yet, the citational inscription of these letters, figured as studied borrowings rather than organic expressions, and their individualized presentation here signal their strangeness in the second English language of the exiled singers. The reaching invocation of the homeland through the anthem comes back to remind the singers of the hollow and fleeting "sound" of their singing rather than of any comforting, even if imaginary, repatriation.

In the specific case of Korean emigrants, this arduous reach across to Korea must also inevitably reckon with the invasions, losses, and transformations of the homeland that have precipitated transnational relocations in this century: "Depletion replete with barraging/Slurred and taken over/Diaspora" (13). Images of "depletion" recur in subsequent poems, most often in reference to the systematic extraction of natural resources, the mass export of Korean bodies for physical and sexual enslavement, and the concerted suppression of Korean language and culture during Japanese colonization.[8] The loss of lives, the massive destruction of social infrastructures and the mass emigrations of Koreans in search of refuge and better opportunities in the conflict-ridden decades following liberation are other historical instances of Korea's depletion. The obverse dynamic of "barraging" also appears frequently in the volume, referring to the legacy of both Japanese colonization and U.S. interventions and impositions in Korea especially, during the war: the incessant falling of "Made in America" bombs from U.S. Air Force jets, the invasive landing of the Marines at Inchon, and in a most harrowing metaphor for the lasting effects of foreign military violence against Korean civilian bodies, "An uncle with shrapnel burrowing into shinbone/for thirty years" (16). These concerted processes have rendered both "Korea" and "Koreanness" into matters of political, military, psychic, and representational struggle, and not some unequivocal fact. Finally, "slurred" and "barrage" also carry negative linguistic connotations. Both the racist, xenophobic slurs and the too quick barrage of difficult-to-comprehend English words directed at the immigrant accompany the loss and "slurring" of one's Korean fluency, impressing upon both the subject of the poem *and* the reader how any resettlement involves a corporeal and linguistic transubstantiation. More than some irrefutable sign of assimilation, the Korean immigrant's *acquisition* and *usage* of English bear the genealogical traces of war and imperial conquests.

The enduring significance of this history in *Under Flag* resists both the pressure of assimilation in the U.S. and the lure of nostalgia for Korea. The poem, "Into Such Assembly," begins with a series of coherent sentence-lines that transcribe the naturalization procedure for becoming American from the point of view of the immigration officer:

Can you read and write English? Yes___. No___.
Write down the following sentences in English as I dictate them.
  There is a dog in the road.
  It is raining.
Do you renounce allegiance to any other country but this?
Now tell me, who is the president of the United States?
You will all stand now. Raise your right hands.

By emphasizing the superficial and arbitrary criteria of language proficiency and rote memorizations of presidential names by which the immigrant would be judged, Kim demystifies the aura of political authority and finality in this procedure.

In stark contrast to its bureaucratic formality and sterility, the following stanza poses a string of sensual images:

Cable car rides over swan flecked ponds
Red lacquer chests in our slateblue house
Chrysanthemums trailing bloom after bloom
Ivory, russet, pale yellow petals crushed

This outpouring of florid details seems excessive, so dense and over-crowded that the evocative force of each word-image becomes displaced and diluted by what immediately follows. Instead of a sentimental rec-ollection, I eventually read the stanza as an impassive and ironic cata-loguing of some of the most sedimented Orientalist signifiers: swan, ponds, red lacquer, chrysanthemums, jade, thatched roofs, and the specifically Japanese *miso*. In this sense, Kim is not so much asserting an absolute and value-laden difference between sterile U.S. bureaucracy and Korean sensuality as juxtaposing two of the several competing dis-courses which impose themselves on the bilingual immigrant. Avoiding the binary trap of each extreme, the next line asserts more directly, "Neither, neither" (29); this speaker would refuse the impossible choice between the bureaucratic imperative of assimilation in the U.S. and the aestheticizing nostalgia for Korea. Concluding the page with the line, "Who is mother tongue, who is father country?"—which can also be a belated question to the doubly negative answer given in the preceding line, Kim thus resists and deconstructs the naturalizing of both language and national identity through their familial metaphorization. The large blank space that follows signals that the question of linguistic and national identity is an orphaned one, without any easy answers.

The next page-section, numbered "2," begins with a set of questions directed at the Korean immigrant that are decidedly different from those posed by the state's representative: "Do they have trees in Korea? Do the children eat out of garbage cans?" (30). Although these inquiries reveal more about the utter ignorance and stereotypical presuppositions of the speakers, that Kim re-cites them here without the disavowing interfer-ence of quotations marks signals how a Korean immigrant subject can-not cleanly repudiate such distorted "American" figurations of Korea and Koreanness. Rather, the subsequent lines demonstrate that they impinge upon and infuse her remembering of the homeland:

We had a dalmatian.
We rode the train on weekends from Seoul to So-Sah where
we grew grapes

We ate on the patio surrounded by dahlias

Over there, ass is cheap—those girls live to make you happy

Over there, we had a slateblue house with a flat roof where
I made many snowmen, over there (30)

These personal rememberings of the sensual contours of middle-class privilege "over there" rub against, without directly countering, the prevailing "American" images of Korea as an utterly alien place of geographic desolation, material deprivation, and sexual servility. Moreover, the present tense declaration that interjects itself into this reverie appears to carry more authority than the simple past tense verbs of the first-person recollection, which marks the completion of this Korean life in an irrevocable past. Childhood memory can only alternate and compete with, rather than simply and finally override, these other versions. Thus, Kim here reinscribes the war in the tensions of identifying as both "Korean" and "American". The identical prefacing of the final two lines with "Over there" allies their two speakers in the same removed location from the place that they speak of—even as its third repetition at the end of the final line emphasizes an even further estrangement for the Korean immigrant subject.

Beyond lamenting an individualistic "identity crisis," the volume locates such multiple and competing determinations of the Korean American subject position in the significant connections and continuities of the geopolitical histories of the U.S. and Korea. The title poem, "Under Flag," opens with a most declarative statement:

Is distance. If she knows it
Casting and again casting into the pond to hook the same turtle
Beset by borders, conquered, disfigured (16)

The period following "distance" is significant, for this punctuation mark appears rarely in the volume, accentuating the doubts and the often disarticulating effects of migration and acculturation. The absent subject of this copula could be inferred from the title to mean precisely the matter of national subjectification, whose guarantee of identity and political protection is posited instead as a displacement and subjugation.

However, the conditional phrase that immediately follows reframes national identification as a problem of knowledge negotiated by a geographically and temporally distanced female subject. The second and third lines locate this struggle over a coherent nationality not only in immigration, but also in the historical inheritance of imperial conquests and internal divisions preceding emigration. The "Turtle Ship" is a potent emblem of anti-imperial resistance and sovereignty in Korean national myth, but the repeated attempts to grasp that ethnic icon from a spatio-temporal distance would be rendered futile by its already deformed and indistinct contours. While poetically colorful, the metaphor of fishing is made strange by the extraordinary and incongruous details of searching for an oceanic creature in a landlocked and diminutive pond. Yet, if we consider the activity of "casting" in a more compositional sense of creating a mold, these lines could describe the bilingual emigrant's frustrating attempts to represent the Korean homeland in a foreign geographical and linguistic context. The figure of national pride becomes unraveled in reckoning with the historical facts of invasion, colonization, and diaspora.

The poem goes on to situate this difficulty within a multilayered critique of U.S. military interventions. The third stanza begins with a cryptic "Above: victims./Below: Chonhui, a typical Korean town. In the distance,/a 155-mm shell has exploded" (16). Countering the ideological and discursive apparatus that foregoes local specificities—"a typical Korean town," as if they were all the same and interchangeable and ultimately disposable—are these descriptions of both familial intimacy and individual bodies that were most likely destroyed by the shell:

Of elders who would have been sitting in the warmest part
of the house with comforters draped around their shoulders
peeling tangerines

Of an uncle with shrapnel burrowing into shinbone
for thirty years (16)

The anguish of war is not assigned to some bygone era in the simple past tense, but articulated here in the awkward and desirous temporality of the conditional perfect, imagining what "would have been" *otherwise* as in the first stanza. The active contemporaneity of "peeling" and "burrowing" further imbues these details with an interminable sense of suspension in their lasting effects. On the next page, the line "Not to have seen it but inheriting it" expresses the psychic significance of these past events and disrupted eventualities for the postwar, diasporic generation of Koreans like Kim.

Countering the pretext of "distance" which enables the disavowal of U.S.-sponsored atrocities against Korean civilians, the poem goes on to impress the active and indeed celebrated involvement of the U.S. by interweaving journalistic accounts that clearly highlight the ("heroic") deeds of the U.S.-Americans:

At dawn the next morning, firing his machine gun, Corporal Leonard H. was shot and instantly killed while stopping the Red's last attempt to overrun and take the hilltop

The demoralized ROK troops disappeared but the handful of Americans, completely surrounded, held out for seven years against continuous attack, until all ammunition was exhausted

General D.'s skillful direction of the flight was fully as memorable as his heroic personal participation with pistol and bazooka (17)

Each of these descriptions attests to the physical *proximity* of hand-to-hand combat, and they figure the "Korean War" as a field for the exercise and display of American masculinity against the alien Red Korean soldiers and the cowardly and less masculine Republican troops. Immediately after the above lines appears a litany of militaristic terms: "Grumman F9F/Bell H-130s/Shooting Stars/Flying Cheetahs" (17). These impersonally technical and cartoonish names belie their devastating capabilities, and they are followed by this ironic line: "They could handle them if they would only use the weapons we have/given them properly, said Colonel Wright." This condescending judgment on the Korean soldier's inability to "properly" use these American weapons ultimately reveals the estrangement of Korean soldiers from "their" own battles, forcing the question, "What was Korean about the Korean War?" and in turn, "What was *not* Korean about the Korean War?"⁹ While Kim thus incorporates these American narrations and technical labels with great ironic and deconstructive force, it is important to note that she does so again without the disavowing gesture of quotation marks, attesting to how they too are an inextricable part of the discursive repertoire of a Korean American writing subject.

Echoing the earlier above/below distinction, "Under Flag" refers to the postwar division of Korea into two antagonistic nation-states and the subsequent period of political suppression and social control in the name of national security. Beginning with a repetition of the declaration of distance, the final two pages are filled with the imagery of mass protests, the tear gas deployed by police, and the self-immolation of student protesters: "Is distance. If she could know it/Citizens to the streets marching/Their demands lettered in blood/The leader counters them/With gas meant to thwart any crowd's ambition/And they must scatter, white cloths over their faces" (19). The nuanced political investments of "Under Flag" go beyond a polemical denunciation of U.S. military imperialism by emphasizing the active role played by (some) Koreans in the sad course of modern history. Against the finite periodization of a "postwar" era, the poem maps an historical continuity between the painful uprooting of bodies by American weapons during the war to the state-sponsored terrorization and the resulting geographical dispersal of Koreans long after 1953. The repeated image of white cloths here suggests both the kerchiefs and gauze masks sported by protesters and other civilians to shield themselves against the tear gas as well as large, billowing political banners at mass rallies. However, rather than the chaos of war, Kim points to the systematic and rehearsed nature of the postwar drills to prepare for the imminent bombing and invasion of South Korea by North Korea:

Every month on the 15th, there is an air raid drill sometime during the day, lasting approximately 15 minutes. When the siren goes off, everyone must get off the streets. An all clear siren marks the end of the drill.

Along with the narrations of American military heroism, these peculiar "instructions" are another of the heterogeneous discourses that inform the Korean immigrant and they interpose any effort to remember and represent the Korean "homeland."

Refusing the officially disseminated paranoia which would justify national division, Kim follows up the instructions with this question: "And how long practice how long drill to subvert what borders are" (18). The subversion in process is not traitorous to the nation but state-sponsored, not so much defending but mystifying the arbitrary absurdities of intranational divisions, especially in the occult spatiality of the *two* Koreas. The following page describes this tragic estrangement of Koreans from Koreans and imagines a possible reconciliation:

> What must we call each other if we meet there
> Brother sister neighbor lover go unsaid what we are
> Tens of thousands of names
> Go unsaid the family name (19)

The compulsory "must," recalling the forceful quality of linguistic identification in the opening lines of the volume, seems inappropriate in light of the subsequent conditional phrase with its unspecified "there." Against the arbitrary designation of the boundary between north and south, Kim refigures this "demilitarized zone" not as an unassailable barrier but as a mid-point, a negotiated place of familial reunions. It is perhaps in an indeterminate Korean American space—removed from both the comforting certainty of native birth but also the immediate paranoia of intranational division—that we can reconsider the rigid binaries of North-South, of Korea-U.S. and stake out some possibilities of home beyond the fantasies of an uninterrupted wholeness.

The historical linkages between a colonized Korean past and a present location in the U.S. take on specific gender inflections in the poem "Body as One as History." The poem opens with matter-of-fact declarations that recall the patriarchal idealizations of woman as life source: "Weight of breasts or milk and all blood/This is a tree. It bears fruit." The two short clipped sentences recite the conventional arboreal metaphorizations of the female body, which work to naturalize its assigned role in socioeconomic reproduction, but their flat tone and terse diction achieve a parodic effect. This cluster of lines concludes on a more resolute denial of any essential feminine abundance and nurturance, asserting instead an active pretense and performance: "This is the body feigning. It is large as I." While this comparison appears at first glance to be an affirmation aligning this bountiful body with the first-person speaker of these lines, it can also be read as further deconstructing this figuration by equating it with the small size and aural brevity of a singular vowel.

From that reduction, the next four lines of the poem take on an increasingly tense and dreary tone: "Time rage, churn of one part and another/Nothing to succor what is dense and fragile at the same time/Inaudible collapse/Given the body's size, size for a grave" (35).[10] The implications of decomposition and death become more and more grotesque and menacing: "Polyps, cysts, hemorrhages, dribbly discharges, fish stink/Skin, registering bruise or touch/But the body streaked black across a red brick wall/The body large as I, larger" (35). The flip side of the idealization of the nurturing female body is the fear and loathing of that same gendered body that associates it with disease and decay. Against both the positively and negatively charged organic associations, the startling final image of body against wall shifts the causes of bodily damage from a natural, biological process to a more deliberate act of violence against women, locating the female body in the realm of history and politics.

The body that is "larger" than the personal pronoun, "I," is not the poet's but precisely the collective body of Korean women as they have lived out this tumultuous recent history. Set off from the beginning by their more dense arrangement, the following three stanzas of the poem traverse a wide spatio-temporal span of Korean women's attempts at survival:

Save the water from rinsing rice for sleek hair
This is what the young women are told, then they're told
Cut off this hair that cedar combs combed (35)

The initial folk remedy of feminine beautification abruptly shifts into increasingly paranoid directives for the young women to purposefully dishevel and de-gender themselves to avoid rape: "Empty straw sacks and hide under them/Enemy soldiers are approaching, are near" (35). As with the "Turtle Ship," any attempt to recuperate some organic ideal of Korean womanhood runs into the ruptures of history, in this case, sexual and physical survival under foreign invasions and civil war.

The following page continues on with this prosaic paragraph structure, but in contrast to the air of alarm about sexual vulnerability in the preceding passage, the references to Korean women here emphasize their fortitude and resourcefulness against the backdrop of war and deprivation:

And in this way she tried to keep them alive—two dried anchovies for each child and none for herself. The train gathering speed. And with no words but a thrust of a fist holding out money the soldiers stroke their penises cup their balls, push stripped plastic dolls with black ink scratched on between the hard twig legs into her face.

This section presents one of the clearest instances of a female subject in the entire volume, but the relationship between the "she" here and the "young women" in the preceding paragraph is not clearly suggested. The courage and self-sacrifice of this mother are also challenged by the gestures of sexual aggression. While the words "stripped" and "plastic" echo earlier references to colonization, war, and civil disturbance, the perverted marking of the dolls and the aggressive gestures of the men in uniform amidst the panic of war evacuation offer up a disturbing illustration of how even such chaotic circumstances are inflected with the uneven operations of gender and sexuality.

From these vivid yet scattered details of war, the poem shifts in time and space to garment production in the U.S., which has been a common line of work for Korean immigrant women:

Treadle needle tread thread. Left armhole, right bodice. Cotton rayon nylon dust. The crouch of the mother over machine over a child's winter coat over a stream rinsing diapers when night falls while the soldiers ranged while the border loomed and she crossed it. Over a blouse 3 cents over a skirt 5 cents and in this way (35)

264

The visually and aurally similar four words at the beginning are linked in their association with sewing, but the paragraph becomes increasingly confusing as to their temporal and geographical referent. While commonly related to the operation of a machine, "treadle" and "thread" also have other suggestive meanings. Treadle can be used as a verb meaning "to tread over." While tread commonly means "to step or walk on," it also has the more active valence of "to subdue, suppress, conquer." In this vein, both words could be related to the historical legacy of colonization, but also to the subordination of women under both Korean and American patriarchal structures as well as to the economic exploitation of immigrant female labor in the U.S. The repeated preposition, "over," collapses garment piecework to child care to domestic work before and during the war. The similarity of "crouching over" a sewing machine and "crossing over" a heavily policed border connects this history for Korean immigrant women who have had to endure the traumas of military invasion, transnational migration, and economic exploitation in the U.S. This is the collective legacy of Korean women to which the "I" will lay claim as the next line asserts a collective "we": "This is the body as we live it. Large as I. Large as." The twice repeated phrase "large as" reads as "largesse," locating the munificence of the female body, not in the biological but in the historical legacy of female survival under war, immigration, and socioeconomic marginalization.

II

Myung Mi Kim's exploration of Korean history through experimental yet exacting deployments of language resonates with Theresa Hak Kyung Cha's remarkable 1982 book, *DICTEE*.[11] Like *Under Flag*, this multiform text expresses a strong investment in the history of Korea's successive colonizations and internal conflicts as it interrelates Cha's own history of cultural and geographical displacement with a series of prior intranational divisions and multinational dispersals of Koreans. Comprised of seemingly discontinuous sections that incorporate the languages of "American" citizenship, French Catholicism, Greek mythology, Chinese philosophy as well as visual images ranging from film stills, historical photographs, maps, and physiological diagrams, *DICTEE* can be read as a painful and skillful exercise in constructing a book-object out of the irreconcilable fragments of one Korean woman's criss-crossed trajectory of dislocations.

The page numbered one in *DICTEE* contains two paragraphs of dictation, the first written in French and the second in English. The passages describe a sparse verbal exchange in French and then in English between a traveler—a displaced female subject—and the "natives." They present the difficulty of proper articulation in a new environment as the woman cannot answer a seemingly innocent query—"How was the first day?" While it may be intended as an innocuously interested question about the inaugural moment of immigration and resettlement, the very fact of asking and any possible response can only reinforce the difference between the transplanted female and the local "families," not unlike the more overtly alienating questions and offensive comments re-cited in Kim's "Into Such Assembly." The narrator's response to the inquiry about her first day is that

> at least to say the least of it possible comma the answer would be open quotation marks there is but one thing period. There is someone period From a far period close quotation marks (1)

In appropriately halting and fragmented fashion, this Korean female migrant in the U.S. and France finds it nearly impossible to talk about her impressions of her new environment without having to assert her foreign origins. But her response ("There is someone. From a far.") simultaneously marks her distance and separation from her putative origins. This "a far" reverberates with the "distance" that repetitiously locates the homeland in *Under Flag*.

As in Kim's poetry, *DICTEE* holds the impossibility of assimilation in constant tension with an acknowledgment of the impossibility of an easy and immediate return to a pure Korean space with its mother tongue. After years of living abroad, the female subject returns only to declare her difference in this originary context: "I speak in another tongue now, a second tongue a foreign tongue" (80). If the acquisition of another tongue is difficult and never complete, neither can the Korean American retain and simply resume the fluent use of an unadulterated Korean native language. Punctuated by suspicious queries and constant misunderstandings, going "back home" is itself replete with silencing and alienating exchanges between the returned emigrant and the "local" Koreans:

> You return and you are not one of them, they treat you with indifference. All the time you understand what they are saying. But the papers give you away. Every ten feet. They ask you identity. They comment upon your ability and inability to speak. Whether you are telling the truth or not about your nationality. They say you look other than you say. As if you didn't know who you were. You say who you are, but you begin to doubt. (57)

There is just another undeniable breach between the female traveler and the English and French-speaking "local" families. Against the assumptions of ethnicity as pre-given, fixed, and affiliated with one corresponding language, the passage powerfully impresses how tenacious associations of language and identity are further complicated and not muted by transnational migrations and resettlements. Rather than some solitarily interiorized "I," the alternately accusatory and hypothetical "you" in this passage interpolates the reader in these unequal and unsettling dynamics of social judgment:

> Not a single word allowed to utter until the last station, they ask to check the baggage. You open your mouth half way. Near tears, nearly saying, I know you I know you, I have waited to see you for this long. They check each article, question you on foreign articles, then dismiss you. (58)

The confusion of pronominal positions here where "you" slips into "I" and "they" slips into and out of "you" echoes the grammatical ambiguities in *Under Flag*. Such contingencies of identity and identification are not cause for a celebration of fluidity but painful states of estrangement and longing, which are often bureaucratically mediated and enforced.

If a literal return to the homeland is thus attenuated, the book attempts a discursive re-territorialization through innovative reinscriptions of Korean history. Sections throughout evoke the period of Japanese colonial rule, the resulting emigration of Koreans to

Manchuria, Japan, and the U.S., the Korean War, and the long period of social and political unrest following the partition. Having indelibly shaped the experiences of her mother as a young exile in Manchuria, her brother's involvement in the student protests for democratization in 1960, and the family's emigration to the U.S., these events are recalled as prominent aspects of Cha's own genealogy. Against the reduction of these historical episodes as having happened to other people at another time, Cha's recountings powerfully testify to their enduring transnational and transhistorical significance, emphasizing the disruptive and alienating effects that continue to shape this Korean immigrant woman writing out of the U.S. in 1982.

What makes *DICTEE*'s writing of Korean history brilliant is that it draws critical attention to itself as a situated discursive production that illuminates and also occludes certain aspects. Like Kim's heterogeneous and paradoxical accountings of the Korean War, the section titled "CLIO HISTORY" works through the historiographical dilemma for a Korean American subject who can gain access to Korean history by way of previously written descriptions and historiographical treatments existing in English. The section includes lengthy citations of three unidentified accounts, all ostensibly written by non-Koreans, describing the Japanese colonial domination of Korea. The second account is set off with two sets of quotation marks, signaling the book's re-citation as a third-hand account. For the task of redressing an episode, event, or person that has been excluded from or marginalized in prior histories, this Korean immigrant historiographer must "take on" those other accountings that have contributed to that erasure. There is no clean detour from this web of writings that she must refer to even as she seeks to contest their documents, each of them a partial production shaped by the specific conditions of their own writing. Furthermore, whatever information is gathered from records, monuments, archives, and primary and secondary texts must be synthesized, ordered, and re-narrated in a *present* act of inscription, which is impelled precisely by the inadequacy of preceding versions. Indeed, the contending narrative about Yu Guan Soon, interjected in the midst of these re-citations, is written in the present indicative tense and utilizes the more intimate and informal first name of the young Korean female patriot: "Guan Soon forms a resistant

group with fellow students and actively begins her revolutionary work"
(30). Such telling imbues these actions and events with a contemporary
vitality, even as its transgression of historiographical conventions draws
critical attention to its own constructedness as well as the naturalized
deployment of the past tense in other accounts.

Cha's critical reflections on twentieth century Korean history are as
much concerned with an effective language of communicating across
geopolitical distances as with memorializing a specific past. A crucial
question raised is the lack of foreign intervention into Japanese colonial
atrocities given the fact that "eye-witness accounts" were available. In
raising that question, she takes this concern about effective communication and the necessity of intervention beyond the narrow geopolitical
boundaries of a solely "Korean" problem:

> To the other nations who are not witnesses, who are not subject to the
> same oppressions, they cannot know. Unfathomable the words, the ter-
> minology: enemy, atrocities, conquest, betrayal, invasion, destruction.
> They exist only in the larger perception of History's recording, that
> affirmed, admittedly and unmistakably, one enemy nation has disre-
> garded the humanity of another. Not physical enough. Not to the very
> flesh and bone, to the core, to the mark, to the point where it is neces-
> sary to intervene, even if to invent anew, new expressions, for this expe-
> rience, for this outcome, that does not cease to continue.
>
> To the others, these accounts are about (one more) distant land, like
> (any other) distant land, without any discernible features in the narra-
> tive, (all the same) distant like any other.

The repeated deployment of the word "distant" works against the
rationale of noninvolvement and the disclaimer of nonaccountability.

Against such generic distancing, Cha would interconnect this history
of Korea to U.S. history, specifically through re-calling the early Korean
immigrant community by full insertion of the "PETITION FROM
THE KOREANS OF HAWAII TO PRESIDENT ROOSEVELT" into
her text. Written in Honolulu and dated July 12, 1905, the letter presents a painfully polite and often awkward written request by the Korean
immigrant community for the Roosevelt administration to intervene on
behalf of Korean independence. We know today that the Roosevelt
administration did not respond positively to this request, instead going

on to sign the Gentleman's Agreement with Japan. The U.S. continued to consider and classify Koreans as "Japanese" nationals, subjecting them to the same immigration laws. Given this implicit affirmation of Japanese colonial rule, it is a most cruel historical irony that the U.S. is figured as one of the "liberators." As much as it is an indictment of such contradictory policies and actions, the most remarkable function of this transnational petition is to reveal the significant overlaps amongst the histories of Korea, U.S., and the "Korean American" community in this century. Cha thus allies her separation from and abiding commitment to the Korean homeland with these early immigrants.

As it contracts geopolitical boundaries, *DICTEE* also troubles temporal distinctions. Rather than accepting the relegation of Japanese colonization and the Korean War into the remote and finite past, these events are reinscribed in terms of their lingering significance in the present. Borrowing from the old journals of Cha's mother, Hyung Soon Huo, the "Calliope/Epic Poetry" section reinscribes the mother's exile from the colonized Korean homeland as an important pretext for the daughter's later emigration to the U.S. Significantly, this narration begins at the moment of the mother's relocation away from her natal family to teach under the dictates of the Japanese imperial regime:

> Mother you are eighteen. It is 1940. You have just graduated from a teacher's college. You are going to your first teaching post in a small village in the country. You are required by the government of Manchuria to teach for three years in an assigned post, to repay the loan they provided for you to attend the school. You are hardly an adult. You have never left your mother's, father's home. (48)

In lieu of the conventionally disinterested or laudatory third-person, past-tense narration, the present-tense, second-person address reads as alternately commanding and imaginary, in both cases significantly problematizing it as a mimetic description of past events. This awkward locution also testifies to the formative inflections and exclusions of gender in historical accountings. Belying the heroic and masculinist self-importance of epic poetry, this telling connects to a multilocational genealogy of female resilience and resistance.

The mother's exilic history and eventual return to the homeland are again invoked in the "Melpomene/Tragedy" section. Written in the form of a letter addressed to the mother on a return visit to Korea eighteen years after emigrating:

Dear Mother,

4.19. Four Nineteen, April 19th, eighteen years later. Nothing has changed, we are at a standstill. I speak in another tongue now, a second tongue a foreign tongue. All this time we have been away. But nothing has changed. A stand still.

It is not 6.25. Six twenty five. June 25th 1950. Not today. Not this day. There are no bombs as you had described them. They do not fall, their shiny brown metallic backs like insects one by one after another. (80)

Recalling two prominently memorialized moments of modern history in the Korean practice of numbering the month and day, these opening paragraphs alternately emphasize the present differences from *and* the continuities with these past events. This Korean daughter's sober and alienated homecoming is set in stark contrast to the mother's hopeful and exuberant return upon "liberation" from Japanese colonization:

You knew it would not be in vain. The thirty six years of exile. Thirty six years multiplied by three hundred and sixty five days. That one day your country would be your own. This day did finally come. The Japanese were defeated in the world war and were making their descent back to their country. As soon as you heard, you followed South. You carried not a single piece, not a photograph, nothing to evoke your memory, abandoned all to see your nation freed. (80–88)

Such expansive dreams of a free homeland would be soon undercut by national division and civil unrest, which imposed the nation's self-alienation all over again. Rather than a linear progression of exile and return, colonization and liberation, the letter goes on to declare a frustratingly recursive stasis:

Our destination is fixed on the perpetual motion of search. Fixed in its perpetual exile. Here at my return in eighteen years, the war is not ended. We fight the same war. We are inside the same struggle seeking

271

the same destination. We are severed in Two by an abstract enemy an invisible enemy under the title of liberators who have conveniently named the severance, Civil War. Cold War. Stalemate. (81)

Within such a collective legacy, the daughter of the exile is also frustrated in her desire for a definitive reconciliation with the homeland. Finding herself in the midst of a student protest for democratization that turns into a violent clash with the U.S.-backed Korean military, the letter recalls the mother's attempts to dissuade the brother from joining the student-led protests of 1960. It then goes on to focus on the tragic irony of Korean military men suppressing fellow Korean student demonstrators:

> The students. I saw them, older than us, men and women held to each other. They walk into the others who wait in their uniforms. Their shouts reach a crescendo as they approach nearer to the other side. Cries resisting cries to move forward. Orders, permission to use force against the students, have been dispatched. To be caught and beaten with sticks, and for others, shot, remassed, and carted off. They fall they bleed they die. They are thrown into gas into the crowd to be squelched. The police the soldiers anonymous they duplicate themselves, multiply in number invincible they execute their role. Further than their home further than their mother father their brother sister further than their children is the execution of their role their given identity further than their own line of blood. (83–4)

The unspecified deployment of "they" and "others" in this passage points to both the anonymity and the convergence of the supposedly oppositional groups engaged in this chaotic clash. The estrangement of the soldiers from their "own line of blood," echoing the displacement of the exile, demonstrates the vulnerability and fluidity of such fixed, biological ties. However, this alienation is not an unavoidable stage of individuation but is a "given identity"—the effect of consciously dispatched orders from above. While the section is critical towards the actions of the police and soldiers, a later passage describes them as acting out of certain patriotic concerns just as the students think of themselves as radical nationalists: "You are your post you are your vow in nomine patris you work your post you are your nation defending your country from your own countrymen" (86). This adversarial positioning of Korean against

Korean, the division of the country in two, the continuing effects of colonization and the immigrant's sense of splitting in displacement are
interconnected.

It is precisely *within* such internal tensions and contestations that
this Korean American subject locates herself most assuredly. In contrast
to the moments of the book detailing the linguistic barriers and bureaucratic mediations that mark her irrevocable estrangement from the
Korean homeland, Cha declares the most confident Korean identification in these terms:

> I am in the same crowd, the same coup, the same revolt, nothing has
> changed. I am inside the demonstration I am locked inside the crowd
> and carried in its movement. (81)

This first-person accounting with its double repetition of "in" and
"inside" offers a stark contrast to the earlier repudiations of the returning
emigrant (57). Under such circumstances, the unified security of a singular "home" is a cruel and untenable myth. Against the linear, bipolar
axis of emigration and return, homeland and host country, *DICTEE* con-
figures a much more flexuous genealogy for this Korean American female
subject. Through this writing of herself inside the reflection upon and the
reinscription of a multiply fragmented Korean history and people,
DICTEE rejects the historicist and exclusive terms of national identification on both sides of the shifting U.S.-Korea border.

III

Theresa Hak Kyung Cha also explored many of these issues of memory,
language, and displacement in her films and videos. As with her critical
engagement with language and textual production in *DICTEE*, Cha's
film/video works attempt to expose the structuring and operation of the
visual media while expressing strong emotional investments and fraught
psychic struggles. In the "Preface" to a collection of essays on film theory
she edited in 1989, Cha wrote:

> The selection of works was made to approach the subject from theoret-

ical directions synchronously with work of filmmakers who address and incorporate the apparatus—the function of film, the film's author, the effects produced on the viewer while viewing film—as an integral part of their work, and to turn backwards and call upon the machinery that creates the impression of reality whose function, inherent in its very medium, is to conceal from its spectator the relationship of the viewer/subject to the work being viewed.[12]

In keeping with such a commitment to the demystification of the naturalizing and suturing powers of film/video, Cha's works deploy a range of experimental practices such as stark imagery devoid of any readily identifiable social context, extreme close-ups, and slow dissolves of repetitious yet nonidentical still images, which challenge the viewer's will for immediate and singular meaning. As Lawrence Rinder writes:

> All of Cha's videos and films are black-and-white and, with a few exceptions, consists entirely of sequences of still images and words. The slow fades and pans by which Cha often moves from one image to the next create a feeling of extreme attenuation in which the viewer's attention is drawn to the spaces and moments in between what is actually perceived.[13]

Even as the works critically engage the unique properties of visual media, they deal closely with both written and spoken languages. Many images are of words—some of them are common and readily meaningful while others are willful distortions of various French and English words—and even single letters that force the viewer's attention to the look of language, the peculiar geometry of the alphabet in different combinations beyond any immediate and obvious sociocultural meaning. By thus estranging letters and words, the films seem to express the Korean immigrant's struggles with a new language while impelling a critical reconsideration of the terms of familiarity and comprehensibility for the viewer, who too must approach these linguistic markings much like a displaced immigrant. *Mouth to Mouth,* made in 1976, opens with a slow pan of the vowels of Hangŭl (the Korean alphabet). It then goes to a watery image of an extreme close-up of the blurred outlines of a mouth, shaping itself into the Korean vowel sounds. In 1978, Cha finished *Passages/Paysages,* a black-and-white video installation on three monitors that incorporates voice-over audio in French, English, and

Korean. A complex meditation on the elusiveness of memory and language amidst the passing of time as well as spatial dislocations, the piece incorporates images of letters and telegrams as well as several voice-over readings of various communications, including one written in Korean by her mother to Cha, expressing the mother's momentarily muted longing for her *kohyang*. A later image shows a hand holding an old black-and-white photograph of Cha as a young girl with her mother at a premigratory moment of togetherness.

Cha's final video/film work, *EXILÉE*, completed in 1981, is most explicit in its exploration of the dynamics of displacement, cast here in the face of an expectant yet doubtful return to the Korean homeland. Revolving centrally around the ambivalent play of memory and anticipation, the piece is a highly fraught and fragmented meditation upon the temporal and spatial disjunction between the U.S. and Korea. It was originally screened as part of a three-channel installation that included a large screen for film projection, a video monitor cut into the center of the film screen, and an audio track of Cha's voice-over.[14] The film screen shows two images, one of a plant in shadow, which draws attention to the play of light and darkness in cinematic projection, and the other image of looking out a windowsill with the white curtains billowing in the wind. Even though the camera is stationary, the movement of the curtains within the frame captures the paradoxical sense of inhibited mobility and unmoored placelessness of exile. While the integration of the three elements—film screen, video monitor, and audio track—alternately complement and compete with each other for the viewer's attention and should be experienced together for full effect, the following explications will focus on the video and audio elements.

EXILÉE opens by asserting the anonymity and the alienating, forceful identifications of transnational migration. The very title of the piece is an odd combination of French and English designations for the displaced personae. On the video monitor, we first see a truncated, "E X I L," which dissolves slowly into " E X I L É"; the exact alignment of these two word-images creates the illusion of the "É" fading into its designated spot. This is followed by a series of other isolated letter-images— "I L E" to a lone "E" to the final slide of "É E" that slowly fades out to a blank whiteness. This perplexing sequence renders strange the very word and figure of modern displacement *par excellence*. At the same time, the deliberately isolated and (re)grouped letters echo the desolate unmooring and multiple fragmentations of the exile as she is subject to a new system of seemingly arbitrary signs and bewildering identifications. The accompanying voice-over unfolds this litany of (un)namings: "before. before name. none other. none other than given. last. absent. first. name. without name. a no name. no name. between name. absent name. named." These varying conditions of identity and anonymity are followed by a stark image of a thick, black brush-stroked X dissolving slowly into another, slightly different X. The X signals the intersection of two distinct and perpendicular trajectories. Taken as a crossing out or a deletion, the X also signals the deracination of the exile over a long period of separation. However, the X can also signify the multiplication of subject-positions in diaspora, beyond a bimodal binary of "home" and "host," native and foreigner. As Cha voices at a later moment, "twice two times two times two. one on top below another one." This endless proliferation displaces the hierarchical binary that privileges one locality as more authentic, more liberatory, more homelike and enforces an absolute choice between two national identifications.

This indefinite multiplicity of identifications is cast in the uncertain spatio-temporal location of the migrant subject, who simultaneously straddles several incommensurable places, cultures, and histories. Consequently, many images and voice-over incantations highlight various examples of liminality. In addition to the curtained window in the film channel, the video monitor projects various threshold images of a paper screen, the doors of a cabinet, a stepped entryway with a carefully positioned row of shoes, and a shot looking in from outside through a pulled-down shade. The window, which permits a certain access to another side yet asserts an equally concrete separation, metaphorically captures the racialized immigrant woman's state of being simultaneously inside and outside several different times and places. The voice-over invokes the spatial markers of "inside," "outside," and "between" throughout, challenging the absolute demarcations of space.

The most resonant images of demarcation and crossing gesture to a transoceanic passage between U.S. and Korea. Several shots of a cloud-filled sky during daylight and at night as well as the still image of a row of pristinely covered but unoccupied seats inside an airplane convey the strange sense of suspension in movement of this trans-oceanic passage. The constantly shifting geographical position of being mid-flight is powerfully captured in the voice-over and the corresponding word-images that steadily count off each of the minutes to arrival:

ten hours and twenty three minuits
sixteen hours ahead of this time

ten hours and twenty two minuits
sixteen hours ahead of this time

ten hours and twenty one minuit
sixteen hours ahead of this time

The strenuously measured anticipation of arrival is regularly undermined by the need to keep in mind the large time difference between Korea and the U.S. The inexplicable spelling of "minuits" and the rendering of twenty-one minutes in the singular imbue a sense of misrecognition to this too eager waiting. The temporal disjunction that remains a constant sixteen-hour difference irrespective of geographical location exacerbates the sense of separation. The paradoxically ambiguous and taken-for-granted designation of "this time" repeatedly brings this traveling subject "backwards" to her point of departure in the U.S. rather than projecting her ahead to the originary homeland of Korea. The doubling movement of "backwards/from the way backwards," pointing to another, preceding transzonal migration from Korea to the U.S., whose accompanying incantation would have been "16 hours *behind* this time," nicely challenges the progressive teleology of immigration to the U.S. In persistently locating the point of departure in the U.S., this chant problematizes any easy definition of "home" and "origin." Finally, within this eccentric time-space of the returning emigrant, when does "this time" shift to "16 hours behind" that other time? At which point is the returning subject more *there* than *here*? The time lag mirrors and reinforces the many years' long time-lag separation of exile.

The anticipatory chant is accompanied by a series of still images on the video channel: laundry drying outdoors, shoes placed on the entry-way steps, an iron tea kettle and matching cup, a white envelope with white powder spilling outside of it, a white rice bowl. Some of these images evoke for me the details of everyday life that linger in my own memories of childhood in Korea. While they can be considered as domestic images, they are not allied with a corresponding female body. Indeed, their decontextualized composition—the images shot often in close-up are devoid of a more clear sense of their location—lacks a sense of vitality. Even though they are signs of a domestic life, there are no traces of persons, accentuating a sense of absence as well as their status as photographic staging, constructed out of both memory and imaginary projection. Some of these aestheticized images, especially the row of shoes, the tea kettle and cup, or the *shoji* screen, could also be considered as rather conventional, even clichéd signifiers of the "Orient" that resonate with Myung Mi Kim's litany of aesthetic nostalgia.[15] Yet, in this specific audio visual milieu of an installation by a Korean immigrant woman, Cha's highly stylized lighting and framing of these objects challenges those earlier naturalistic reproductions of the "Orient" and provokes a reconsideration of the complex history and cultural politics that have rendered them as such stereotypically "Orientalist" images. Another possible reading would be to cast them in the context of a Korean immigrant, who can gain access to the past through this strange web of memory, desire, and the narratives and images available to her through the occluded and distorted American cultural projections of the Orient: "the only scene from the outside was imagined. was shaded in. was left unmarked. was dreamed. was erased. was fantasy. was phantom."

As in *DICTEE*, *EXILÉE* expresses a difficult tension between erosion and tenacious survival of this attachment in the face of lengthy separations; there is an equal, simultaneous emphasis on "effacement," "abolition," and "ablution," on the one hand, and "trace," "remnant," and "souvenir" on the other. Even while she is thus eagerly anticipating her return arrival, *EXILÉE* is also careful to remind the viewer that this Korean female is traveling with a U.S. passport. Images of each of the following identifications are slowly dissolved into and out of each other: "name-nom," "sex-sexe," "permanent residence–lieu de residence," "birthplace–lieu de naissance," as well as for "husband-wife" and for "minors." That this return must be thus bureaucratically authorized in the two adopted languages of English and French shows how this Korean emigrant has been irrevocably transformed in the interim period and returns as a different subject. The voice-over chants—"moved on towards time. continued to disappear little by little in parts from limb to limb. just to the end and towards the end. over again. little by little. in pieces." It soberingly marks both change and loss and ultimately interrogates the memories and expectations behind the desire for reunion expressed so viscerally in the earlier part of the film. The film ends with the frames of two phrases: "RE NAME" and "TWICE over." The declaration of mediations and reconstruction will themselves be called into question again, as the entire sequence is itself repeated a second time. While seemingly identical, there are significant differences, additions, and omissions in the second half. The accenting and ordering of the incantations and images are rearranged, so that there are new silences to be contemplated and new connections to be gleaned, pointing out the unreliability of memory.

While both *DICTEE* and *EXILÉE* persistently point to the manifold inaccessibility of a Korean home for a Korean American immigrant woman, their mournful reflections risk dissolving the specificities of the Korean history of colonizations, divisions, and global scatterings into a generic discourse of war, postcoloniality, diaspora, exile, and postmodern fragmentation. Even the deeply moving account of the emigrant's return to a still divided and violence-filled Korean homeland and her repudiation by local residents and officials in *DICTEE* tends towards a level of abstraction, wherein the complicated and unequal international and domestic political economy that undergirds the entire return experience is not considered. For example, the interactions of native Koreans and returned Korean Americans turn on many other socioeconomic axes beyond ethnicity and language and take place in a variety of strained and incommensurable settings beyond the customs gate.

On this note of socioeconomic difference, I turn finally to Kim Su Theiler's 1993 experimental film, *Great Girl*, which locate the struggles of return and remembrance in varying material circumstances that highlight socioeconomic inequalities of gender, class, and sexuality amongst Koreans and, even more specifically, amongst Korean American women.

IV

As an emerging filmmaker, Kim Su Theiler is of that generation of diasporic Koreans whose cinematic frame of reference bears the influential traces of filmmakers such as Theresa Hak Kyung Cha and Trinh T. Minh-ha. The experimental techniques of Theiler's stunning 1993 16mm short film *Great Girl* could also be attributed to its subject matter, of a Korean American adoptee attempting to piece together a tenuous connection to Korea from the fragments of memory, crude anecdotes, hearsay, chance encounters with strangers, bureaucratic documents, and American popular culture. The elusiveness of a Korean identity in such a context of near total severance of cultural and familial connections is expressed in the film's heterogeneous and often disorienting form, which combines jarring cuts, colored tints, dramatic stagings of select movements against stark backdrops, obviously artificial model landscapes, and disjunctions between the audio and the images. An actress, Anita Chao, credited as "K. aka Cho Suk Hi," performs the roles of two central female figures in the piece. K. is a young adult with long hair, made-up face and brash speech and mannerisms, the initial possibly a veiled reference to the filmmaker's first name. Cho Suk Hi is portrayed with a shoulder-length bob much like the photo in an adoption document and dressed in a series of clothing reminiscent of young Korean girls. Referencing the lower spatiality of everyday Korean life and the viewpoint of a child, the camera is usually positioned at a low angle. Despite these self-conscious and alienating deployments of the cinematic apparatus, there are also evocative moments that attest to the power of memory and the desire to locate a Korean identity and home. In one sequence of the little girl playing by herself on some steps, the voice-over reinforces the girl's isolation by declaring that the "other kids didn't like me," only to be followed by a haunting rendering of a common Korean childhood ditty, "San-to-kki."

Great Girl opens with a blue-tinted shot of fabric flapping in the wind. This curious image, replayed several times throughout the film, is revealed later as the curtains of a bus in motion. The fluttering curtain and the row of seats, covered at the top by white fabric, are reminiscent of the images of Theresa Hak Kyung Cha's *EXILÉE,* but unlike the stark placelessness of Cha's imagery, the moving window allows glimpses of the passing landscape. The second and more referential image is the adoption document of a young Korean girl, which identifies her as having, among other physical characteristics, a "Yellow" complexion and also notes her "Discovery Place and Date." The title of the film is then flashed in three languages; besides the English "*Great Girl*," there are the Korean characters Sok Hee and the commensurate Chinese characters.

The Korean adoptee's separation from the homeland is a peculiarly fraught one, in which the possibility of "return" is laden with uncertainty and struggle. The audience learns of her return and attempts to retrace her past first through confusing voice-over conversations between a young, English-speaking woman, her Korean translator, and a group of Korean residents about her possible identity and their confused and contending memories of who she could be and where she could have lived as a child. In the earlier inquisition with a Korean man, about the orphanage she possibly stayed in before emigrating, the translator tells the adoptee in broken English, "There's not exist, so not important" to which she responds, "But it exists in my mind . . . you know . . . it's the only documentation." In a later exchange, two Korean women attempt to recall whether she could be the girl that they once knew as a child. When the Korean American adoptee expresses her frustration and difficulty of comprehension, all that the translator relates to her is this puzzling but suggestive phrase, "You were very white and white." The women also say that she was called by different names, Suk Hi and Soon Mi, further exacerbating her confusion and the linguistic gulf that separates her from these other Korean women.

Accompanying these unseen conversations are shots of K. performing two activities differently associated with Korean womanhood. In the first scene that follows the opening titles, K. is sitting on the floor peeling apples on a low Korean *pabsang* covered with pages of a Korean newspaper. She proceeds to cut the apple into bite-sized pieces and place them on a serving plate. This activity commonly associated with a refined Korean femininity is performed with an awkwardness—the peelings are thick and the pieces are misshapen—that suggests both her desire and inability to "be a Korean woman." The lone, stark setting of this performance denaturalizes these tasks, and not just for the culturally estranged Korean female adoptee. The second sequence of actions

begins with an overhead shot of K. cutting off her hair, eventually showing the entire floor space around her to be covered by the shorn locks.
It then proceeds to a low-angle close-up of K. sweeping the hair up.
Suggesting the fragmentation, loss, and recuperation of a Korean female
identity for the adoptee, these images could be taken to signify various
things, including the practice of poor Korean women who cut and sold
their hair in the postwar era of poverty as well as a later reference to the
mother's job as an *ibalsa*.

The film's following sequence occurs in an interview setting with
Cho Suk Hi, here dressed in what looks like a schoolgirl uniform of a
white blouse and black blazer, which offers a clear contrast to the stark
white backdrop. While the framing is a conventional medium close-up
of the interviewee's head and shoulders, the decontextualized setting and
the slightly asynchronous audio track recall the experimental techniques
of Trinh Minh-ha's *Surname Viet, Given Name Nam*. The distant and
echo-like voice-over begins: "My name was Cho Suk Hi. I went to
Tongduch'ŏn to see if I can find out information about my orphanage
and my mother." Although she addresses the camera directly, her hesi-
tant tone of voice and nervous mannerisms betray a vulnerability. The
voice-over goes on to describe a series of new clues from various people
as well as new frustrations in the attempt to gather information. A city
reporter leads her to the gardener of her orphanage who leads her indi-
rectly to the vice president of a hotel who "thinks he knows a woman
who could be my mother." But this too proves to be more confusing
than enlightening:

> When this woman and I meet, we don't recognize the other. Just to
> make sure, she circles around to see the other side of my face. Her
> daughter had gotten a scar from a bicycle accident.

In the accompanying close-up shot, Cho Suk Hi does not mouth the
words but begins to brush her hair to one side as the camera circles
around to the viewer's left. While this camera movement mimics the
motion of the woman-mother, rather than intensifying identification
and emotional investment, this moment of (possible) rediscovery and
reunion is revealed as a cinematic construction as the film's camera crew
is now slowly brought into our field of vision.

In profile, K. recites various occupations in Korean and in English as she looks forlornly off into space. When she says, "doctor," she looks down to check a cheat sheet in her hands, betraying a lack of fluency in Korean as well as a doubtful attitude about this respected profession in particular. The shadowy lighting and half-turned face reinforce the mood of uncertainty. This shot is intercut with a frontal head shot of K. under harsh white lighting, with a lone bulb hanging to the right. Speaking with more confidence, she begins, "Well, when I would tell people, friends, where my mother and I lived, what she did . . . ," thus giving a context for the strained litany of occupations in the preceding scene. The film abruptly cuts back to the previous recitation scene as she states: "doctor. *ŭisa*. businessperson. *sirŏpka*. scholar. *hakja*." Then, after a moment of slight hesitation while she silently plays with her hair, K. utters the word, "*ibalsa*." She does not translate this last into English, revealing a slippage along both class and gender lines, which could not be discerned without some knowledge of Korean language and society. Meaning barber or haircutter, *ibalsa* is also a euphemism for women who work in barbershops where sexual favors can be purchased. The hint of shame or denial in this refusal/inability to make this particular translation is immediately covered over when the camera cuts back to a more confident K. describing people's uncomfortable and insensitive reactions to the disclosure of her personal history:

> They would pause. Then they would tell stories like the one about the cab driver who bombed the beauty shop. The girls hadn't treated him properly. Or the one about the Korean American boy who had heard that he can get a hand job with a shave. He had to check it out, so he went and when he opened his eyes in mid-shave, he found out that the barber was giving him his erotic massage and not—what?—the delicate young maiden he expected. I don't know what people are thinking. What is on their minds?

Rather than simply internalizing the sexist and elitist terms of derogation of those women who must work at the barbershops, Theiler shapes the sequence in such a way as to effect a frank critique and interrogation of a broader social context that implicitly condones the misogynist exploitation of and violence towards Korean women's bodies. The grainy night footage of the streets of Korea that fills the middle of this soliloquy also suggests a larger geographical context but the frontal face shot of K. returns at the end to punctuate the mocking and critical tone of the words.

K.'s relating of the barbershop anecdote marks the differential experiences of return to the "homeland" for Korean Americans. This anecdote is humorously circulated among Korean Americans, especially males, who exploit the experience of returning to Korea as a chance to purchase sexual labor from local women, aided by favorable dollar exchange rates and shielded by distance from their "homes" in the U.S. But the film recites the anecdote here to mark the heterogeneous desires and stakes invested in the return to the homeland, which are organized around inequities of class, gender, sexuality, and, for the adoptee, ethnicity as well.

Even though she retains only scattered images and incidents from her childhood in Korea, there are several allusions to the low socioeconomic status of her biological mother. In addition to the hair-cutting sequence, the connection between domestic poverty and an international political economy built upon poor women's bodies is strikingly depicted in a scene in which the female figure tapes two American dollar bills to her naked belly, beneath her shirt. This act signifies both the adoptee's status as a commodity and also paranoid hoarding as a response to the economic impoverishment that caused her transnational adoption.

Other sections suggest that K.'s mother was a sex worker for an American military clientele. The orphanage was supposedly located in Tongduch'ŏn, an infamous site of U.S. military-related prostitution in South Korea. In the sequence immediately following the scene of the taped dollar bills, the young Cho Suk Hi is slowly awakened from sleep by a flirtatious bilingual conversation wafting in from the next room. An American male voice says, "I've never played this. I play poker all the time with the guys on the base, but I've never seen these." A Korean woman's voice speaks to him teasingly, and it becomes evident that she is teaching him to play *hwat'u,* a Korean card game associated with the lower classes and with "fallen" women in particular. The girl's eyes are wide open by the end of the scene, when the woman's playful giggles dissolve into the sounds of a jet plane taking off—a premonition of the girl's later transcontinental flight to the U.S. In the following scene, the young girl is shown sitting on the floor and shuffling the *hwat'u* cards when the older woman, noticing her actions from off camera, asks in Korean: "Oh, Sook Hee, you too want to play *hwat'u*?" This third, slightly different name should be noted. When the mother concedes that she will teach her "just this once," the young girl responds in Korean, "Mom, teach me like you did for your friend." The lingering memories of motherly affection are qualified by the indelible marks of U.S. military presence and the resulting commodification of women's sexual labor for purchase by American men in South Korea. These qualified and imagined memories of the Korean homeland elicit comparisons with Myung Mi Kim's poem, "Into Such Assembly." *Great Girl* also suggests critical differences between the middle-class Korean American female subject of Kim's poem, who can afford a shred of distance and self-differentiation by calling up an alternative set of childhood memories to the racist and sexist declarations about Korean women's sexual commodification and the orphaned Cho Suk Hi, for whom childhood memory and U.S. military prostitution are inextricable.

Re-membering the Korean homeland inevitably forces this Korean American subject to reckon with her own corporeal status as a transnational object of exchange. Making reference to her bureaucratically processed and reconstituted subject position as a transnational adoptee, a shot of a meat-processing plant with an audio track of an insistent buzzing, eerie music is intercut with an extreme close-up of Cho Suk Hi's head, as the sounds of heavy, plodding footsteps and barely discernible shadows show a male figure methodically encircling her as if performing some kind of clinical examination. Abruptly, she is knocked backwards and out of the frame. The following moving shot of a blue-tinted terrain with a shadowy presence hovering above further extends a sense of vulnerability and dread. In the next scene, the young girl sits in front of some stage steps in a colorful dress, once more against a white backdrop. She is blowing bubbles with her own saliva when an unidentified male approaches and stands before her on the right edge of the screen, the low-angle of the frame showing only his legs next to her crouched figure. She must look up at him. The unequal position of these two figures represents the power differentials between girl-child and male adult. He hands her a piece of paper, which she proceeds to rip into pieces and eat. This sequence vividly enfigures the transnational adoptee as a product of institutionalized paperwork.

Great Girl ends with an old, faded color photograph of the narrator-filmmaker as a young girl, what she refers to as "a photo taken of me to give to my parents." Aside from her adoption documents and passport, the photo is one of few clues to her irretrievable identity: "My American mom gave it to me some years later. It wasn't enough, so I went back to Korea in a way to create my own documents and memories that exist now only in my mind." The identification of her "American mom" imbues a distinct nationality to motherhood, denaturalizing the homologies of mother and motherland, family and nation. The piece ends with the image of a young Korean female, possibly the filmmaker herself, sweeping and mopping a small room inside an obviously working-class home. A map of Korea hangs on the wall, with only the southern half visible to the camera, which is placed outside of this room. Acting not as leading frontispiece but as a closing reminder or echo, this truncated image of the "homeland" connects the history of national partition and the subsequent military build-up of the South with the aid of the U.S. to this immigrant female subject's irretrievable Korean identity, which is an effect of international economic disparities and foreign military occupation. This, then, is the "home" that she has provisionally constructed.

*　　*　　*

Distinguished from but also suggesting a reverberating echo in their desirous yet sober invocations of the Korean homeland, these four cultural productions by Myung Mi Kim, Theresa Hak Kyung Cha, and Kim Su Theiler banish the rigid binaries of U.S.-Korea and present-past that undergird the xenophobic command to repatriation. By exploring the mutual yet uneven embeddedness of "Korean-American" relations in twentieth-century geopolitics, they chart an elaborate and criss-crossed web of domination, suffering, privilege, and complicity, which spans *distance* and precludes absolute designations of belonging and authenticity. With its deliberately complicated and mottled formal construction, each work takes up the challenge of representing this convoluted historical legacy and political terrain for a Korean American female subject. The artists' renderings of their particular alienation from the homeland, and their frustration as they attempt to recall and present it, gesture toward a broader interrogation of the terms of belonging and estrangement by which *any* body lays claim to an unequivocal home on such difficult grounds.

NOTES

I would like to thank the fabulous Korean women who participated in the "Articulations of Korean Women" conference at Berkeley in April 1994, where I presented a first version of this essay.

1. My deployment of both "Korea" and "home" in the rest of the paper bears consideration of such multiple valences, but I will only use the quotation marks when I intend an additional emphasis.

2. As Anne McClintock notes, "No nationalism in the world has ever granted women and men the same privileged access to the resources of the nation-state." ("'No Longer in a Future Heaven': Women and Nationalism in South Africa." *Transition* 51 (1991) McClintock elaborates on the "gendering of the national imaginary":

> All too often in male nationalisms, gender difference between men and women serves to symbolically define the limits of national difference and power between men. Excluded from direct action as national citizens, women are subsumed symbolically into the national body as its boundary and metaphorical limit: . . . .Women are typically construed as the symbolic bearers of the nation but are denied any direct relation to national agency (62).

("Family Feuds: Gender, Nationalism and the Family." *Feminist Review* 44 [Summer 1993]: 61–80.)

3. See Biddy Martin and Chandra Talpade Mohanty, "Feminist Politics: What's Home Got to Do With It?" *Feminist Studies/Critical Studies,* edited by Teresa de Lauretis. Bloomington: Indiana University Press, 1986, pp. 191–212. See also bell hooks, "Choosing the Margin as a Space of Radical Openness," Yearning: Race, Gender and *Cultural Politics.* Boston: South End Press, 1990.

4. Writing about the location of the Filipino writer in the U.S., E. San Juan, Jr., calls for a similar reconfiguration of past and present, Asia and the U.S.:

> And this cannot be done without evoking the primal scene coeval with the present: the neocolonial situation of the Philippines and its antecedent stages, the conflicted terrain of ideological struggle which abolishes the distinction/distance between Filipinos in the Philippines and Filipinos in the United States. Continuities no less than ruptures have to be articulated for an oppositional practice to emerge. . . . Of all Asian-American groups, the Filipino community is perhaps the only one obsessed with the impossible desire of returning to the homeland, whether in reality or fantasy.

(E. San Juan, Jr., "Mapping the Boundaries: Filipino Writers in the U.S.A." *The Journal of Ethnic Studies.* 19: 1 [Spring 1991]: 123–124.)

5. The formal and stylistic aspects of each of these works merit a more thorough consideration than I can provide within the limited scope of this paper. While some find these works overly elliptical and inaccessible, their sparse and fragmentary compositions manifest uncertainty about their relationship to a Korean homeland and a displacement of the representational conventions of mimesis they have inherited as Korean American subjects.

6. Walter Benjamin, *Illuminations*. New York: Schocken Books, 1968.

7. The choice of the anthem is powerful and appropriate for several reasons: 1) it serves a metonymic function in relation to the nation-state; 2) it is an obvious site for the meeting of nationalism with language; and 3) it is an important pedagogical tool for the cultivation of patriotism in the young and impressionable.

8. "Under Flag" contains these lines: "Drilled at the core for mineral yield and this, once depleted,/never to be replaced" (17). The lines "A face hauled away and a small flag of the country nearby/They were stripped" (24) from the poem, "Food, Shelter, Clothing," refer to the forced relocation of Koreans for physical labor in Japan as well as in other outposts of the Japanese empire.

9. As Chungmoo Choi so cogently asks, who is the invisible subject of the intransitive verb "partition"? Choi notes that

> the dominant narrative of South Korean history long acknowledged liberation as a gift of the allied forces, especially of the U.S.A., since Koreans were excluded from the liberation process itself. . . . Such a narrative has delegitimated the Koreans as valid agents of both nation-building and the subsequent military and economic dependence on the Cold War superpowers, although to a differing degree in the North than in the South. The transitive verbs "to liberate" and "to partition" presuppose a subject (or subjects), who is external to the action and yet administers it, and a passive receiver (the object) upon which such actions are performed.

See Chungmoo Choi, "The Discourse of Decolonization and Popular Memory: South Korea," *positions* 1:1 [Spring 1993]: 80.

10. Both "time" and "rage" can function as either noun or verb, opening up the first phrase, clearly set off by the comma, to a host of competing meanings: 1) it could be a grammatically incorrect recitation of the colloquial phrase, "Time rages on," to express the irrepressibility of temporal progression; 2) it could connote a certain anger against history; and 3), it could also be a directive to more methodically "time" the expression of rage that must be actively suppressed according to the patriarchal prescriptions of feminine passivity. As a noun, "churn" names "a vessel in which milk is stored to make butter," which would connect it to the "milk" in the first lines of the poem. It can also indicate "an agitated state (as of water)" or, as a verb, "to agitate"; both possibilities are appropriate to the poem's problematization of the essentializing figurations of the female body as well as Kim's disruptive and contestatory poetics. Finally the word can also mean "to produce by vigorous, continuous mental activity," which challenges the physiological reduction of the female body.

11. Theresa Hak Kyung Cha, *DICTEE*. New York: Tanam Press, 1982. See also *Writing Self, Writing Nation: Essays on Theresa Hak Kyung Cha's DICTEE*. Edited by Elaine H. Kim and Norma Alarcón. Berkeley: Third Woman Press, 1993. My essay in the volume, "The Liberatory Voice of Theresa Hak Kyung Cha's *DICTEE*," touches upon some questions around identification and representation but is somewhat diffuse. This essay seeks to clarify and rethink some of the concerns raised there and, more importantly, to place Cha's work in conversation with other Korean diasporic women's cultural productions. Myung Mi Kim's own early interest in Cha's work, and specifically *DICTEE*, can

be seen in an essay she wrote titled "ERASURE/RESTORATION: Theresa Hak Kyung Cha," which appeared in the October 1988 issue of the journal of feminist avant-garde poetics, *HOW(ever)*. In this essay, excerpts from *DICTEE* are re-printed.

12. Theresa Hak Kyung Cha, ed. *Apparatus Cinematographic Apparatus: Selected Writings.* New York: Tanam Press, 1981.

13. Lawrence Rinder, exhibit brochure for a show of Theresa Hak Kyung Cha's works at the University Art Museum/Pacific Film Archives at the University of California, Berkeley, California, July-September 1990.

14. *EXILÉE* has now been shown twice in this three-channel form: on November 8, 1994 and then again on March 6, 1995, both at the Pacific Film Archives, University Art Museum at the University of California, Berkeley.

13

HELEN LEE

A Peculiar Sensation:
A Personal Genealogy of Korean American Women's Cinema

Her hair is wrapped smoothly in a possibly comfortable bun, higher than seems right but that was the style then. She is perched on a rock, near flower bushes, smiling. My mother clutches a small handbag with gloved hands, her legs neatly arranged. Like my father, she wears a crisp suit. I don't know what color because the image is from a black and white photograph, not a memory. They are about the same age as I am now.

As adults, I think we are haunted by an image of our parents in their youth, a time we never knew them. For child immigrants, these images of the past also come from another place. Not here. A place far enough away that a telephone call occasions worry first, not joy. My parents left Seoul when I was three years old. A year later, my sister and I joined them in Toronto, Canada. Our young tongues, trained in Korean food and language but unschooled and now unhomed, were soon eager for french fries and making friends in English. I think that age especially, around three and four (just prior to grade school, when private home life becomes formatively public), was critical when I try to recall where photographs end and memory begins. It isn't clear.

It is a kind of curse, I think, to leave your birthplace when you are young enough to lose your mother tongue but old enough not to forget the loss. For my generation, Korean American/Canadian women filmmakers who were born there but raised here, the utter contemporaneity of our experiences means "back there" and "back then" as much as right now. As someone who writes and makes images about such tongue-tying experiences, I would like to try to remember this particular haunting of representation and subjectivity, where language is the spine of memory. Through our images, the faded pictures of our mothers speak with new force, saying something about our lives here. I am certain we all became filmmakers as soon as we stepped off the plane.

For now, let's put away those childish wishes for assimilation and discover a new desire for affinity. This article represents the desire to look at the work of my peers, other Korean American women filmmakers,[1] and discover the connections among their work and also the films I have made. I wondered if there was anything specific about the efflorescence of media work over the past few years which represented commonalities of location. How did our experiences as *kyop'o* (overseas Korean) women inform our aesthetic practices? How did these works function from the perspective of cultural displacement and feminist intervention, where race and gender identifications were prominent? How did the imbrication of Korean diasporic sensibilities (our "*kyop'o*-ness" or identities as overseas Koreans), and our multivalent positioning and constant negotiations as women and artists of color in this new world, reflect in our work? What kinds of representational strategies were being deployed, and what did this new visual culture signify[2]—simply, what were we saying, and how were we choosing to say it?

First, I am quite struck by the fact that most Korean American filmmakers are, in fact, women. For a generation destined, according to classical immigrant narratives of social and economic progress, to be brilliant doctors and lawyers (and by patriarchal imperative, good wives to boot), this is a startling find. Given the male-centered legacies of cinema history, theories of the cinematic apparatus, and the world of film production itself, it is also extraordinary. Was the desire for self-representation so intense as to supersede all the traditional barriers which usually placed women and people of color as outsiders looking in? Or, in the case of Korean American women filmmakers, did our peripheral status accord a privileged view—a "double vision"?

I imagine a girl standing before a mirror, or a woman holding a camera to her eye. Slowly, she turns to behold her image reflected back at her, like a doubling or twin. Not identical, different but same. She sees herself, as if for the first time.

A kind of "double consciousness"[3] is available to us, as minority women in the white-dominant culture of North American society. In an American context, we are Korean. In a Korean context, we are women. These media works embody an ambivalent and contingent status of American/Korean, white/other, here/there, and very often a place in-between. Issues of race and gender are impossible to ignore when their privileges and oppressions affect dimensions of everyday life, not to mention the critical and artistic expressions we try to bring to it. Aptly named a "triple bind"[4] by Trinh T. Minh-ha, alluding to competing allegiances to different communities, this unique equation of subjectivity—Korean/woman/artist—can also prove immensely enabling. Could it be that patriarchal expectations for the son have, ironically, liberated the daughter? (Sometimes I do wonder if I would have engaged in such an unstable profession as filmmaking if I'd been expected to be the family breadwinner.) More likely though, the Korean daughter became a feminist with something to say.

Our issues are different from what I imagine our female contemporaries in Korea, immersed in anti-colonial, nationalistic discourse in conjunction with feminism in a neo-Confucion context, might take on. In the '80s, while Korean students were taking to the streets, the business of assimilation and dreams of professional prosperity were occupying Korean American youth. Immigrant success meant moving into ivory towers, not smashing them. But this is a crude simplification (especially now, with government gestures toward political reform stymieing former student movement members of the '80s, we are faced with a Korean society as economically stratified as ever in the post-Korean war era; as well,

Asian Americans are coming to the economic and political fore as never before). Ultimately, for individuals and organizations devoted to progressive change, the question of what comprises socially committed, critically informed work is answered by where we are located. While cut from the same anti-imperialistic cloth as our Korean colleagues, I think we're more likely to critique ideals of western democracy and liberal society as illusions, than to claim them. Too many encounters with racism make it impossible to be a chest-beating American nationalist (and for a Canadian, it is downright anachronistic). Still, for mostly middle-class Korean Americans, the seduction of capital usually overrides considerations of class and sometimes even race. That's why when I speak of "identity," it is less a personal one (though it may be that, too) than a socially constructed, politicized identity which needs to be "earned" or declared. Although I have always been Korean, becoming "Korean American" or "Korean Canadian" was a longer, self-examining process. Acts of community in the context of racism and acute marginality are, in this way, themselves political.

These films and videos by Korean American women are highly conscious, artistically and theoretically mediated works (all produced by filmmakers with full benefit of college educations or art/film school, usually both). They are not "naive" in any sense, taking part in this highly politicized arena with strategies of reinvention and resistance. Much of the groundwork laid by feminist cinema and Asian American media has informed our filmic practices and we, in turn, extend those histories.[5] Fortified by debates around political and "third"[6] cinema, the rigidities of realist filmmaking and pressures to produce only "positive images" of the community, we roundly reject the banality and victimology associated with "minority" filmmaking. Mere oppositionality, stereotype-fighting documentaries, or simplistic "identity" films ("I am Korean American, and this is a portrait of me") do not constitute this oeuvre. Like some nationalistic Korean, I am proud of this. A fierce and prodigious discursivity is at work; like a persistence of vision, these plural or multiple forms of consciousness pervade our films. The combined forces of our immigrant family pasts, the lingering effects of Korean male patriarchal traditions, Korea's own colonial national history, they all feed into our contemporary North American perspectives. Sometimes there's time to kick at the can of postmodernity and cultural theory, too. As signposts of new knowledges and new subjectivities, these media works represent complex and personal articulations of race and gender, representation, and the politics and aesthetics of identity formation in film.

> Born with a veil, and gifted with second-sight.
> — W.E.B. DuBois

If there is a "godmother" to this recent flowering of work, it is the late Theresa Hak Kyung Cha. Her profound, luminous legacy of critical and poetic writing, performance art, and film and video work has left its traces. Although few of the film/videomakers discussed here would regard Cha's influence as a direct one (I knew only her name when making my first film), the themes and formal concerns of her media work during the '70s and early '80s surface again and again in these contemporary films. Cha's semiotic explorations of language, memory, and subjectivity in the context of feminism and Korean colonial history are especially prescient. While the feminist, postcolonial writings and films of Trinh Minh-ha gripped me as a cinema studies undergraduate during the mid-'80s, I didn't yet know of Theresa Hak Kyung Cha before her. Like Trinh, Cha can be at once poetic and interrogative in her unusual forms of address, which are almost oracular. As a body, Cha's work rematerializes the site of Korea-as-cold-war-victim, and re-maps the emotional and cognitive terrain of "Korea" into something tangible for *kyop'o* understanding, a groundswell of critical fictions, diasporic imagination, and genuine political struggle.

Talk about marginal. Until a few years ago, an identity as specific as "Korean American" filmmaker was an impossibility in the American cultural consciousness, even in its alternative quarters. When I made my first film, *Sally's Beauty Spot* (1990) and was living in New York, the prevailing term, politically and organizationally, was "Asian American." For someone from Canada coming to the States, even Asian American sounded great. To encounter organizations such as Asian CineVision in New York, Visual Communications in Los Angeles, and the National Asian American Telecommunications Association in San Francisco was a revelation. This history of Asian American filmmaking, I discovered, was predominantly Chinese American and Japanese American, and consisted primarily of documentaries. These organizations, devoted to supporting the production, promotion, and exhibition of media work by Asian American film/videomakers, also mounted annual film festivals. I decided I was going to make a film to show specifically at ACV's New

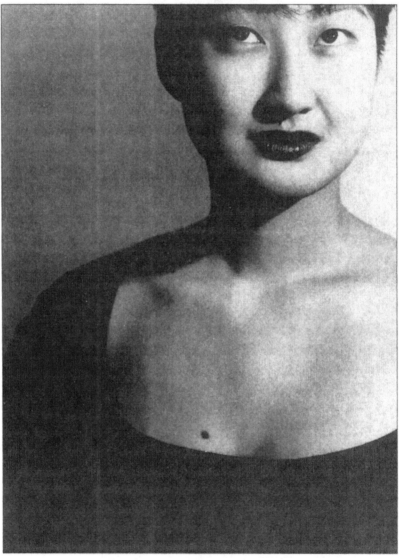

From stereotypical object to sexual subject: *Sally's Beauty Spot*

York festival. The film wouldn't be documentary and wouldn't be earnest, but elliptical, theoretical, feminist, and hopefully, funny and accessible. This Asian American audience would be my primary audience. Besides, how could they turn me down; just how many Asian American filmmakers were out there, anyway?

Enough, I guess. I showed the selection committee a silent cutting copy, which kept falling apart in the projector. They turned down the film. Come back next year, they said, when it's finished. I did.

Sally's Beauty Spot is an image-and-idea-driven film. Rather than focusing on character or story, the deconstructionist tendencies of the film and its hybrid aesthetics were inspired by a personal excitement with theory. Using a despised black mole on a young woman's breast as a metaphor for the threat of cultural difference, the film explores western notions of Asian femininity and idealized romance. Sally tries rubbing, scrubbing off, and covering up the skin blemish. Made without a script per se, the piece collages together my interest in postcolonial and feminist film theory with pop cultural elements. At the time, I was researching the representation of Asians in the history of American film and television. In the postwar period, a spate of Asian/white romances had emerged from Hollywood, what I call "miscegenation melodramas." Ubiquitous among them, and my clear favorite, was *The World of Suzie Wong*, starring William Holden and Nancy Kwan. Revisionistically speaking, I should spit out this bit of colonial candyfloss I know, but in truth I've loved eating it since childhood. The film was shown regularly on TV, and Kwan's prostitute was one of the few popular images of Asian women around. This kind of obsessive, acculturated form of spectatorship was interesting in itself: Korean girls in Canadian suburbs, glued to California sitcoms and old Hollywood movies on the tube; we were not exactly the intended audience for this once racy bit of entertainment. True, during all those times of looking, rarely did any of these images look back at me. But this one did.

Kwan's Suzie Wong was dragon lady and lotus blossom rolled in one, but caught in a racist time warp, could you really blame her? She was beautiful, fiesty, and deserved reclaiming. Homi Bhabha's seminal retheorization of the stereotype[7] was the trick. Instead of arguing the derogatory or false nature of racial and sexual stereotypes, Bhabha reconceptualized them as "arrested" forms of representation. Stereotypes should be viewed "relationally" according to other representations, he suggests, rather than held up to any picture of reality, thereby releasing it from burdens of truth or moralism. My "Suzie Wong" was a total fiction, pulp romance. As a Korean growing up in North America, it was impossible to be a real essentialist. No one knew where Korea was, so what could they really know about you, if they didn't even know where you came from? In this way, I became an Asian American before I became Korean American. Pillaging troves of Hollywood fare such as these "mixed race" dramas, I found all the Asian characters were Japanese or Chinese anyway (though I don't want to fight for Orientalist crumbs, this problem of the lack of a popular Korean signifier still dogs me to this day). Although Suzie Wong herself is from Hong Kong, the main character in *Sally's Beauty Spot*, while played by my sister, Sally, is not specifically named as Korean, Chinese, or Japanese, to underscore the shared dimensions of Asian American women's experience.

Sally's Beauty Spot tries to give a pulse to these linchpins of racial and sexual identity, in tandem, as inseparable preoccupations. The discourse of race in the United States was, and still is, overpoweringly white versus black. If Asians are admitted into the dialogue, it is almost exclusively in relation to white-dominant culture. Such a status quo–reinforcing focus on the white/other dynamic is not only supremely irritating, but it reflects the workings of power, not our multiracial society. Personally, I haven't been interested in representing Asian/white couplings. The predominant relationships in my films have been between Asian and other Asian, black or Native characters, and then only marginally, whites. In *Sally's Beauty Spot*, Sally's vacillation between white privilege and the prospect of a liaison with a black man (a pairing you'd be hard-pressed to find in Hollywood), reflects the tension of broaching an Asian presence in the stratified minefield of American race relations. On the soundtrack, different musical idioms and numerous abstracted voices interrogate this terrain. Clips from *The World of Suzie Wong*, photographs and voices of other Asian women, and images of Sally's body punctuate this narrative of discovery and subjecthood. The film maps this progression of psychic and theoretical attachments to the body, spectatorship, and voice with a simple story about an unwanted mole.

When I showed the film to Homi Bhabha, one of the critical inspirations for the film, he remarked how the mole or "beauty spot" on Sally's breast functioned as the *punctum* of the piece. Roland Barthes used the term to describe how a peripheral detail in a photograph may "prick" or unsettle the viewer in ways unexpected from the photograph's more conventionally coded meanings. The punctum's effect is startling, like a "sting, speck, cut, little hole." Registering a visceral effect, "It also bruises me," Barthes writes, "is poignant to me."[8] Such a compelling detail may give a clue to how we come to "remember" an image or photograph, through the body. My sister, Sally (who by the way has no neurotic impulse towards her mole), had an immediate but different response to Bhabha's suggestion. To her, the *punctum* was not the mole but the stretch marks on her breasts. The film's final images are of a black man's lips dissolving into Sally's own, radiant smile.

> She heard faintly the young girl uttering a sequence of words, and interspersed between them, equal duration of pauses. Her mouth is left open at the last word. She does not seem to realize that she had spoken.
> —Theresa Hak Kyung Cha

During the mid-'70s, Theresa Cha began producing work as a student at the University of California, Berkeley. The sheer formalism, elegance, and occasional opacity of her text constructions, in writing and media, reflect an excitement and curiosity about French poststructuralist ideas which were then gaining importance on this side of the Atlantic. For the theoretically uninitiated, Cha's work can be daunting. Embracing a conceptual indeterminacy characteristic of avant-garde performance aesthetics, their meanings are often created provisionally in the encounter between the text and reader. The specificity of the reader as a social subject is always a precondition of performing the meaning. But different from her Euro-American intellectual peers, her thoughts were as much about Korea, which was marginal even to a western understanding of "the Orient." Problems of language embody this sense of cultural displacement. The word, Cha implies, is not a universal or neutral signifier, not always in English or French. By a specific somebody, words are read, spoken, and breathed around, sometimes with considerable strain. In *mouth to mouth* (1975), the Korean language can offer the assurance and comfort of one's mother tongue, or is slippery as a cipher—depending on the viewer and her positioning. Cultural location, however, does not always guarantee a linguistic one. Language, once a repository and reliable signifier of culture, becomes contingent and fragile in the context of displacement.

mouth to mouth opens with a continuous left to right panning movement over a series of written characters: simple vowel letters from *hangul*, the Korean phonetic alphabet. The movement fades into black, then fades up to a video snow effect, accompanied by static noise. This is followed by an image of a woman's mouth framed in close-up, superimposed over this snow/static. Her mouth widens ever slowly, but we don't hear her. Fade out. Fade in with another close-up of the same, her mouth forming a different, voiceless vowel. The video follows this pattern in a highly composed, almost ritualistic manner, with variations in sound treatments (static, water, bird sounds, sometimes silence) and the occasional camera movement. As in her other film and video work, the piece's formal austerity extends from the visual to the aural dimensions of the piece.

Although *mouth to mouth* references the populist, physiognomic origin myths of *hangŭl*,[9] the functioning of language for the *kyop'o* speaker is not nearly so transparent. The supposedly neutral text of written language is gradually overturned by the arduous, subjective aspiration of speech. This tension between the text and speech mirrors the disintegrating relationship between sound and image in the videotape. While the disembodied voice may function as a radical, even liberatory tool for her feminist avant-garde contemporaries,[10] Cha's voiceless body suggests other problems of cultural legibility and knowledge. Here, the disconnection of voice and body alludes to the oscillatory nature of native/non-native tongues where the transparency and certainty of language is suspended. The use of the vowel as a structuring absence of the word, as opposed to the positivity of consonants, underscores its supplementary but elemental nature. Significantly, two vowels are missing from the written text (compound vowels aren't even included here). The incomplete set suggests a child or beginner's first apprehension of the language, or the imperfect recall of a native speaker whose mother tongue is lost. Cha's mute mouth, forming familiar/unfamiliar vowels, "performs" the Korean language with a desire for speech. The vowels' "absent" nature indicates the materiality of language, as building blocks. Where language itself is homed, however, is another question.

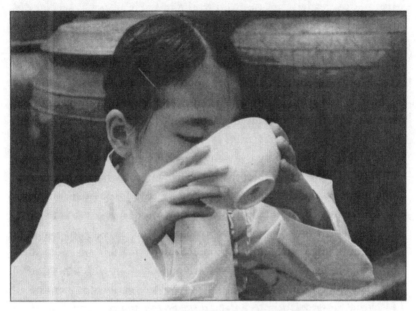

Remembering *DICTEE: Mermory/all echo*

Cha's long-standing interest in negative space and silence is shared by the work of more recent video artists, most directly in Yunah Hong's work. Hong's first videotape, *Memory/all echo* (1990), is based on Cha's seminal poetic text, *DICTEE*.[11] The book itself is a complex document combining written text with graphic components, and covering topics ranging modern Korean history, Catholic ritual, and cinema spectatorship, to topographies of the human body. Hong's video gathers together archival material from the Korean war and dramatic reenactments filmed in Korea and the U.S., with visual montage elements such as computer-generated effects and photographic stills. Using *DICTEE* as a base text, the voice-over is comprised solely of selections from the book. But Hong's style is more allusive than illustrative of Cha's writing.[12] Rather than attempting an exhaustive, literal adaptation of the book, the video focuses mainly on themes related to Korean and American identity and issues of cultural and linguistic displacement, underscoring the interpretive possibilities and elliptical phrasings of the translation process itself.

Like the book, *Memory/all echo* attempts to engage the viewer in a self-reflexive, readerly relationship to the text. Hong tracks several discursive levels at once, extending the video's montage aesthetic to a multi-layered presentation of voice. Three narrators with different accents (signifying varying levels of acculturation to the English language), adopt several forms of address. In one segment, Cha's eyewitness retelling of her brother's decision to join a 1962 student demonstration against their mother's will is narrated in third person. The video dramatizes this sequence, collapsing Cha's real-life experience with the story of a fictional character (played by the same actor). The use of the pronominal shifter (you/I; she/he) enables the subjective interplay between historical and autobiographical accounts locked by the accrual of time and memory. The sequence, although filmed in slow motion and extreme close-up, employs an arch, gestural performance style that drains the confrontation of any conventional dramatic intent or emotional identification. Linking her brother's anti-government position with a portrait of Yu Guan Soon [Yu Kwan-sun], the martyred nationalist heroine of 1919, the narrator/author/character traces the politics and history of modern Korean resistance to locate it within a personal, familial framework. The space between—tensions of nation and family, gaps between history and autobiography, the ellipses of story and memory—is transformed into a language of loss, displacement, and exile.

In Kim Su Theiler's *Great Girl* (1993), the haunting of cultural loss takes the form of a search for origins. The film's departure point is Theiler's own trip to Korea to find information about her birth mother. But this search doesn't function as a transparently autobiographical document or an effortless return of the subject to the mother/land. Laid out as a series of vignettes, the piece unfolds rather cryptically: a roomful of black hair, American dollar bills bandaged to a young girl's belly, an ambivalent childhood encounter with a U.S. serviceman (perhaps her father?), neutral adoption documents, uneasy travelogue footage of a hometown that existed before only in her mind. Like secret layers of a memory long repressed by familial and cultural silence, the discursive curiosity of this search unearths a place—Korea—sedimented by the absences and persistence of memory and silence in stark and unsettling ways.

Theiler's film begins with an extreme close-up shot of a black and white image, accompanied by music and a regulated scraping noise. The image is magnified to the point of illegibility. It is similarly difficult to locate the source of the sound, or its relationship to the image. This disjunctive relationship between the visual and aural is a primary stylistic

In search of the mother/land: *Great Girl*

trope of *Great Girl*, where sound is used contrapuntally or non-synchronously towards a redefinition of the subject, who is variously named in the film ("K," Sun-Mi, Cho Suk-hi, and implicitly, Kim Su Theiler). This non-realist use of sound, including voice-over, represents an interventionist strategy which feminist film theorists such as Kaja Silverman and Mary Ann Doane have deployed against classical realist cinema's reinforcement of male subjectivity and the illusion of a unified, coherent subject. The seamlessness of realist sound/image production masks "the potential trauma of dispersal, dismemberment, and difference,"[13] and the spectator's imagined plenitude or insufficiency of the image/subject. As the mirror opposite of realist filmmaking, identity-production seeks to expose its material workings. In *Great Girl*, Theiler's deconstructive task is to uncover the past trauma of dispersal (adoption and immigration), dismemberment (separation and loss of the mother), and difference (the *kyop'o*'s return to Korea).

In a key scene of the film, "K" is being interviewed about the trip and her experience meeting hometown folks who can give her information. The sequence is reenacted by an actress (Anita Chao) wearing a suit and coiffed hairstyle, and sitting obediently behind a desk. Strangely, her lips move out of sync with the monologue, followed by a slight echoing effect. As she moves into a story about how a scar on her body could definitively identify her, "K" detaches the microphone from her lapel and leaves the desk, as the camera follows her walking into another part of the room. She talks about meeting a woman who "could be my mother." The beating noise (the dislocated sound from the film's opening) is almost thunderous. But no one provides the right answers ("I looked nothing like the pictures"). Engaged in what Cha has called a "perpetual motion of search," the film's discursive explorations of self-identity and self-knowledge render an asymptotic relationship to "truth": the closer she comes, the more inaccessible and irrecoverable her past is. The carefully staged testimony of "K"'s faked performance undermines the documentary-like presentation of a unified, spontaneous, "authentic" subject. The film's visual and conceptual fragmentation, and the interpolated nature of the filmmaker's investigation—chance meetings, faulty memories, nasty rumors (the townspeople's suggestion of her mother as a prostitute with no prospects but American adoption of her biracial, illegitimate child), and implied wishes for a happy ending—reveal the impossibility of a transparent search for cultural and biological origins. Later in the film, the initial, illegible black and white close-up shot is widened to reveal the image's contents: sails of a boat caught by an intense wind.

> The effect of mass migrations has been the creation of radically new types of human being: people who root themselves in ideas rather than places, in memories as much as in material things; people who have been obliged to define themselves - because they are so defined by others - by their otherness; people in whose deepest selves strange fusions occur, unprecedented unions between what they were and where they find themselves.
> —Salman Rushdie

The "in-betweenness" that characterizes films about immigrant experience, especially when faced with the physical or metaphoric possibility of return, is a persistent wound of the diasporic imagination. What is interesting is how these ideas take shape, depending on the form. The more free-wheeling language of experimental film and video can be immensely enabling in conveying a discursive complexity. It's possible to pack a film with dense ideas and a radical aesthetic, and be all the richer for it. The rules of narrative film, however, are far stricter. Still, the principle of diminishing audience (the more experimental your film is, the smaller your audience) plagued me as I contemplated a shift to narrative filmmaking. Why not try to communicate hitherto marginalized stories and characters through a more accessible form? At the same time, other models of contemporary innovative and subjective filmmaking that identified marginalized characters and the interplay of difference—cultural, psychic, sexual—showed it was possible to locate these ideas in a narrative context.[14]

My second film, *My Niagara* (1992), features a Japanese American/Canadian[15] protagonist, a 20-year-old woman named Julie Kumagai. In continuing my exploration of displacement and assimilation, and racial/sexual representation in film, I wished to collaborate with another Asian writer on a film about an Asian/Asian relationship. This didn't come about innocently. One of my guiding lights, videomaker Richard Fung, had an interesting reaction to *Sally's Beauty Spot* and the Asian/black dialectic it sought to set up. "So, you think that's radical, Helen?" he challenged (very gently, of course). "The Asian and black thing is provocative but you know what's really radical? Yellow on yellow."

An inaccessible interiority: *My Niagara*

My Niagara is a story of maternal loss and intercultural discovery. Written with novelist Kerri Sakamoto, the film explores the inner world of Julie Kumagai who, on the cusp of adulthood, faces choices to move her life forward. At the film's outset, she is breaking off with a boyfriend and contemplating a trip to Europe with her best friend, Enza. Julie lives at home with her incommunicative father, and her life is shadowed by the death of her Japanese-born mother (who, on a return trip there when Julie was a small girl, died in a drowning accident off the coast). At Julie's workplace, a stately water filtration plant by the lake, she meets a young man, Tetsuro, who, recently emigrated from Japan but of Korean origin, is obsessed with all things American. They make a connection, but Julie ultimately cannot escape her listless state; life goes on. While this is the plot proper and *My Niagara* is a drama, the film is essentially minimalist and counter-dramatic in design.

The central relationship that Kerri and I wanted to portray was Julie and Tetsuro's, and their evolving realizations of cultural difference. To us, the picture of an assimilated Asian in America was a *sansei* (or third-generation) Japanese Canadian/American. But Julie's background also resembled my own upbringing in a predominantly white suburban environment. What were the differences between being a settled Asian person in North America, and a recent immigrant; what were the similarities? What kinds of dynamics and perceptions existed among Asians of differing nationalities living here? Also, how does the fantasy of Japan in Julie's idealized memories (as a place of origin and the site of her mother's birth and death), change when confronted with Tetsuro's experiences of discrimination as a Korean in Japan? Although these were our didactic considerations in creating the story and our characters, we were also dead-set against making an earnest "race relations" drama. Once established, cultural identity would be a given, not constantly "rehearsed" for an assumedly "white" audience; our audience would already be knowledgeable and informed. As well, there would be no obvious or Orientalist signifiers (for instance, although we assume Julie's father, as a *nisei* or second-generation Japanese, had an internment camp experience, this never comes up in the film, not as much because the story isn't his but that this would be the most obvious filmic representation of a *nisei* character. He was just an emotionally bottled-up dad, for personal as well as cultural reasons). Enza and Dominic (not coincidentally, both ethnic whites) have their own quirks, and Tetsuro his Memphis stylings.

Julie (Melanie Tanaka), Tetsuro (William Shin) and Mr. Kumagai (George Anzai) are played by non-professional actors, not because of the dearth of Asian actors, but because of a particular "non-performative" performance style which I had hoped to experiment with. Different from documentary-like naturalism, the style I was searching for was a convergence of real-life personas and scripted characters toward non-psychological portrayals. Reduced and flattened, they could suggest an inaccessible state of interiority. I thought their alienation wouldn't be properly served by gutsy, positivist performances. Muted or held-in, their canted expressions of emotional discord and cultural displacement alluded to theoretically based notions of absence and negativity. Suspicious of models of identification that relied on audience absorption, I hoped for some critical distance (was it possible to be both emotionally engaged and critically aware at the same time?). Similarly, the progression of the story is obliquely presented and ultimately subverted. Julie's own passivity is mirrored in the film's languid expository style. In the ending, Julie's momentary communion with her father (she finds a charged but constipated gift of a wooden box he's crafted himself—touching, but also oddly paralyzing), also denies specific narrative closure. But it is less a refusal than a deferral. The film's final notes, the daughter's dutiful gesture of filling her father's rice bowl, and an image of her mother's watery grave, suggest another chapter of a continuing story.

Also dealing with families and parent/child dynamics, other narrative films by Korean American women filmmakers avoid a deconstructionist approach in favor of a realist, reconstructionist tone and spirit. These works feature critical dilemmas faced by Korean American families with female protagonists, interestingly all daughters, at their center. While issues of national culture and the family still coalesce around language, critical discursivity is transformed into dialogue and dramatic conflict.

Problems of language and cultural difference encountered by second-generation Korean Americans, compounded by biracial identity, are the subject of Kyung-ja Lee's *Halmani* (1988). Kathy is born of a Korean mother and U.S. serviceman father. Her home life is an example of middle-class assimilation, idyllic and erased of any signs of ethnicity. Living outside of an urban center (and therefore outside a community of Korean Americans), Kathy's white-as-norm American comfort is uprooted by the arrival of her very Korean grandmother, Halmani. Oriental signifiers start to proliferate: gifts of a ceramic vase and traditional *hanbok* dresses, yucky foods, odd customs, and an unrecognizable language. Her mother's assurance that "Korea is a long way away" is threatened by Halmani's newfound presence, and a reminder of not the foreignness "over there" but of the difference within.

Kathy speaks only English, and Halmani only Korean, so grandmother and granddaughter literally cannot speak to one another. Halmani's Korean is left untranslated, reinforcing Kathy's sense of estrangement (and curiously, the viewer's; I craved for Halmani to be on equal footing but Lee decides not to subtitle Halmani's dialogue). Instead, their method of communicating transfers to the body, and

oscillates between the physical connection/repulsion of Kathy's own biological and cultural ambivalence. Still, their bodies can correspond. The
film's framing often places Kathy and Halmani within the same two-
shot, emphasizing their shared physical stature. "Halmani noticed that
you're left-handed, too," her mother says. It's when Halmani does something strange and visceral, like squatting on the earth, chanting while
polishing the vase, or praying as she burns paper, that Kathy's alienated
Americanness seeks to excise any display of alterity.

East meets southwest: *Halmani*

When asked to draw a self-portrait in class, Kathy models her fingers
around her face and is stymied; the drawing's a mess, and she runs away.
After her father brings her home, Kathy proclaims, "She's disgusting. I
hate her," and smashes the precious vase to the ground. Halmani's reaction is swift and perfect: fury and true disgust. This a moment when
Halmani's identity, throughout the film positioned as "authentic" and
unknowable, won't be denied. The film's resolution, Halmani's forgiveness and Kathy's penance, plays out the banality of cultural compromise:
Kathy eats her words after Halmani takes the blame for the broken vase,

and she dons the *hanbok* for her family. Through the verbal and non-verbal communion of the film's final scene, a long shot of Kathy and Halmani together against a desert sunset, Kathy willingly accepts not just the signs of cultural difference, but the language itself. "*Kamsahamnida*, Halmani," she thanks her grandmother, her tongue humbled by the native.

Sexual liberty as personified by Mae East: *Be Good, My Children*

The desire for assimilation takes a decidedly adventurous, sardonic turn in Christine Chang's *Be Good, My Children* (1992). At the film's outset, Chang boldly asks of her characters, "Why did you come to America?" A musical-comedy-drama, the film satirizes the saga of a struggling Korean immigrant family in New York City: Mom is a "Jesus freak" who works at a Harlem clothing store, Judy aspires to be an actress but tends bar on the sly, and Jimmy is failing out of school (the father is notably absent). Mom still hopes for mainstream professional success for her children, who opt for white boyfriends and wished-for car dealerships in LA. Their entanglements and conflicts form the basis of the film's plot, but it is the extra-diegetic levels, in the form of two "narrators," which subvert our expectations of the conventional family drama.

The film opens with an Asian woman wearing impeccable make-up and a huge blonde wig languishing on top of a bed, clutching a teddy bear. This is Snow White (played by Chang herself). She addresses the camera directly, introducing the family via a photo album and acerbically decrying this "mean world." Snow White functions as an omniscient narrator, like a guardian angel to the family, but more devilish than angelic. In an early episode with Jimmy, she dribbles chocolate candies to lure him, fairytale-like, into a lesson of simple economics, NYC-style ("These are pennies; we throw them away. These are nickels; we give them to beggars"), before releasing her authority as the film's driving force ("Say it! I have absolute power"). Another figure, Mae East, who is first introduced as daughter Judy's alter ego but soon enters the story as a character in her own right, provides the main musical numbers. It's high camp, with Mae East's torch songs and the sexually charged persona of Snow White, part sex kitten/part dominatrix, releasing the drama from the realist confines of the typical immigrant narrative.

Toying with the conventions of a morality tale, Chang discards the myth of hard-working, model minority citizens in an explicit critique of the American dream and the white norm. Offset by the sheer jazziness of the musical interludes, the family's parables offer a deeply ironic perspective of Korean immigrant life (for me, marred only by some of the actors' inauthentic Korean accents). One of Mae's musical numbers is even set in a California drive-in theater in the middle of an earthquake. In another sequence where Judy recounts a dream to a psychologist, several Asian women with names like Cherry Blossom, Miss Butterfly, and Lady Dragon first display themselves as stereotypical submissives but end up beating up on the white males, yelling, "That's not my name!" Later, the same women, including Judy, rally together in a self-affirming musical number led by Mae East's rebel femininity. By presenting an unequivocally sexual image of the Asian woman in a campy musical or melodramatic context, the film avoids essentializing the Asian American experience or "fixing" the stereotype as false/true. The film's radicality lies in this refusal to reinforce dramatic realist presentations of what Korean women are "really like." Its parody of Hollywood happy endings similarly denies escapist tendencies of the immigrant narrative. When Jimmy and Judy steal the church offerings from their mother's church to hail a cab to "somewhere over the rainbow," and Mom launches into the

L. A. Woman: *La Senorita Lee*

show tune of the same name, you know that Snow White (and Chang herself) is smirking. "Oh my, just the lullaby I needed," she says. "But forget it. This ain't no time to dream."

The dysfunctional family and personal compromises made to sustain the illusion of perfect nuclearity also propel the narrative of Hyun Mi Oh's *La Senorita Lee* (1995). The film follows the choices made by Jeanie Lee, a vivacious young woman ending an affair with Tomas, a Mexican worker who has left her pregnant. She feels pressured to marry Harry Kim, a childhood friend and young doctor, in order to bail out her mother and grandmother. The backstory is the financial ruin of the family's business during the L.A. riots, and the father's subsequent abandonment of his wife, mother, and daughter (even in a household containing only women, patriarchal pressures still assert themselves). Oh presents Jeanie's personal crisis as an example of the complex positioning of this generation of Korean American women in Los Angeles, poised on the edge of a continent bordered by desiring bodies, clashing cultural realities, and a "prodigality of tongues."[16]

The film's structure is circular, beginning and ending with Jeanie (also played by the filmmaker) lying on a highrise rooftop, moments after fleeing her traditional Korean wedding. The strains of a Korean folk song and the vivid colors of her *hanbok* and *chokturi,* set against the smoggy backdrop of downtown L.A. and the sound of helicopters in the distance, portray the conflict almost iconically. We enter the story through Jeanie's vision, a close-up shot catching her half-conscious state as she passes through dream, sleep, and memory. The film's flashback structure effectively internalizes the site of Jeanie's dramatic conflict into her body, so that the drama unfolds as part of Jeanie's consciousness and her subjectively-drawn world. Struck by pregnancy cramps in the bathroom of a hotel room she's sharing with Harry on a whim, Jeanie's thoughts move to an idyllic scene on the same rooftop where she and Tomas speak Spanish to one another, and share a night of lovemaking. Later, on the operating room of an abortion clinic, the threat of terminating her pregnancy conjures up an image of a small girl—Jeanie herself as a child. This jolts her into a moment of self-apprehension, and she runs. Jeanie's "wildness" and its repression are also reflected in the film's structure, a continuous sublimation of her sexual identity into the filial role of dutiful Korean American daughter and now, mother.

When Jeanie's feminist will and new world freedoms are overtaken by considerations of the family's future (ruled by the interdependency of different immigrant generations and, ironically, a continuation of patriarchal structures supported by women), her marriage to Harry is a sign of defeat. But Jeanie's radical decision to keep Tomas's baby shows the exact price of compromise. "I don't believe anymore," she tells a small Mexican boy on the rooftop in one of the film's last scenes. The "cosmopolitanizing of humanity" in a place like Los Angeles (which Tomas calls "the loneliest city in the world"), can also signal what Rey Chow has named a "vanishing of human diversity."[17] Difference is subsumed by forces of urbanization, assimilation, and homogenization. At the film's closing, various spoken lines from the film create a voice montage over a single shot of Jeanie's quiet face, ending on a freeze-frame of her eyes opening, wide awake. Of the different languages which haunt her —Korean, Spanish, English—which will her child eventually claim?

Hyun Mi Oh's script was a kind of revelation when I first read it several years ago. Encountering its cultural sophistication and astute writing recalled a time years earlier, when I first saw Pam Tom's seminal film, *Two Lies* (1989), a beautifully made black-and-white film about two Chinese American sisters and the psychological aftermath of their mother's eyelid operation. With strongly enacted characters and a compelling story, it struck a perfect balance of cultural identity exploration and expertly crafted narrative. The film spoke to me, and it spoke well. The film also made me laugh, the better to spit out, not swallow, the bitter pill of racial assimilation. For a fourth-generation Chinese American filmmaker like Tom, the question of language isn't such an issue (all the dialogue is in English). But for 1.5 generation filmmakers such as Oh and myself, language functions as a kind of primal site of conflict, a site which signifies torment, misunderstanding or loss. Perhaps it is because I am now struggling with Korean language lessons, or crave certain foods to which I do not know the names, or cannot discuss intellectual topics in real depth with my parents, that I make the films I make, to recover this sense of loss.

The confluence of language and crisis surfaces in my third film, *Prey* (1995), a drama about a young Korean Canadian woman who falls for a shoplifter in her father's convenience store the morning after an overnight robbery. Taking place over the course of one day (but a day that will determine what the next days are like), Il Bae's everyday family routine is upset by this handsome Native stranger, Noel, who insinuates himself into her life and apartment. Is he to be trusted? A surprise visit by Halmoni, her grandmother who doesn't speak English, forces her to choose alliances, but Il Bae's defense is poorly negotiated by the fact of Noel's ethnicity and his disheveled, possibly dangerous appearance, as much as by Il Bae's unsure command of the Korean language. These problems of miscommunication and cultural perception are heightened by circumstance when Halmoni meets him not only post-coitally shirtless but also in possession of a gun (echoing a specter of violence familiar to Korean American store owners' lives). In the film's conclusion, a late-night confrontation set in their convenience store, Noel proffers this gun to Il Bae's father as a safeguard against future robberies. But to the father, Noel couldn't be anything but a robber, and he mistakes the gesture as a hold-up. Il Bae's final introduction ("Dad, this is Noel. Noel, this is my dad.") is in some ways just the beginning.

The meeting of Il Bae (Sandra Oh), a young Korean Canadian

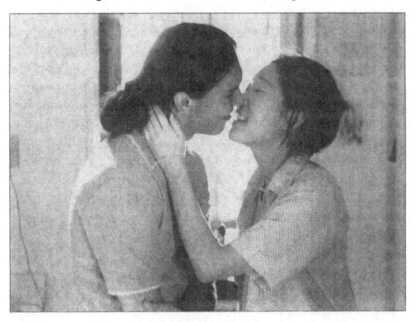

All you need is a girl and a gun: *Prey*

woman and Noel (Adam Beach), a Native man, creates an unexpected alliance. While they each come from totally different social spaces, there are also aspects which are shared—the same high school, a sense of cultural displacement, and lives shadowed by personal loss (the death of Noel's sister, Lucy; Il Bae's absent mother). I think of their relationship as a completely contemporary one, a phenomenon of the late twentieth century that allows such encounters between Asian immigrants and indigenous people to be possible. Since Koreans emigrated in significant numbers only in the past two decades, it's historically unlikely that Il Bae and Noel would have met until now. Native people, who suffer the same invisibility as Asians and other racial minorities in mainstream media, are practically unknown to the Korean American/Canadian community. It was important to me to explore how a Native character could impact on a Korean family who may have never before acknowledged the Native presence in their adopted land. Halmoni refers to Noel as a "foreigner," not suspecting the irony of her words. While Il Bae and Noel are familiarly cast as star-crossed lovers, this "new world" narrative also creates an emotional space where ideas around ethnicity and belonging can be as meaningful and dramatic as cinematically coded elements like trust, desire, and gunplay.

In conceiving the film, I wanted to avoid reinforcing certain dualisms that I thought typified some Asian American filmmaking. The binaristic opposition of tradition (old, backward "Orient") and modernity (progressive western ideas and attitudes) particularly unnerved me. Although traditional perspectives play a large role in our lives, I don't believe that Korean identity played in simple conflict with living in North America. It wasn't an either/or choice; we live an incredibly hybrid existence. In the film, both English and Korean co-exist, however fragilely, a balancing act of language and identity for 1.5 or second generation immigrants of any nationality. Hyphenated existence (Korean-Canadian, Korean-American) from an adult perspective as opposed to the assimilating impulse of childhood affords the distance and desire, and sometimes necessity, for both tongues to exist in simultaneity. A typical convenience store was the perfect stage to enact this drama, a place where so many Korean Americans have spent their lives (my own movie-watching hours are just recently outpacing my days behind a retail counter). Il Bae's father, circumscribed by this setting, is a barometer of this tongue-twisting dance of language and race. Even he, as imperfectly "bilingual" as his daughter, misunderstands—his daughter, Noel's intentions, the unending drone of labor at the expense of love. By the film's end, Il Bae does not make an either/or choice, but mediates her father's position into a place of forced compromise and personal release.

The script for *Prey* was originally written for Sandra Oh and my mother's sister, In Sook Kim, to play the roles of Il Bae and Halmoni. I knew this would be an interesting process of not only pairing a highly trained actor like Oh with my aunt, who'd never performed before, but also because Oh, like the character, didn't speak Korean and my aunt doesn't speak much English. Since I cannot really speak Korean either, a process of translation was integral to the project. At every stage, from rehearsal to shooting to editing, the interpreter, Jane Huh, stuck close and ready. I wasn't prepared for the cultural wrangling over specific attitudes and sayings that I thought were authentic or convincing, but Jane insisted were off-mark. True to form, my aunt, herself a prolific essayist and poet, refused to play the role of the grandmother (who was initially written as very accepting of Noel and Il Bae's liaison) and demanded changes. My aunt wanted Noel out of Il Bae's apartment and out of her life. While I never thought I'd take identity for granted, especially in a film about cross-generational differences, here I was making my own cultural assumptions. Ultimately, developing Halmoni's character was a collaboration between my aunt and myself, a creation of the Korean and *kyop'o* imagination. I doubt the film would exist without her.

No one today is purely one thing.
—Edward Said

From our "simultaneously split and doubled existence"[18] as Korean American women, we have learned to become adept, sophisticated readers of images. From this minoritized position, we had learned to focus on subversive readings and peripheral details, seeing how the *punctum* satisfies. Now, we take up the whole frame; as writers and film-makers, we have created new images, enlarged those details. Can the

317

production of an image of identity lead to the "transformation of the subject in assuming that image"?[19] The representation of Korean women is complex, figured by and interpolated through a variety of discourses, but each frame of these moving images elucidates us, bringing the image of the colonial subject one step closer toward self-identification. The ideas of home, memory, language, and desire obsess us; we try hard to translate these collective thoughts in ways never imagined for us. These narratives of the tongue, voice, and body, they all speak with newfound specificity. The velvet grain of Mae East's voice, Sally's crooked smile, the flaring of Jeanie Lee's *hanbok*, Cha's silent lips—all engaged in a "perpetual motion of search," these explorations signal a kind of *kyop'o* arrival. While the question of identity is never guaranteed, this new clamoring of images suggests other, curiously beautiful ways of traveling in a strange land.

SELECTED FILMOGRAPHY

This listing includes films and videos made by and about Korean American women, available through the following distributors or filmmakers:

Be Good, My Children, Christine Chang, 1992, 47 min. 16mm. Women Make Movies, 462 Broadway, #500, New York, NY 10012, 212–925–0606.

Camp Arirang, Diana Lee and Grace Yoon Kyung Lee, 1995, 28 min. video. Third World Newsreel, 335 West 38th Street, New York, NY 10018, 212–947–9277.

Comfort Me, Soo Jin Kim, 1993, 8 min. video. 201 Wayland Street, Los Angeles, CA 90042, 213-550-1772

Daughterline, Grace Lee-Park, 1995, 11 min. 16mm. Grace–Lee Park, 6104 N.E. Sacramento, Portland, OR 97213, 503–223–2243.

Distance, Soo Jin Kim, 1991, 13 min. video. Soo Jim Kim (see *Comfort Me*)

Do Roo (Circling Back), Soon Mi Yoo, 1993, 14 min. 16mm. Yellow Earth Productions, 3900 Cathedral Avenue N.W., #501A, Washington, DC 20016, 202–338–9577.

A Forgotten People, Dai-Sil Kim Gibson, 1995, 59 min. 16mm. Crosscurrents Media, NAATA, 346 9th Street, 2nd Floor, San Francisco, CA 94103, 415–552–9550.

Golden Dreams, Alice Ra, 1995, 9 min. 16mm. CrossCurrents Media.

Great Girl, Kim Su Theiler, 1993, 14 min. 16mm. Women Make Movies.

Halmani, Kyung-ja Lee, 1988, 30 min. 16mm. Pyramid Film & Video, 2801 Colorado Avenue, Santa Monica, CA 90404, 310–828–7577.

Here Now, Yunah Hong, 1995, 32 min. 16mm. Yunah Hong, 223 East 4th Street, #12, New York, NY 10009, 212–677–8980.

An Initiation Kut for a Korean Shaman, Diana Lee and Laurel Kendall, 1991, 37 min. video. University of Hawaii Press, 2840 Kolowalu Street, Honolulu, HI 96822, 808–956–8697.

In Memoriam to an Identity, R. Vaughn, 1993, 5 min. video. Katharine Burdette, 15308 Alan Drive, Laurel, MD 20707, 301-725-0472

Korea: Homes Apart, Christine Choy and J.T. Takagi, 1991, 60 min. 16mm. Third World Newsreel.

La Senorita Lee, Hyun Mi Oh, 1995, 26 min. 16mm. Cinema Guild, 1697 Broadway, #506, New York, NY 10019, 212–246–5522.

living in half tones, Me-K. Ahn, 1994, 9 min. video. Third World Newsreel.

Memory/all echo, Yunah Hong, 1990, 27 min. video. Women Make Movies.

Mija, Hei Sook Park, 1989, 30 min. 16mm. Visual Communications, 263 South Los Angeles Street, Suite 307, Los Angeles, CA 90012, 213–680–4462.

mouth to mouth, Theresa Hak Kyung Cha, 8 min. video. University Art Museum and

319

Pacific Film Archive, University of California at Berkeley, 2625 Durant Avenue, Berkeley, CA 94720, 510–643–8584.

My Niagara, Helen Lee, 1992, 40 min. 16mm. Women Make Movies.

Permutations, Theresa Hak Kyung Cha, 10 min. 16mm. University Art Museum and Pacific Film Archive.

Prey, Helen Lee, 1995, 26 min. 16mm. Canadian Film Center, 2489 Bayview Avenue, North York, Ontario, M2L 1A8, Canada, 416–445–1446.

Red Lolita, Gloria Toyun Park, 1989, 6 min. video. Gloria Toyun Park, 3064 Cardillo Avenue, Hacienda Heights, CA, 91745, 818-336-6141

re/dis/appearing, Theresa Hak Kyung Cha, 1977, 3 min. video. University Art Museum and Pacific Film Archive.

Sa-i-Gu, Christine Choy, Elaine Kim, Dai-Sil Kim Gibson, 1993, 36 min. video. Crosscurrents Media.

Sally's Beauty Spot, Helen Lee, 1992, 12 min. 16mm. Women Make Movies.

Through the Milky Way, Yunah Hong, 1992, 19 min. video. Women Make Movies.

Translating Grace, Anita Lee, 1996, 20 min. 16mm. Nagual Productions, P.O. Box 364, Station P, 704 Spadina Avenue, Toronto, ON M5S 2S9, 416–588–6976.

Undertow, Me-K. Ahn, 1995, 19 min. video. Asian American Renaissance, 1564 Lafond Avenue, St. Paul, MN 55104, 612–641–4040.

Videoeme, Theresa Hak Kyung Cha, 1976, 3 min. video. University Art Museum and Pacific Film Archive.

What Do You Know About Korea? R. Vaughn, 1996, 7 min. video. Katharine Burdette (see *In Memoriam to an Identity*)

The Women Outside, Hye-Jung Park and J.T. Takagi/Third World Newsreel, 1995, 60 min. 16mm. Third World Newsreel.

NOTES

I wish to thank Elaine Kim and the editors for their encouragement, all the filmmakers who supplied tapes, photographs and comments, Abraham Ferrer for additions to the filmography, and also to Esther Yau, Richard Fung, and Cameron Bailey for their usual fabulousness.

1. Although I refer to "filmmakers," videomakers are also included here. Also, I use the term "Korean American" although it is properly "Korean North American," which includes Canada as well as the United States. To talk about the differences (and similarities) of Korean American vs. Korean Canadian identities and histories would comprise another article, so excuse my predominant use of the former.

2. "New" is relative, and everything is context. While the "history of cinema" recently celebrated its centenary, the respective histories of Asian American and feminist cinemas date back only some twenty odd years. In this particular context, anything called "Korean American" would have been begging company, or collapsed into other definitions. Only in the last few years has this work reached a critical mass to be so named. In this sense, film and video work by Korean American women is still a cinematic project in its infancy, and this survey is provisional at best. For reasons of space and focus, this discussion centers around a selection of experimental and narrative works, not documentaries. Refer to the filmography for a more complete list of works by Korean American women filmmakers.

3. W.E.B. DuBois's concept of "double consciousness" is useful in cultivating possibilities for considering cultural difference in non-dualistic ways. Allowing the co-existence of objectification and subjecthood, he writes about "this sense of always looking at one's self through the eyes of others." This turn-of-the-century model of decolonization for post-emancipation blacks uncannily resembles the tricky balance between identification and alienation marking the post-colonial, migratory experiences of the late twentieth century. See DuBois, W.E.B. *The Souls of Black Folk*. New York: First Vintage Books, 1990.

4. Trinh, T. Minh-ha. *Woman, Native, Other: Writing Postcoloniality and Feminism.* Bloomington: Indiana UP, 1989, 6.

5. One striking note is the dearth of filmmaking by Asian American lesbians, including Korean Americans. I can't speculate why, but the absence is astonishing considering the strength of lesbian work in feminist cinema, especially in recent years.

6. "Third cinema" (versus Third World cinema), was first coined by Argentinian filmmakers Fernando Solanas and Octavio Getino during the late '60s as a rallying cry for anti-colonial, revolutionary cinema. During the late '80s, a renewed concept of third cinema was debated, especially among black British theorists and practioners, to signify the work of diasporic, politically and theoretically minded filmmakers who were starting to see themselves increasingly in terms of a community. See *Questions of Third Cinema.* Jim Pines and Paul Willemen, eds. London: British Film Institute, 1989.

7. Bhabha, Homi K. "The Other Question: Stereotype, Discrimination and the

Discourse of Colonialism," *The Location of Culture.* London: Routledge, 1994, 66–84.

8. Barthes, Roland. *Camera Lucida.* New York: Hill and Wang, 1981, 27.

9. *Hangŭl,* developed under the reign of King Sejong (1418–1450), was designed to replace Chinese characters and achieve widespread literacy. The consonants are said to be based on the shape of the human tongue, mouth, and throat when forming these letters.

10. See "Disembodying the Female Voice: Irigaray, Experimental Feminist Cinema, and Femininity" by Kaja Silverman, *The Acoustic Mirror: The Female Voice in Psychoanalysis and Cinema.* (Bloomington: Indiana University Press), 141–186. Silverman examines the work of Yvonne Rainer, Sally Potter, Patricia Gruben, and Bette Gordon in relation to the asynchronous use of the female voice and female subjectivity.

11. Cha, Theresa Hak Kyung. *DICTEE.* New York: Tanam Press, 1982, 168.

12. See also Walter Lew, *Excerpts from: Dikte, For DICTEE* (1982). Seoul, Korea: Yeul Publishing Co., 1992. His book offers another example of a critical collage based on Cha's *DICTEE.*

13. Doane, Mary Ann. "Ideology and the Practice of Sound Editing and Mixing," *The Cinematic Apparatus,* ed. Teresa de Lauretis and Stephen Heath. New York: St. Martin's Press, 1980, 47.

14. Although I watched Korean movies whenever possible, they weren't a prime source of inspiration because, with the exception of a few works, the exported films I saw during the '80s and '90s were typically staid melodramas or slight comedies. Because I was interested in a subjective cinema, middle-aged male perspectives (from which the directors invariably worked) about Korean women and their representation in Korean cinema struck me as idealized or, again, marginalized or tokenistic.

15. Japanese American or Japanese Canadian, the interchangeability was intentional because the co-writer, Kerri Sakamoto, and I believed the social and political histories were so similar, why not the personal ones? This story was meant to transcend an arbitrary national border and acknowledge the similarities between the experiences of people of Japanese descent in North America.

16. Ella Shohat and Robert Stam, "The Cinema After Babel: Language, Difference, Power," *Screen* 26 (May–August 1985), 35–58.

17. Chow, Rey. "Where Have All the Natives Gone?" *Displacements: Cultural Identities in Question,* Angelika Bammer, ed. Bloomington: Indiana University Press, 1994, 137.

18. Jameson, Frederic. "Modernism and Imperialism." *Nationalism, Colonialism, and Literature.* Terry Eagleton, Frederic Jameson, Edward Said, eds. Minneapolis: University of Minnesota Press, 1990, 51.

19. Bhabha, Homi K. "Interrogating Identity: Frantz Fanon and the Postcolonial Prerogative." *The Location of Culture.* London: Routledge, 1994, 66–84.

Contributors' Notes

Chungmoo Choi is Associate Professor of East Asian Studies at the University of California, Irvine. She has edited a special issue of *positions: east asia cultures critique*, titled "Comfort Women" and is now completing *Frost in May: Decolonization and Culture in South Korea* for Duke University Press.

Hyun Yi Kang is Assistant Professor of Women's Studies at the University of California, Irvine. Her book, *Compositional Subjects: Enfiguring Asian/American Women,* is forthcoming with Duke University Press.

Elaine H. Kim is Professor of Asian American Studies at the University of California, Berkeley. She recently authored *Writing Self/Writing Nation: Essays On Theresa Hak Kyung Cha's DICTEE* (1994) and co-edited *East to America: Korean American Life Stories* (1996) and *Making More Waves: New Writing By Asian American Women* (1997). She is currently working on *Fresh Talk/Daring Gazes: Contemporary Asian American Issues in the Visual Arts* for the University of California Press.

Hyun Sook Kim is Assistant Professor of Sociology at Wheaton College. She has written on state repression and national liberation struggles in post-World War II Korea. She is currently writing *Displaced Bodies: The Politics of Nationalisms, Ethnicities, and Sexualities of Diasporic Korean Women,* which is about the dominance of nationality and ethnicity principles over sexuality in the lives of Korean women in China, Japan, Korea, and the U.S.

Helen Lee is a Toronto-based independent filmmaker. Her works include *Prey* (1995), *My Niagara* (1992) and *Sally's Beauty Spot* (1990), which have been screened at numerous festivals and events internationally. She is currently working on a film adaptation of Chang-rae Lee's novel *Native Speaker.*

Yong Soon Min is an artist and Assistant Professor of Studio Art at UC Irvine. Her work has been exhibited both nationally and internationally. She is a recipient of NEA Artists Grant in New Genre (1989–90). One of her current public art projects is a Percent for Art commissioned window design for a new public library in Flushing, New York.

Katharine H.S. Moon is Assistant Professor of Political Science at Wellesley College. She teaches courses on gender and women in world politics, particularly women and war. Her focus is mostly on women in East Asia. Her book, *Sex Among Allies: Military Prostitution in U.S.–Korea Relations, 1971-76*, will be published by Columbia University Press.

Seungsook Moon is Assistant Professor of Sociology at Vassar College, where she also works with the Women's Studies program. She has published articles on masculinity, the state and gender politics, and Eurocentrism and social theory. She is currently a book titled *Modernizing Gender Hierarchy: Militarism, the State, and Industrialization in South Korea, 1963-1992.*

Hyun Ok Park is a Visiting Assistant Professor of Sociology and a Postdoctoral Fellow in the Korean Studies Program at the University of Michigan, Ann Arbor. She has published essays on nationalism, class formation and diasporic identities of the Korean Chinese in Manchuria, and collectivity and differences of women, especially regarding the experience of motherhood. Her current book project focuses on transformation of nationalism in twentieth-century Korea, theorizing colonialism, Korean transnational migrations, and the changing contours of the Korean nation.

You-me Park is Assistant Professor of English at the George Washington University. Her essays on Korean culture, gender, and (post)coloniality have appeared in *positions: east asia cultures critique and In Pursuit of Contemporary East Asian Culture*. She is currently completing a book manuscript on Korean/Korean American women's writings.

Hyunah Yang is currently a Ph.D candidate in Sociology at the New School for Social Research. Her dissertation is on Korean family law, particularly in relation to questions of tradition, modernity, and feminist jurisprudence.

CPSIA information can be obtained at www.ICGtesting.com
Printed in the USA
LVOW05s0020300713

345284LV00013B/197/P